The Process of Editing

The Process of

Editing

R. Thomas Berner

The Pennsylvania State University

Allyn and Bacon

Boston • London • Toronto • Sydney • Tokyo • Singapore

Series Editor: Steve Hull
Editorial-Production Service: Editorial Inc.
Cover Designer: Suzanne Harbison
Cover Administrator: Linda Dickinson
Composition and Manufacturing Buyer: Louise Richardson

Library of Congress Cataloging-in-Publication Data

Berner, R. Thomas.
      The process of editing / R. Thomas Berner.
        p.   cm.
      Includes index.
      ISBN 0-205-12694-4 (alk. paper)
        1. Journalism—Editing.   I. Title.
  PN4778.B4   1991   90-19206
  070.4'1—dc20   CIP

This textbook is printed on recycled, acid-free paper.

Credits

On page 140, the four rules of consultative editing are taken from *How I
Wrote the Story,* Second Edition, and are copyrighted by the *Providence
Journal-Bulletin.* On pages 141–142, the thirty-two suggestions are taken
from *How I Wrote the Story,* Second Edition, and are copyrighted by the
Providence Journal-Bulletin. On pages 322–323 the story on Major Nichol-
son is by Anndee Hochman and is from the March 31, 1985 *Washington
Post,* and is copyrighted by the *Washington Post.*

Other copyrighted material is acknowledged where it appears.

Printed in the United States of America
10 9 8 7 6 5 4 3 2 1   95 94 93 92 91 90

For Blair M. Bice (1914–1989),

who was a friend first

and a publisher second

Contents

Preface

A memorandum soliciting applicants for the editing internship program of The Newspaper Fund begins, "The need for newspaper copy editors is greater than ever." That memorandum was written in the late 1970s. Since then, the need for copy editors has increased. College graduates are learning that they can step from the classroom to the copy desk without first working as a reporter.

Copy editors are also getting some public credit, although not on a widespread scale. One newspaper, the Springfield, Mo., *News-Leader* publishes in each section the names of the copy editors, headline writers and page designers responsible for that section. "Clean copy, clear headlines and jazzy layouts require just as much sweat and tears as good reporting and photography," the managing editor, Kathy Kozdemba, says. "Agony is agony, whether it's over the perfect lead, perfect headline or perfect layout."

Copy editing skills can be transferred. The person who can write a clear sentence in a newspaper can do the same for a television or radio station, for a magazine, for a newsletter or for an advertising agency. Each medium may have different technology and different goals, but each first must communicate, and words play a large part in the transaction. The message is all-important, and it is the copy editor who sees to it that the message is clear.

Even though the emphasis in this book is on newspaper copy editing, the reader should understand that the skills and concepts explained are applicable in many jobs. Some of my former students do not work for newspapers, but they still edit for a living and they are quite happy. I have worked as a consultant to, among others, newspapers, advertising departments and book publishers. I once worked as a writing coach for the author of a psychology textbook. I predict that when I retire in 2004, I will easily be able to find freelance work as a copy editor, if I want it.

This book focuses on editing for newspapers. In some places I discuss concepts as well as skills. Copy editing is an art, not a science, and what the beginning copy editor needs is the conceptual framework as well as an understanding of the basics. I have long argued with students who want courses in sports reporting, consumer reporting and court reporting that reporting is reporting is reporting; once understood conceptually, it can be applied to any subject. The same is true of editing.

Speaking of reporting, various journalism professors over the years have surveyed newspapers to find out if they tested job applicants and what the tests were like. Even when applicants were seeking reporting positions, they had to demonstrate some ability in editing. So even if reporting is your goal, some editing ability can come in handy.

This book originally appeared as *Editing* (Holt, Rinehart and Winston, 1982). The present edition is a major update and revision. Much rewriting and reorganization have occurred. The people who helped me rewrite and reorganize are Shawn C. Balthrop of the University of Missouri; Dennis Cusick of the California State University, Sacramento; Martin Gibson of the University of Texas, Austin; Justice Hill of Ohio University; Paul Jess of the University of Kansas; and Carl Sessions Stepp of the University of Maryland. They spent a great deal of time evaluating the original manuscript and provided me with invaluable direction. Some other people also provided help in ways I cannot elaborate. Let me recognize colleagues and friends Leola A. Johnson, Karen Freeman, H. Eugene Goodwin, Donald L. Smith, John N. Rippey, John S. Nichols, Sally Heffentreyer; Jeff Price of the *Philadelphia Inquirer,* the best copy editor I have ever known; Donald H. Black, who made me aware of the value of photographs and who is now an editor; Raleigh C. Mann of the University of North Carolina, for his helpful review of *Editing.* I can't come up with the names of all the students who have over the years sent me examples of good and bad editing; their contributions appear anonymously throughout.

While I was working on this book, two of my former publishers died. One of them had been an absentee publisher and I hardly knew him. The other, Blair M. Bice, came to the office every day and worked late into the night, especially during the early years when we were struggling to get a newborn newspaper going. A decade later I began to realize the influence this publisher has had on my professional and personal life. I dedicate this book to him.

Chapter 1

The Copy Editor

The Role of the Copy Editor

Copy editors are in great demand. Wherever editors gather, eventually the talk turns to finding a way to woo young people into considering a career as a copy editor. No editor can publish a newspaper without copy editors. Reporters may come and go, get laid off or fired, but even in the most perilous economic times, newspapers need copy editors. As David Hill reported in the *Washington Journalism Review,* when the *Colorado Springs Sun* folded in 1986, the copy editors found new jobs much faster than the reporters. An editor in Pennsylvania called me one day to tell me that in a massive reorganization of the newsroom, he had laid off two reporters but wanted to hire four copy editors. Did I know of anyone?

Unlike some editors whose jobs have been immortalized by Hollywood and Broadway, the copy editor remains anonymous. The public image of the intrepid reporter or the barking editor belies the reality of newspaper publishing, for it is the unglamorous copy editor who puts the paper together day in and day out. The fearless investigative reporter can uncover a scandal of national import, and the editor can issue directions on how the story is to be played, but it is the copy editor who polishes the reporter's words and turns the editor's directions into reality. Without the copy editor (or deskperson, as the jobholder is sometimes known), the newspaper would be a ragged collection of good intentions, and good intentions do not result in good newspapers.

The copy editor assumed a greater role when newspapers entered the electronic age. Once thought of as the last person who could catch a mistake, the copy editor of old actually enjoyed superb backstopping from printers and proofreaders who were often as skillful as the copy editor. But today those reserves are gone, victims of automation and modernization. The copy editor now bears responsibility once divided among three or four people. As Robert H. Williams of the *Washington Post* explained the work of the copy editor: "Copy editors come to be the institutional memory of a newspaper, the ones who know where bodies are buried inside the organization and outside of it, the ones who know when the last near-fatal policy errors were made and what they cost. Copy editors know that World War II came before the Korean War and that it wasn't David who went into the lion's den, but Daniel, and they are forever amending such bizarre mistakes in reporters' stories. Copy editors become terribly proficient in the industrial science of producing a newspaper and in the art of making words work together."

Benefits come from all of that. The copy editor is generally better paid than a reporter, and at most newspapers no one rises through the ranks without doing some desk work. Newsroom promotions from the middle to the top level usually come from the desk, not the reporting staff.

An old advertisement for *The New York Times Manual of Style and Usage* proclaimed, "As a writer you're judged by your consistency and accuracy of style and usage." It could also have said, "As a copy editor you are judged by your ability to catch a writer's inconsistent and inaccurate style and usage." Writers up against a deadline make mistakes that in more leisurely circumstances they would not make. Deadline aside, every writer's copy needs an editor's eye to smooth the pace of words and parade of facts for the reader.

The copy editor must know not only how to use language well but also how to fix a writer's story without destroying the writer's style. A copy editor must spot errors that lesser mortals would never see, must see that the story's unvoiced questions are answered immediately, must write accurately and with sparkle (a favorite word in copy editor job descriptions). The copy editor must select stories with unerring regard for reader interests, must design an attractive page around the selection, must see that the tone, style and flavor of the newspaper are maintained, and must write headlines that (again) sparkle. In evaluating copy editors, one newspaper examines their ability to identify important story elements, organize stories, edit copy tightly, spot legal and fairness issues, meet deadlines, identify the best headline angle and write headlines with flair. (*Flair* is a substitute for *sparkle*.) In outlining the many virtues of good copy editors, Kenn Finkel, then of the *Dallas Times Herald*, told an American Press Institute seminar for journalism educators that a copy editor should have a "healthy skepticism that asks questions and tries to make a story answer them; [a] burning desire to release no story that has vagueness or unanswered questions."

For that, copy editors, who do not get bylines, take their gratification internally. They are secure in the knowledge that they have helped produce a first-rate newspaper. They know that their sharp eyes may have saved the publisher $1 million in libel damages. They are, above all, humble.

The copy editor serves as a professional reader for the good of a very special client, the reader of the newspaper. Even when reading about a favorite subject, the copy editor, despite being well read and knowledgeable, simulates ignorance to ensure that the final story will be clear to the reader.

The copy editor respects the reporter. In fact, between good copy editors and reporters mutual respect for high standards serves the reader, because the copy editors and reporters see themselves as working together. Decades ago a beginning reporter praised a column written weekly by his city editor. "It would be a lot better if I had a copy editor," the city editor replied. Then there is the story of the late Peter Kihss of *The New York Times*. Kihss was highly regarded for his accurate reporting and quit three times when editors introduced errors into his copy. Good copy editors respect reporters like Peter Kihss. Good copy editors engender rapport with reporters. To that end, they do not make changes in copy for the sake of change. "I'd write it differently" is no reason for a copy editor to change a reporter's story. A copy editor remembers that a change can just as easily make a story inaccurate as accurate. Copy editors are not infallible.

Those who aspire to the copy desk should know that today's newspapers hire copy editors directly out of college instead of making them serve an apprenticeship as a reporter, as in previous times in journalism. The copy desk today is not a place where worn-out reporters are tossed. Would-be copy editors must prove their potential, often by taking a series of tests that show not only ability with the language but also the instinct to sense errors. Told to edit a story, one journalism graduate on a job interview asked, "Where's the city directory?" He knew some of the tools of the trade. He went on to pass the tests and get the job. Within four months he was news editor; within two years, managing editor. His assistant, who during college served a Newspaper Fund internship on the desk of *The Boston Globe,* moved on to become a copy editor for *Advertising Age* within a year of graduating from college. The closed door to early advancement is now wide open.

Copy editors need not feel cut off from writing opportunities either, for though they seldom get a chance to cover hard news, they do have time to produce work hard-pressed reporters don't. Copy editors bent on doing some writing find pleasure in writing editorials, columns, reviews or features for Sunday use.

A Variety of Editors and Their Duties

Copy editors are but one type of editor. Given the number of editors any one newspaper might have, an outsider could get the impression of too many bosses and no workers. In newspapers, though, the tendency is to put someone in charge of something and then call that person an editor. Thus, the person who writes play reviews might be called the Arts Editor or the Culture Editor on the basis that the person is a specialist and deserves to be so tagged. And despite the notion that some news executives give subordinates titles rather than pay raises, many newspaper editors perform necessary functions in the day-to-day operation of the paper.

Editors make things happen. Editors generate ideas. Editors lead by example. The person responsible for the news and opinion content of a newspaper is the executive editor or editor. Under that person is the editor responsible for overseeing the daily operation, the managing editor. If the newspaper is large, the managing editor usually has more contact with reporters than the editor or executive editor, who must also deal with corporate responsibilities and long-range planning. As Charles W. Bailey II, former editor of the Minneapolis *Star and Tribune* put it: "The editor must represent the community, the public constituency inside the newspaper building as well as outside. He must regularly remind his staff of its responsibility to that community. And once in a great while, he must be prepared to remind his publisher of that responsibility."

At some newspapers the person holding the title of editor is the editor of the editorial page only. If the paper is large enough and has an op-ed (for opposite-editorial) page, that page has an appropriately titled editor. Top editors have associates and assistants, listed under those titles or called by different titles such as news editor, city editor, metro (for metropolitan) editor, national, foreign, sports, feature editor. Newspapers in non-metropolitan areas often have county editors who are responsible for seeing that news in the less-populated sections of the newspaper's circulation area gets covered. Give a newspaper a specialty and an editor will be named to oversee it. A printer once quipped that if he walked into the newsroom at his newspaper and said, "I need an editor out back," everyone in the newsroom would follow him to the shop.

More and more women and minorities are filling positions of responsibility in newsrooms of all media as publishers and station managers discover that a person's sex or race does not correlate with a person's abilities. Some gains by women and minorities have not come without court suits, and future editors would do well to ensure that today's gains are not lost tomorrow. Still, during the 1980s, women and minorities have moved into a variety of responsible positions as editors and bureau chiefs. The Gannett chain, especially, ranks as one of the most progressive employers because of its willingness to put women and minorities in executive positions.

The advancement of women and minorities is good for the news media. They bring to newspapers and broadcast outlets new points of view, so necessary to ensure that the news media understand their audiences. Besides the fact that they enlarge the pool of competent workers who can bring a new perspective to world events, they may be able to provide an insider's view of issues like prejudice in education and employment, and social relationships. Some journalists believe that day care issues get better coverage in the news media because women journalists have helped their male counterparts understand the issues from a woman's point of view.

If the top editors of all news media have failed in any field, it is in the skillful handling of their subordinates. Time and time again journalism school graduates on their first job complain that "nobody tells me how I'm doing" or "nobody edits my copy." One of the long-standing problems of journalism is that in a field predicated on communication, some of its practitioners cannot talk to each other. No matter what their level, editors must participate in the communication process.

One breakdown occurs in the hiring process when the news executive fails to describe the job clearly. The result is that after a person has been hired or promoted, the executive says, "Oh, by the way, I also want you to do such-and-such," tasks the person has no interest in doing or for which the person is not qualified. Had the executive defined the job clearly at first, the problem could have been avoided.

The good editor recognizes that the newspaper's success depends on the staff. The good editor hires people who are not only bright but brighter than the editor. If editors who are weak writers hired only those people who wrote at the editor's level, the newspaper would surely fail. Editors who hire shouldn't feel threatened by talented people; in fact, they should heavily recruit the best.

Once a talented staff is assembled, the good editor primes it for success. In such a newsroom, no recent journalism graduate can whine about not being told how he or she is doing, because the good editor sees that the top editors routinely, albeit sometimes informally, meet with reporters to explain what they're doing wrong—and right. On a daily basis, copy editors ensure high morale by explaining to reporters why stories had to be cut or held. Nobody's left in the dark. By the same token, reporters should talk to editors and not wait for them to initiate every discussion. At some newspapers, in fact, reporters have initiated their own writing workshops as a way of improving each other's writing. Good editors encourage such initiatives. (See Chapter 7, "Consultative Editing.")

The editor continues staff training beyond that first day when the new reporter received a copy of the newspaper style guide and a list of office personnel and their telephone extension numbers. Formal and informal training sessions, including in-house critiques, continue throughout the reporter's career, and at larger newspapers, reporters are sent back to school for updating or to workshops to pick up information on a specialty.

Good editors pay attention to the development of their staffs. They strive to involve staff members in decisions. After all, subeditors and reporters are really middle managers and should be involved in making decisions that affect them. Good editors encourage staff members to improve their professional skills and to pursue other interests that will help round out the staff members.

In the training process, the good news executive is looking for managerial talent, people who not only possess qualities of leadership but also want to lead. Not every person of leadership talent wants the promotion, and not every person who wants the promotion should get it. A classic example of poor management is the transfer of a very good reporter to the copy desk, there to fail because the reporter's interests lie in reporting. If kept there too long, the reporter suffers the stigma of being a loser, and the editor finds it more difficult to solve the problem. Making the copy editor a reporter again appears to be a demotion, even in the reporter's eyes.

When not functioning as executives, the many editors in newspapers perform a variety of duties not always foretold in their titles. The managing editor at a small newspaper might unlock the door in the morning, clear the wire, edit copy, write headlines, lay out Page One, hire and fire staff—and make coffee. At large newspapers, the managing editor ensures that the newsroom budget includes money to buy coffee.

At some newspapers, the city editor, often portrayed in the movies as a gruff-talking person, has final responsibility for all local copy. The city editor might check each story for content and then assign it to an assistant for editing and headline writing, or the editor might process the story on the spot.

Other people working with the city editor are the wire editor, who at some newspapers is responsible for the state, national and international news sent by the wire services; the news editor, who might be in charge of dummying Page One; the photo editor, who might be a photographer in charge of the photo department or the person responsible for the cropping and sizing of all photographs; and the copy editor, who edits and headlines stories under the direction of a chief copy editor or the city editor.

The Newsroom Hierarchy

The editors just mentioned and others must fit into a hierarchy. The following briefly describes the hierarchy of a composite medium-sized daily (75,000 circulation) that also publishes a Sunday edition.

At the top is the editor, who ranks as an equal with other newspaper department heads such as the advertising director and the circulation manager. The editor answers to the publisher. (On a larger newspaper, the executive editor would have overall authority.) The editor, while exercising overall control, does not sit on the desk or edit copy. The editor ensures overall quality by coordinating the work of the many assistants through the chief assistant, the managing editor.

Working under the managing editor are five assistants, who at some newspapers might carry titles such as chief copy editor, state editor, news editor, wire editor, local or city editor. At this composite daily, these people are assistant managing editors.

The primary concern of the first assistant is the quality of headlines and copy editing. This assistant managing editor not only supervises the universal copy desk (explained presently) but also evaluates the writing in the paper and works with individual reporters who are having writing problems. One of this editor's duties is frequently assembling and writing critiques of the newspaper. (One of the best-known collections of critiques is "Winners & Sinners," which the late Theodore M. Bernstein wrote for *The New York Times*.)

The second assistant managing editor oversees coverage of state news, that is, news that occurs in the state but outside the paper's immediate circulation area. This editor also oversees the newspaper's bureau in the state capital and any other bureaus the paper may have within the state. All correspondents work under this editor, who also oversees the production of the paper's state edition.

The third assistant managing editor coordinates special projects, overseeing, for example, all election coverage. In such a case, this editor would work with the state editor to avoid conflicts, overlaps and duplication and to produce a smooth election package of preview stories and results. The third assistant also oversees the newspaper's special investigative reporting team. The virtue of having an editor oversee investigative reporting cannot be stressed enough. Some newspapers with investigative reporters forget that the editing of such work needs as much care as the reporting. When newspapers fail to free an editor to coordinate investigative reporting, a harried editor with too much to do must take on the additional work of checking the investigative report. Not having been in on the story from the start, the harried editor begins work in ignorance.

Pressed because daily work awaits, he or she rushes through the investigative work and misses holes. A special editor works with the team from the start and avoids those problems.

The fourth assistant managing editor oversees all news received via the wire services. This job is more than just sign on, read and route. This editor must make sure that stories are distributed to the right desks and that updates and corrections get to the right editors. Automatic sorting systems do not replace this editor. They help the editor do a better job. At some dailies this editor is responsible for designing Page One.

The fifth assistant managing editor assigns stories within the newspaper's circulation area. Although the managing editor can generate story ideas, it is this assistant who sees that a reporter gets the assignment and the time to do the assignment.

Subordinate editors on this composite newspaper include graphics (is responsible for overall appearance of the paper but does not lay out each page), photo, sports, business and lifestyle/leisure. Where appropriate, these editors select the stories to go on their pages and then design the pages within the framework established by the graphics editor. Some newspapers have an operations desk that is responsible for laying out the local and wire news sections of the paper.

One other editor oversees the Sunday edition, making sure that the content for the special sections gets in type throughout the week instead of at the last minute. News and sports sections in the Sunday edition fall outside this editor's purview; they are usually the responsibility of the editors mentioned before.

Depending on the newspaper, copy is edited at a universal desk or at individual department desks. In a universal system, all copy except sports is edited by the copy editors at that desk. A universal desk ensures consistency of writing and style much better than individual departments can. At newspapers where individual departments edit their own copy, minor stylistic and editing differences explode into newsroom warfare, and the main purpose of the newspaper is forgotten as the lifestyle editor and the business editor feud over, say, the use of last names in second references. As silly as it may sound, such internecine debates can stymie quality work.

Sources and Resources

Bailey, Charles W., II. "The Changing Role of Editors." Speech to the Minnesota Newspaper Foundation, Minneapolis, Minn., Nov. 5, 1982.

Currie, Phil. "Why Bother with Staff-Development Programs? Attraction, Retention, Invention, Exhilaration, Cooperation." *Editorially Speaking* 35, no. 8 (August/September 1982).

_____. "Editing in the '80s: Adding a Minority Perspective to a Single-Dimension Staff." *Editorially Speaking* 35, no. 9 (October 1982).

_____. "Editing in the '80s: Staffers Seek Formal Feedback; Here's a Plan to Provide It." *Editorially Speaking* 36, no. 5 (May 1983).

_____. "Getting Your Act Together: Gannett Editors Offer Helpful Hints on Being Organized." *Editorially Speaking* 40, no. 6 (July 1986).

_____. "A Tribute to John B. Bremner: His Words, His Lessons, His Inspiration." *Editorially Speaking* 41, no. 7 (September 1987).

Dulaney, William. "New Employee Evaluation Techniques Involve Staffers in Personal Growth, Job Development." *PNPA Press* (October 1981): 6.

_____. "What Motivates Newsroom Personnel?" *PNPA Press* (April 1982): 6.

Gwin, Louis. "Prospective Reporters Face Writing/Editing Tests at Many Dailies." *Newspaper Research Journal* 9, no. 2 (Winter 1988): 101–111.

Hill, David. "Wanted: Copy Editors." *Washington Journalism Review* (July 1986): 8.

Kozdemba, Kathy. "By-lines for Copy Editors Give Credit to Unsung Heroes." *Editorially Speaking* 43, no. 4 (May 1989): 8.

Mullins, Ed. "Newsroom Training." Speech to Southern Newspaper Publishers Association, Smaller Newspapers Seminar, San Antonio, Texas, Sept. 29, 1983.

Thornburg, Ron. "City Desk Editing Seminars Offered Survival Kit for 'Life in the Wind Tunnel.' " *Editorially Speaking* 41, no. 8 (October 1987).

Williams, Robert H. "Giving Copy Editors Their Due." *Presstime* (December 1988): 34–35.

Chapter 2

The Copy Editor and Technology

The Electronic Evolution

Important to understanding the significance of the copy editor's role is knowing how the production tasks of putting out a newspaper have changed since the computer age began. The use of the computer has affected many departments and jobs in the newspaper, but perhaps the job most affected has been the copy editor's.

Countless stories could be told, but all would come down to one word, speed. Producing a newspaper doesn't take as long as it used to. A reporter still takes a certain amount of time to write a story, and an editor still takes a certain amount of time to edit the story, write a headline for it and position it on the page. But even those processes have been subtly speeded up by electronic editing equipment. Meanwhile, the gain in speed from the editor's desk to finished type must be measured by the speed of light. A laborious mechanical process has yielded to the electronic age.

In 1978, a small plane crashed into a jetliner over San Diego little more than an hour before the first-edition deadline for the San Diego *Evening Tribune*. More than 40 staff members went to work immediately and put together a Pulitzer Prize-winning package that delayed the first edition by only 10 minutes. The editor had expected a delay three or four times longer. The editor credited the *Tribune's* electronic system for making the process so fast. He credited the people on his staff for winning the Pulitzer Prize.

In Providence, R.I., Eliot Jaspin of the *Journal-Bulletin* analyzed 30,000 state mortgage files and uncovered a scandal in the state's mortgage agency. In Atlanta a couple of years later, a similar analysis revealed that whites were five times more likely than blacks to get a home loan with the same income. The result: a four-part series and a Pulitzer Prize for the *Atlanta Journal* and *Constitution*. Back when it wasn't so common, Thomas J. Moore of the Chicago *Sun-Times* used a personal computer to analyze the federal budget and figured out which classes of people would be affected most by budget cuts. For another story, he was able to search the records of Nexis, an electronic database, and figure out how much aid Libya had given to Nicaragua. Back in Rhode Island, the *Journal* analyzed computer files of school bus drivers to establish that several of them had bad driving records. On the West Coast, the *San Jose Mercury News* identified the secretly owned properties of Philippine dictator Ferdinand Marcos by sorting through computerized information. In all parts of the country, newspapers have begun using computers as reporting tools.

In another time, reporters and photographers covering an important story might keep in touch with each other using walkie-talkies. In a still earlier time, reporters would have used inconvenient telephones or, worse still, remained out of touch with each other. But today, a reporter covering, say, a congressional hearing can whip out a pocket telephone and call in the story from the hearing room rather than making a mad dash for a limited number of pay telephones in the hallway outside the room.

Portable computers show up everywhere. They first appeared as 20-pound behemoths in press boxes around the country on football weekends. Sportswriters would produce their stories in a couple of hours after the game and then transmit them to the home office hundreds of miles away via telephone in a matter of minutes.

Today reporters routinely carry a lightweight portable computer, usually a rectangular flat object with a small screen. Whether in press boxes or city council chambers, whether 300 miles from the home office or only 3 miles, reporters find the latest laptop computers as necessary as pen and paper.

Take Ken Ficara of the *Centre Daily Times* in State College, Pa. Ficara works for a morning paper and has a normal deadline of 11 p.m. When he attends municipal government meetings that start at 7:30 p.m. and seldom end before 9:30 and that could be the basis for three or four stories, Ficara knows that he won't have the time at the end of a meeting to get all his writing done. So when there's a break in the action, Ficara writes his first story and, if he has enough time, goes to another room with a telephone and sends his first story to his editors a few miles away. Any lull in a meeting enables him to work on still another story. He has become more efficient and productive, thanks to the laptop computer he routinely totes.

No more running back to an office to write a story, no more tangling with traffic, no more dictating over a telephone. A reporter with a portable terminal is a traveling bureau that can move around a beat unfettered by the need to get back to an office to write. A telephone provides the link from the portable bureau to the main office and its computer.

The cellular telephone has changed the process even more. In 1989, Robert Reinhold of *The New York Times'* bureau in Los Angeles heard about an assassination attempt 125 miles away in San Diego. He immediately drove off, using the cellular phone in his car to round up assistants. On site and with only an hour until deadline, he gathered information, wrote the story on a portable computer in a nearby parking lot and then transmitted it to New York City over his cellular phone in time for the first edition. This is a mixed blessing for the desk. Editing on a computer gives copy editors more flexibility than pencil and paper did, but as reporters with laptop computers push deadlines, the pressure will mount on copy editors. Stories written on deadline are not necessarily the most graceful and usually require extra attention on the desk.

In the newsroom, the introduction of VDTs (as video display terminals are called) has turned the typesetting duties performed by printers over to reporters and editors. That has meant fewer printers at a newspaper but more editors who find themselves as the only checkers of a story. (Printers were reliable backup editors.) Because the computer will have typeset whatever the editor allows on the screen, editors function as proofreaders, another position disappearing from newsrooms. Computers don't make mistakes; they amplify them. The greater responsibility should translate into higher wages, because the reporters and editors are now performing additional tasks. The higher wages, unfortunately, haven't always come with the increased responsibilities.

The storage capacity of a computer provides newspapers with a variety of opportunities to publish a more personal and local newspaper.

Newspapers have long published zoned editions, but now that the newspapers are free of the pokiness of the Linotype, they can divide their product into more zones, from parts of a county to neighborhoods. Obviously, a page or a section devoted to one neighborhood will carry more detailed news than would the same section devoted to a larger area. It is not impractical to store a lot of information on a computer with its mammoth storage space. The speed of the equipment, of course, contributes significantly to the growth in zoned editions, because it has made them easier to produce quickly. The copy desk, in tandem with the operations desk, produces the zoned editions.

The storage capacity of a computer allows a newspaper editor to use a story in one zoned edition, withhold it from a second, but reuse it in a third with a different headline (rewritten by a copy editor) and in a different format (such as a different type size and width). Doing the same thing in the past would have taken more time than it was worth. One college daily stores its local stories for reuse in a weekly newspaper sold by mail to alumni. Even the mailing lists are kept in a computer in ZIP code order.

My office computer contains *The Associated Press Stylebook*. At first, having an alphabetized reference book on computer doesn't sound like much. After all, a human is capable of looking up entries in the stylebook. But its virtue on the computer shows up when the editor or reporter doesn't know which entry to look for and instead types in a keyword. For example, type the word *address*. The computerized stylebook reveals that *address* or some version (e.g., *addresses*) shows up under the following entries: abbreviation, addresses, alley, Associated Press, avenue, boulevard, Churches of Christ, drive, f.o.b., capitalization, plurals, nonspecific references, highway designations, Mailgram, No., figures or words, passenger lists, pope, road, State of the Union, street, terrace, United Press International. The word *sex* or related forms show up under AIDS, animals, brunet, brunette, chauvinism, chauvinist, Equal Rights Amendment, hurricane, names, sex changes, spokesman, spokeswoman, transsexuals, typhoons, women.

A reporter can apply the same principle and check cross-references in a database. Librarians at the *San Francisco Chronicle* searched the electronic version of *Who's Who* to learn who was a member of the secretive all-male Bohemian Club. They used the key word *Bohemian* to learn who belonged to the club and discovered that one of its members was Caspar

Weinberger, then secretary of defense. Such a search done by hand would have taken eight years, and what the search uncovered wouldn't have been news anymore.

Another tremendous advantage of the storage capacity is the library service it can offer a newspaper. Forget the bound editions of the paper or the yellowing and dog-eared clips in a file; the modern copy editor looks information up in the newspaper's electronic library, which is available through the keyboard of a VDT. It became available because every day all stories published are automatically stored in the newspaper's electronic library. Depending on the sophistication of the system, the copy editor can find information through various means. One of the best allows the copy editor to command the computer to produce all stories mentioning, say, *rezoning* within the past year. In that way, the copy editor gets a broad picture. Less sophisticated systems require more searching time but are nevertheless faster than a reporter turning page after page of old newspapers or rooting through files. The computer not only speeds up the search time, it does the searching too.

The library function goes beyond the newsroom, for the newspaper's information can be sold and resold to anyone who wants it. Newspapers, in other words, are extending their short shelf life by increasing the availability and accessibility of their contents. The daily newspaper formerly satisfied readers for a short time and then was easily discarded. That still happens in the electronic age, but the information on the printed page can now be stored for later accessing for a fee.

One such service is called Dow Jones News/Retrieval. The service provides world and sports news, business and financial reports, weather and even daily coverage of major Japanese institutions. Subscribers who want to check back issues can access the service's reference library, where they can get, among other things, the full text of articles from the *Wall Street Journal* and the *Washington Post*. Also available are Associated Press stories and articles from regional newspapers, *USA Today* and the Gannett News Service.

Subscribers can also track various companies and get a variety of stock market quotes, current to within 15 minutes. If the market indicates a good portfolio, the subscriber can access an airline schedule and make a reservation for a flight to a vacation paradise. Portable computer in hand, the subscriber can access the service from the island paradise and get reviews of movies and books.

Among the first to recognize the long-range potential of usually short-lived news material was *The New York Times,* which created The New York Times Information Service Inc. That service allows subscribers to retrieve information from a computer storage base. The users of such a service are not only other newspapers but corporations and libraries that want the information easily available but do not have the time or space to gather and store it themselves.

In addition, the Associated Press joined with the *Times* to produce the Associated Press Political Databank, used by subscribers in 1980 to keep up with the presidential campaign. Daily the AP updated the stored information to provide subscribers with current facts on the candidates, issues, strategies and changes. The service also provided background information. All the information went to subscribers on high-speed wires, making it available in seconds. Thus, any copy editor can check current and detailed information on the presidential race. Routinely, now, the Associated Press establishes special databases for certain events. Election coverage has gone beyond the presidential to include a database of stories and analyses from Associated Press reporters in every state and in Washington, D.C. Other news services and newspapers have followed suit.

The implications go far beyond the corporation, library or newspaper needing information. Given that many individuals in the United States have personal computers and terminals, what is to stop a college professor in Laramie, Wyo., from purchasing access to an information computer at *The New York Times* or the University of North Carolina and retrieving information on rural poverty? Nothing. The technology already allows for that. With costs going down, more people have bought home computers. In fact, some newspapers allow people to access their main computers to submit columns, letters and obituaries. This means the newspaper is open 24 hours a day, although people may not be on duty all that time.

Some newspaper watchers suggest that what has just been described foreshadows the death of the printed page. Why buy a newspaper that is susceptible to late delivery, to getting blown off your porch on a windy day, or to getting soaked in a rainstorm when your newspaper can appear story by story on a television screen in the comfort of your livingroom, on time and dry? Perhaps newspapers will disappear. Other people contend that the average reader will not want to spend time sitting at a computer terminal to select and read that day's news. After all, if the average reader gives a newspaper no more than 20 minutes, why would a video substitute fare better? Theoretically, it should fare worse. The beauty of the newspaper as we know it is that it provides news preselected by editors who try to publish what they believe readers want. They separate the wheat from the chaff. A video "newspaper," on the other hand, would offer everything, and the reader/viewer would have to select what to read and what to ignore. In other words, the modern newspaper also does 90 percent of the reader's work. But with the right software, someone with a computer at home can program it to select certain stories automatically, by story type or dateline or keywords.

Second, because of the way a modern newspaper is designed, the reader knows some stories are more important than others and will ignore some stories because of their small headline size or low placement on a page. The video screen treats coups and tea parties alike typographically; not much to distinguish one from the other.

These problems can be overcome, but that still leaves the one enduring quality of a newspaper, the printed page. The emphasis on literacy has ennobled the printed page. It contains detailed information in black and white; it is there tonight, tomorrow and next year. It can be consulted. It can be kept on a shelf; it can be stored in a family album. An account of someone's wedding looks better in a newspaper, clustered as it is among other wedding stories, than it would as a single item on a computer printout. A family album of computer printouts lacks the command presence of the printed page.

The computer does the work for the human, but the human decides what work has to be done. Customized software gives editors an electronic selection process of stories based on keywords. The computer program knows the keywords and indexes all stories containing those words. This makes life more efficient for the small copy desk.

One newspaper has programmed its computer to quickly figure out batting averages, saving the sports department much time. Another newspaper's computer alphabetizes long lists of sports scores, allowing readers to find their favorite team whether it won or lost. If Nebraska loses to Florida State, 21–10, the score will be found under Nebraska 10, Florida State 21, and under Florida State 21, Nebraska 10. For casual fans who

might have forgotten whom their favorite team played during the weekend, finding the score is easy.

The right computer married to the right printer can create just about anything. Computing batting averages and alphabetizing a weekend's worth of scores from athletic events are elementary tasks compared to the advanced graphic elements a good system can produce through human input. A copy editor needing a three-dimensional map showing population distribution in the United States can quickly retrieve a U.S. map from a database and plot information on it as necessary. The database also includes a variety of other maps, from local voting precincts to the statewide ecosystem. Such a database provides the newsroom with opportunities to tell stories more graphically even when up against a tight deadline. Some newspapers subscribe to services that provide custom maps and color separations that can be downloaded onto a personal computer. Putting together a breaking story of words, photographs and other graphics has become practical because of the computer.

Tools to an End

The usual cry raised against technological change is that it dehumanizes any system. "Machines are replacing people," the doom sayers warn; "people don't count any more." The truth is, the electronic changes in newspapers have hurt some people, primarily printers who have lost their jobs to machines that do the printers' work better, faster, cheaper and without going on strike. Many publishers, however, did not fire printers made obsolete by computers but instead trained them for other work or offered them large financial settlements to retire.

By the same token, some in the newsroom and the darkroom complain that the computer hinders their creativity and replaces their thought processes. That is nonsense. For example, when manufacturers developed cameras that automatically determine lens speed and aperture size, good photographers realized that the camera's so-called brain was not replacing their brain but was taking over mechanical functions. Photographers still control the creative aspect of the photograph, its substance and content.

The newsroom computer has not changed the fact that humans must gather, write, edit, evaluate and package news for other humans. The editor who pushes a button on a VDT and removes a word from a story is no different from the editor in a non-electronic newsroom who does the same thing with a pencil. Only the process is faster now. The brain determines redundancy, not the computer.

No computer can decide if a story is libelous. Only a person, someone able to ask "How would I feel if this story were about me?" can sense the nuances of a story that might wrongly harm someone for life. A computer can enhance any photograph, but it cannot evaluate the photograph for creativity or news value. A computer cannot judge a photograph in terms of taste or ethics. A human can.

A computer is a tool that is as good as the user, and no better. The electronic gadgetry in a newsroom is not mere wizardry installed by the publisher as a tax write-off; the equipment serves the people in the newsroom.

The VDT

VDTs are not perfect. One major concern is their impact on health. The issue of whether radiation from VDTs causes severe eye problems such as cataracts may never be resolved to everyone's satisfaction, but the fact remains that some users perceive that they suffer health problems, and that alone represents an ethical concern for manufacturers and publishers. VDTs do emit radiation, according to the National Institute for Occupation Safety & Health, but not at levels hazardous to humans. But subsequent information suggests that women who work around VDTs have problem pregnancies or miscarriages above the normal rate, although the VDT's link to that is unclear, and some VDT users have installed shields over their screens to block out some radiation.

One study found that VDT users complained about headaches, eye strain, deteriorated vision, low back pain, neck pain and shoulder pain. Optometrists believe that VDT use may aggravate vision problems, and they urge VDT operators to take 15-minute breaks every two hours. People who use VDTs for long periods of time, such as copy editors, and who wear glasses may discover that they need a different set of glasses for work.

To a lesser extent, improperly lighted rooms that house VDTs can create glare that tires eyes and causes fatigue. Strenuous copy editing of any kind can result in eye fatigue if a room is not properly lighted, but it appears that a VDT needs a more diffused light than would be tolerable in a pre-electronic newsroom. Polarizing filters that can be simply installed have been developed to help increase contrast and reduce eye fatigue. More modern personal computers come with the capability for a user to change brightness and contrast, to tailor them to the individual. In any case, users should have their eyes checked regularly and should rest if their eyes tire. The health benefits are obvious, but the advice carries a practical message—tired eyes don't do a good job of editing.

Another problem is RSI, repetitive strain injury, which has crippled some VDT users. RSI is linked to the continuous use of the hands, arms or shoulders. Some of the afflicted have undergone surgery for nerve damage in their hands and wrists. The American Newspaper Publishers Association has several suggestions for avoiding RSI. They include making sure chair and desk are at the correct position so that thighs are horizontal, neck straight, head centered above the spine, arms at a 90-degree angle, hands and wrists extended straight out, feet flat on the floor.

A poorly planned system can frustrate a user. Such frustration usually arises when an editor strikes a key and the computer takes 10 or more seconds to execute the command. The delay signals an overtaxed computer that needs to be upgraded. An editor who experiences a brief delay may execute the command a second time, believing the system is not working. Some VDT systems, however, will execute any given command in time, meaning that a command given twice might be annoyingly executed twice.

The VDT can serve as a note file for reporters who, before writing a story, transcribe their shorthand notes into longhand. Since each reporter can be given a queue or workspace in the computer, the notes won't get mixed with someone else's. By the same token, reporters and editors do not write anything personal for VDT storage because it is unprofessional, because the personal work takes up storage space the computer needs for working data, because no one has a guarantee that what is written won't be found by someone else, and because what is written might accidentally show up in print. Imagine how foolish everyone felt when the following note to an editor appeared as the ending of a story: "I have attempted to revise the lede of thi sty to fit the current policy of the Clearwater Sun, i.e., that this is the best of all possible worlds. Bull shit. Still, I love you." (The newspaper apologized.) Some systems offer private files and invisible sign-on passwords, but they don't provide absolute privacy. Anyone who uses a VDT system long enough begins to understand how it works and can divine passwords and other secrets.

Each VDT system is different; where one system's command to call up a story might be OPEN another's could be FETCH or LOAD. But the principles behind the different words are the same, and new users should remember that as they learn a system. Reduced to newsroom needs, a VDT system is merely the typical newsroom, but with electronic circuits instead of pencils and paper.

Sources and Resources

Eisenstein, Elizabeth L. *The Printing Press as an Agent of Change*. Cambridge: Cambridge University Press, 1979.

Meyer, Philip. *Precision Journalism*. Bloomington: Indiana University Press, 1973.

Miller, Tim. "The Data-Base Revolution." *Columbia Journalism Review* (September/October 1988): 35–38.

Preble, Laurence D. "A Healthy Interface." *The Rainbow* (February 1988): 118–121.

Rykken, Rolf. "Repetitive Strain Injury." *Presstime* (June 1989): 6–8, 10.

Slesin, Louis. "VDT Radiation: What's Known, What Isn't." *Columbia Journalism Review* (November/December 1984): 40–41.

Smith, Anthony. *Goodbye Gutenberg: The Newspaper Revolution of the 1980s*. Oxford: Oxford University Press, 1980.

Technology and the Future: A Guide for Editors. Reston, Va.: American Society of Newspaper Editors, 1989.

Truitt, Rosalind C. "PCs: Newspapers Are Finding New Uses for Personal Computers. And There's No End in Sight." *Presstime* (April 1987): 18–20.

———. "New York Times Is Latest Metro to Embrace Large-Scale PC System." *Presstime* (September 1988): 72–73.

Underwood, Doug. "The Desktop Challenge." *Columbia Journalism Review* (May/June 1989): 43–45.

Walker, Tom. "Computers Give New Life to Morgues." *Presstime* (December 1982): 4–9.

Chapter 3

The Editing Function

A Job with Many Duties

Copy editors are responsible for all manner of things during the editing of a story. At small newspapers, copy editors not only edit copy but also write the headlines and design the pages. At really small newspapers, copy editors can be called upon to take stories over the phone when no reporter is available.

Copy editing can be broken into macro and micro editing. In micro editing, the copy editor checks the parts of the story, while in macro editing the copy editor ensures that the parts fit together. Chapters 3 to 6 discuss many aspects of both kinds of editing. Copy editors must consider copy flow and deadlines, writing style and tone; they must look for holes in stories and challenge stories that seem airtight. Libel is also a major concern for copy editors. So, too, are matters of fairness and balance. Copy editors must ensure that words are used correctly and that the arithmetic adds up. They also need to ensure that copy does not disparage someone because of sex, race or ethnic background.

The copy desk is no place for the indecisive. Copy editors are expected to make quick, and correct, decisions. They must also know how to say no firmly when yes would be easier. Finally, some practical advice for copy editors: Many errors tend to be repetitive and the better copy editors learn that early in their careers. Knowing the typical error created by a certain situation, the copy editor can quickly fix the mistake and spend more time seeking out the atypical. In fact, copy editors need to be sure that they don't spend all their time looking at the parts of the story and fail to notice if the parts make a whole story. As an unidentified editor once said at an American Press Institute seminar: "A good editor approaches copy as though it is a proposal worthy of consideration, but guarantees no more than that. Too many stories get published just because they get written."

A copy editor should read each story three times. In the first reading, the copy editor reads for the sense of the story, doing no editing other than fixing a misspelled word or taking out an extra comma. The copy editor makes sure the story develops as promised in the lead, that it contains no unanswered questions, that the transitions work. On the second reading, the copy editor edits. The third time, the copy editor makes sure no mistakes were edited into the story. Figure the minimum time for the process at a minute an inch.

Beginning copy editors should remember the advice given to doctors: Do no harm. Unfortunately, when copy editors do harm, their mistakes appear in print for all the world to see.

General Duties

Here are some of the general duties of the copy editor.

The Story Conference and Copy Flow

Most of the editors meet daily for the story conference, at which time they tell what major stories they have and make a pitch to the managing editor for their biggest story to appear on Page One. The managing editor makes the final decision on Page One content.

The conference is usually held about four hours before deadline or, in the case of a multiple-edition newspaper, before the first deadline. All section editors appear with enough copies of their budgets (lists of top stories) for everyone at the meeting. Stories are described in a few sentences and, where known, their length is given. Is art (photographs and graphics) available? The budgets tell that. The photo editor's budget, by the way, is the finished photograph.

The editors agree on where the stories will go. One of the important functions of this coordination is to ensure that two sections of the paper will not use the same or similar stories and thus compete with each other. Overlap is avoided.

Also present at this meeting are the makeup editors. They learn what the lead stories will be for each section and the relative value of all other stories in the section. Because they also know the estimated length of the stories, they can return to their desks and begin designing pages. The photo editor sits at the operations desk, deciding what size to make each photo.

Throughout the day, reporters have been filing stories with their respective assignment desks. On those desks, the editors evaluate the stories in preparation for the story conference. They also check to make sure the reporter has covered the story well and hasn't missed the lead.

The assignment editors then release the stories to their respective copy desks. The chief copy editor (known as the "slot") assigns each story to one of the several copy editors. They in turn read the stories carefully, make corrections, talk to reporters about unclear sentences and bad organization, and then send the stories back to the chief copy editor, who checks the work of the reporters and the copy editors.

Once a page is designed, photocopies of the page go to the respective copy desks. There copy editors check headline assignments on the stories they edited. They then pull up a copy of the stories they edited and write headlines. Again, the chief copy editor checks the work before sending it to the production department for pasteup. Copy editors also write captions for all photographs and graphics and read page proofs.

Maintain Copy Flow

The copy editor is a primary mover behind the story. The copy editor fits into a chain usually started when the city editor orally assigns a story to a reporter. At that point the city editor might record in an electronic diary to whom the story was assigned and when the reporter is expected to turn it in.

The reporter, of course, gathers the information and writes the story, sometimes consulting first with the city editor if problems develop. In other cases, the city editor may have to prod the reporter to write the story, not because the reporter is lazy but maybe because the reporter is checking out one last fact. The city editor, given dispassionate distance from the story, can see that the reporter can still write the story and insert the fact later, something that will speed production in the end.

At the time the city editor expects the story, he or she checks the reporter's file to see if the story has been done. The city editor may check over the story, although not edit it, then assign it to the chief copy editor, who assigns it to a copy editor for editing. Before assigning it, the city editor may decide which page the story will appear on and what size headline the story will get. Those instructions are placed at the beginning of the story.

All copy editors know they can find work in a special file, and once finished with one story and its headline, the copy editor automatically checks that file to see what other stories remain to be edited. When finished, the copy editor may assign the story to a second file or may return the story to the same file, from which a second copy editor will retrieve it for a final reading. All copy editors know which stories to read first because the city editor has told them which pages will be set in type early and which pages will go late. If Page 4 is an early page and Page 6 is a late page, copy editors will read all Page 4 copy before proceeding to stories for Page 6. If no other copy exists, Page 6 copy is read. A copy editor doesn't forgo editing a story just because it is for a late page or a later edition. Work cleared early in the shift eases the pressure before deadline.

At some newspapers, the city editor can learn the status of any story in the system merely by signing into a particular file and checking its directory, which tells how long the story is, its page number, its headline size, how many times it has been edited and whether it has been sent to production. The story is assigned to production by the chief copy editor. By executing the correct commands, the chief copy editor drives an electronic typesetter that will produce the story and its headline in a few seconds. From there, a production employee takes the story to a makeup bank. If the story is assigned from one VDT to another, it is also sent to a special file, and the people in production know that stories in that file are ready to be printed. The production people then give the commands that drive the typesetter.

Meet Deadlines

Everyone who has a deadline in a news operation should meet that deadline to help produce an orderly product. Newspapers and newscasts put together at the last minute because someone missed a deadline announce their roughness to the impatient and easily dissatisfied readers and listeners. Although a newspaper's arrival in the home is not as precise as the beginning of a broadcast medium's news program, readers still expect their newspaper to arrive around the same time every day. Given that readers spend so little time with the product, a later newspaper may mean that day's issue goes unread because the time normally reserved for reading the paper has passed.

Copy editors need to worry about cash flow as well as copy flow. Missing deadlines has economic implications. Many people on a newspaper have certain jobs to do at certain times, and they report to work at times beneficial to printing and distributing the newspaper. The people who drive the circulation trucks begin work about the time the newsroom is closing. Those people are paid from a certain starting time even if the newspaper isn't off the presses. It is not productive to pay people not to work. Eventually, missed deadlines that set back production result in overtime pay, which in excessive amounts could create financial problems for the publisher. It is incumbent on every employee of the newspaper to work for the economic well-being of the newspaper lest the newspaper fold and jobs be lost.

Frequent overtime is not only hard on corporate profits but also on people's morale. The people who must work overtime grow tired of their jobs and aren't as sharp. As a result, they don't produce a sharp product.

Meeting a deadline is more than turning in all the assigned work at the deadline. Reporters and editors should strive to avoid peaks and valleys in workloads by working steadily. Copy editors who sit around chatting when work exists create their own pressure when the work piles up. The city editor and copy editors can also avoid peaks and valleys by assigning equitable workloads and by staying on top of the news flow. If some reporters are dealing with late-breaking stories, the desk should advise other reporters on routine stories to get them in sooner.

Most of the time a copy editor works in an almost pressure-free environment. Sure, there's work to be done, but if the pace is steady, the pressure is less. Pressure does mount toward deadline, which should not be used as an excuse to do poor work. The best copy editors shrug off the maddening pressure, do their finest work, and still meet deadlines.

Story Parts

Deflate Pomposity

A reporter will not always realize that he or she is quoting the gobbledygook of bureaucrats or the empty sentences of politicians or the jargon of academicians. The phrase sounded good at the time and the reporter didn't bother to analyze it. But now the story is before the copy editor and analysis begins.

Pomposity defies clear-cut rules, but generally it appears in direct quotations that the copy editor should paraphrase into something clear. For example, an academic report says, "First, many respondents indicated the desirability of understanding the relationship between the level of tuition and its impact on enrollment." That means: The report said it was important to understand what a tuition increase did to enrollment. Regrettably, the sentence still does not make clear who has to do the understanding.

Politicians are notoriously pompous, often because they want to sound as though they're saying something when they're trying extremely hard not to commit themselves to anything. Thus, this sentence:

> The senator said his proposed new infusion of assistance is needed "to offset the erosion in the value of aid caused by our inflation over the past two years."

Note how the reporter got caught up in the fog of pomposity by using "infusion of assistance." What the sentence means, and the desk should create through rewriting, is:

> The senator said his proposed aid is needed to offset what inflation has done to the value of aid in the past two years.

A bureaucrat once proposed that the best way to get the public's opinion on a proposed rate increase was to schedule "public input sessions," whatever that means. And then there was the college football coach who once said, "The element of surprise is used best when it's not expected." The desk should challenge such inane statements.

A copy editor may also find that many pompous sentences are better deleted than rewritten. But when rewriting is the answer, the copy editor should show the rewrite to the writer to ensure accuracy.

Put Life into Breathless Prose

Newspapers are no longer written for, as an editor once put it, "people who move their lips when they read," but that doesn't excuse this 57-word stifler:

> One department spokesperson who was asked about the figures that showed Americans had to work longer to eat last year than in 1974, while the average in other countries declined, said that "no doubt inflation rates were higher in the other countries last year" and speculated that wages probably rose higher than food prices in other countries.

The reader who finishes such a sentence is no doubt left breathless. The copy editor who let the sentence go into print could have created two sentences, such as:

> One department spokesperson was asked about the figures that showed Americans had to work longer to eat last year than in 1974, while the average in other countries declined. The spokesperson said that "no

doubt inflation rates were higher in the other countries
last year" and speculated that wages probably rose
higher than food prices in other countries.

The resulting two 29-word sentences still make no sense, meaning the
copy editor must query the reporter for an explanation. Some long sentences, though, can be repaired easily:

A government spokesman said the departure had
been delayed but would not say why, and unofficial
sources said authorities were awaiting assurances from
Libya, the eventual destination, that the hijackers would
be granted asylum before dispatching the aircraft carrying the hostages.

Broken in two:

A government spokesman said the departure had
been delayed but would not say why. Unofficial sources
said authorities were awaiting assurances from Libya,
the eventual destination, that the hijackers would be
granted asylum before dispatching the aircraft carrying
the hostages.

For quick reading, the best sentences are on average 17 to 20 words
long, but a copy editor should not automatically divide every long sentence into shorter ones. A good sentence derives its beauty from the
rhythm of the words, not the number.

Fill in the Holes

Sitting before a VDT pondering a story, a copy editor puts a story to a
test it must pass before getting forwarded to the reader. As the copy editor
reads, questions arise. If the story does not provide the answers, back it
goes to the reporter. And if the reporter is not available, the copy editor
turns reporter and gets answers.

Some of the questions are obvious. In a story about the suspension of a police officer for one day without pay, the question is, How much pay did the officer forfeit? Other questions might not be as obvious. A story reporting that the city council has lowered property taxes should include an explanation of what the action means to the reader in dollars and cents.

Filling in for the reader, a copy editor examines a story about a legislator calling for a law that would require couples to wait six months after filing a marriage application before getting married. The story appears complete, but several questions arise in the mind of the copy editor. Why does the legislator think this law is necessary? More important, what is the constitutionality of such a law? The copy editor returns the story to the reporter to track down the legislator and ask the questions. But if the reporter is not available, then the copy editor should call the legislator and ask. And if the legislator is unavailable, the copy editor should call some legal expert for an opinion, because the reader deserves the answers with the questions.

The day after a general election, the Associated Press filed a story with this lead: "U.S. Rep. Tom Foglietta, in a race to keep his congressional seat Tuesday, also found himself in a race to apprehend a purse-snatcher." The next six paragraphs of the seven-paragraph story detail how the congressman witnessed a purse-snatching and chased two youths. They were not caught, but they did drop the purse. The story also gives the name and age of the victim. But one thing the reader does not learn is whether Foglietta kept his congressional seat. Even though a wire service copy editor missed the hole, the local editor shouldn't have.

And there's the story about the man who became the founder and president of a frog collectors' club. The lead says:

> It all began when his girlfriend, who later became his wife, purchased an orange, yellow and green shower curtain. To coordinate, she picked up a toothbrush holder, soap dish and hand towels—all displaying frogs with bright orange and yellow eyes.

Two paragraphs later: "Twelve years later, he added, 'I still have the frogs but not the wife.' " In the six paragraphs that complete the story, the reader never learns what happened to the wife. Divorce? Death? Did she croak? Did she leave him? What happened? The desk needs to ask.

And here is the first paragraph of a two-paragraph obituary:

> Molly Price, the author of "The Iris Book," generally considered the definitive work on the subject, died of a cerebral hemorrhage Friday at Good Samaritan Hospital in Suffern, N.Y. She was 81 years old and lived in New City, N.Y.

The other paragraph details her survivors. Meanwhile, what exactly is the subject of *The Iris Book?* The eye? Flowers? The desk needs to ask.

Other holes in stories often result from carelessness. An address given only as "Meadow Lane" needs a number with it. Check the telephone book. A story contains a name with "nmi" (no middle initial). Check the city directory or some other source. A suspect's age is missing. Call the police. A direct quotation does not match the speaker's previous stance. Call the source to clarify the quote. In a story announcing that the city is hiring a new public works director, nothing was said about what had happened to the former director. Whatever the story's shortcomings, the copy editor sees that they are corrected.

Question Facts

It is not unfair to expect copy editors to know when the facts aren't facts. Copy editors are often thought of as trivia experts and as being knowledgeable in all fields, not just the humanities in which they are usually bred. One legendary editor found an error in a complicated equation done by Albert Einstein.

Internal clues should tip the copy editor to a fact error. For example, the obituary of a man who died in 1981 says he was a 1940 graduate of the University of Notre Dame. The obituary also says the man was 54. Assuming that the man was 21 when he graduated in 1940, in 1981 (41 years later) he would be 62. Since the story doesn't say the man was a child prodigy, you can't account for the eight-year discrepancy by saying he graduated when he was 13.

In 1981, *The New York Times Magazine* published an article that the author later admitted was in part plagiarized from a novel. Daniel Burstein, then a freelance writer, raised some questions about how the story got by the *Times'* editors. He noted that in one sentence the author claimed to have seen someone on a distant hillside through binoculars and that "the eyes in his head looked dead and stony." In the next sentence, Burstein notes, the author says, "I could not make him out in any detail." As Burstein observed, no one had to be an expert on the subject to see the contradiction and ask questions. The internal clues were self-evident.

Another story with conflicting internal clues comes from the society pages, where a bride is described as having received a certificate in dental assisting and being employed as "an orthopedic assistant." She worked for an orthodontist (teeth), as certified, not for an orthopedist (bones).

Then there is the example of the reporter who wrote that the date of the next general election was Nov. 10. But since the general election always falls on the first Tuesday after the first Monday, the latest a general election can occur is Nov. 8.

Sometimes, though, the error is not so clear-cut. What is the fact error in a story saying that a state's Supreme Court ruled that the state police may not reveal a suspect's prior record? The case involved an action taken by the state police, but the decision really applied to all police in the state. Realizing that, a copy editor called the wire service that produced the story and shortly after received a correction.

Such fussiness not only gives the reader a better product but also serves historians, who frequently rely on newspapers as a starting point for research. A historian can lose precious time chasing a false start provided by a newspaper. Corrections often don't help because they receive less prominent display than the error.

Get the Facts Straight

The suspicious minds that edit newspapers do not know everything, but they know enough to recognize their limitations. Good copy editors are smart enough to know what they don't know.

A story that says a jury ordered testimony stricken from the record should raise the eyebrows of a high school student in a civics class and should move a copy editor to change *jury* to *judge,* the only person in a trial with authority to order testimony stricken. The same copy editor knows that referring to the senators who represent the 50 states in Congress as state senators confuses them with the senators who convene in state capitols. A senator in Washington is a U.S. senator. Similarly, the copy editor knows that the headline "Soviet ambassador appointed" suggests someone from the Union of Soviet Socialist Republics, not the U.S. ambassador to the Soviet Union who the story is about.

Eyebrows go up again when a reporter turns in a crime roundup story and writes in one paragraph that someone forged the name of Irene Zepanski on a check and three paragraphs later that someone damaged a bicycle owned by Irene Zepanski. Either it's a lightning-strikes-twice story that needs a new lead or it's a case of reporter carelessness. The copy editor must ask.

In that category of suspicious editing is the story about the columnist who referred to wasps, hornets and yellow jackets as bugs. Checking with a dictionary and an entomologist, the newspaper's in-house critic learned that wasps belong to the superfamilies *Vespoidea* and *Sphecoidea;* yellow jackets are small wasps and belong to the family *Vespidae;* hornets belong to the genera *Vespa* and *Vespula.* Bugs, on the other hand, belong to the order *Hemiptera,* which is none of the preceding. Unfortunately, the error appeared in print because a copy editor decided to make a guess rather than check it. Said the entomologist, "All bugs are insects but not all insects are bugs." He said nothing about copy editors.

Watch for New Words Made by Typos

Many typographical errors leap out at copy editors when they're reading the newspaper, which is the wrong time. They should have been caught before publication. Some of the more serious errors are those that create new words, usually turning an otherwise serious story into a funny one. For example, when Gerald R. Ford was president in the mid-1970s, this headline appeared: "110 refugees hit by Ford poisoning." (The story was about food poisoning.) The headline writer either was making a political statement or not thinking. And from time to time, the birth announcements have listed the birth of a male child, "the sin of Mr. and Mrs. . . . ." Occasionally a newspaper will announce a "pubic meeting," which may be where the "sin" came from in the first place, instead of a "public meeting."

Countless other typos include the infamous *not* of "not guilty" being turned into *now,* and those that refer to "closet friends" or "closest friends." Then there's the bluegrass music columnist whose reference to a "mandolin picker" came out "pecker." With the copy editor now the only backstop between reporter and reader, vigilance to catch errors must be tripled. Computers don't proofread stories.

Gang Up on Double Entendres

It has been said that if anyone on a newspaper staff needs a dirty mind, it is the copy editor, who must watch for two-faced sentences. One of the double meanings is usually salacious, and that's usually the meaning the reader remembers. These headlines—"Prostitutes appeal to pope" and "Police can't stop gambling"—may get by, but a reporter who writes about a police officer who "relied on intuitive judgment when he exposed himself to an armed suspect" invites smirks and maybe an angry telephone call or two.

Copy editors must be alert for a reporter who writes "the climax of the meeting arrived with a bang when a spectator's chair broke and the person fell to the floor," because the reporter is obviously trying for the double entendre. The columnist who began his essay on turkey callers with this quotation knew he would raise eyebrows: " 'Put it in your mouth and blow,' he said as he handed the little moon-shaped object to me." The reporter who wrote, "Idi Amin is holed up in Libya with his two wives and a concubine" may have missed the subtle double meaning, but so did the newscaster who read the sentence over the air.

Many double entendres are not only salacious but also sexist. From a wire story on the Mummer's parade, a New Year's Day tradition in Philadelphia: "Women first cracked the all male Mummers ranks about five years ago." A copy editor changed the verb to "entered." A photo caption of a boat crew composed of a female coxswain and seven male rowers reported, "It was the first time both universities were coxed by women." While *coxed* is the correct verb, one wonders if it is the appropriate one. The caption writer could have easily stated that it was the first time both crews had female coxswains. Then there are these sentences from a newspaper story:

> She said the man sat on the bench in only his boxer
> shorts for about five minutes and exposed himself.
> "It wasn't long, but it was long enough," she said.

Since the direct quotation adds nothing to the story, delete it. If it had contained worthwhile information, it could have been paraphrased.

Challenge Profanity

Profanity should not be used unless it is part of a direct quotation and then only if necessary to tell the story. People who speak in a continuum of profanities show a mental defect, an inability to select original words. Remove such a person's cursing streak and the copy editor may find nothing was said at all.

One of those necessary times for printing profanity arose when the Watergate tapes of the mid-1970s were released. The profanities revealed a mentality impossible to depict without publishing the foul words of a president and his aides. The wire services marked the stories so that newspapers and readers would know the stories contained profanities. Television newscasters blipped the foul words, but as they read a direct quotation, all the words, even the ones not spoken, appeared on the screen. Those were unusual times and called for unusual approaches.

In its entry on "obscenities, profanities, vulgarities," *The Associated Press Stylebook* advises: "In reporting profanity that normally would use the words *damn* or *god,* lowercase *god* and use the following forms: *damn, damn it, goddamn it.* Do not, however, change the offending words to euphemisms. Do not, for example, change *damn it* to *darn it.*"

Put Precision into Sentences

Sentences constructed with misused words and phrases quickly fall apart, leaving behind only a rubble of imprecision. The copy editor who allows such contradictions as "about 26.5 percent" or "some 17 people" permits ambiguous phrases to becloud a sentence's intent. Generalities don't convey information the way specifics do. Faced with this phrase—"Acting on a tide of amendments at the special two-day meeting, the bishops . . ."—

a copy editor reached deeper into the story to find the number of amendments and inserted it, thus giving a more precise "Acting on a tide of nearly 100 amendments, the bishops . . . ."

The reporter who refers to the U.S. House of Representatives as "Congress" and the copy editor who does not fix it both need a civics lesson. "Tossle-capped children" may conjure up for the reporter an image of children frolicking in the snow, but the reader sees nothing because *tossle* is not a word. (The writer meant *tassel.*)

Watch out for the oxymoronic, the contradictory, as in this sentence: "The test was ended because one student did not want to be required to take an optional swimming test." If it's optional, how can the student be required to take it?

Given a public not as skilled with the language as journalists are supposed to be, letters to the editor can present challenges for the desk. A letter writer who was angry that she had missed a deadline for paying a traffic ticket complained about the delay of "receiving a traffic violation in the mail." What she got in the mail was a ticket for a traffic violation, traffic violations being hard to mail. Finally, what of the reporter who wrote that "the controversy erupted last week when the chairperson requested her to respond to published reports about her absences in writing"? How is one absent in writing? The sentence should have said: "The controversy erupted last week when the chairperson requested her to respond in writing to published reports about her absences." These and other examples throughout this book build a case for precise reporting and writing and thorough copy editing.

Do the Arithmetic

Any time numbers appear in a story, the copy editor should do the arithmetic. A reporter once claimed that a litigant in a small claims case had stopped payment at $600 on a job that totaled $1,344.67 because he felt the $810 labor charge was too high. But if you add $600 and $810, you get $1,410. How do you account for the $65.33 difference between $1,410 and $1,344.67? Another reporter explained how 35,000 square feet of office space was going to be used: all-purpose room, 1,400 square feet; kitchen, 200; restrooms, 300; activity room, 850; game room, 600; office, 150. That totals 3,500 square feet, not 35,000 square feet. The reporter mistyped the total square footage. The copy desk caught the error because a copy editor did the arithmetic.

One of the seldom thought-of basic tools of copy editing is the calculator, which allows a copy editor to easily check a reporter's arithmetic. If a story says snow removal costs are up 5 percent over last winter, the copy editor should do the arithmetic to make sure.

If the unemployment rate last month was 10 percent and this month it is 5 percent, the decline is 50 percent, or 5 percentage points, but not 5 percent. Also, the 50 percent figure says so much more than the 5 percentage points and is the preferred way to express employment statistics. Only with interest rates does an increase or decline expressed in percentage points mean more to the reader, since interest points can be translated into dollar amounts. As for the stock market, percentage declines mean more than point declines, as *The New York Times* once reported. When President Eisenhower had a heart attack, the market declined 31.89 points, or 6.54 percent. Thirty years later, the market declined 86.61 points, or 4.61 percent. It's all relative, which is what percentages show better than points on the stock market. The desk should be alert for any story in which the insertion of percentages will make the story clearer. Election returns expressed in whole numbers alone are not always as meaningful as when they are accompanied (not replaced) by percentages.

When a story says five people were arrested, a copy editor should count the names listed. A reporter could easily forget to list a name or two. Also, the desk should check reporters on how they have come up with unusual figures. One editor tells about the reporter who claimed that thousands of people had entered a new store in one hour. "How did you arrive at that figure?" a copy editor asked. "Well," the reporter said with pride, "I counted the number of people who went through the door in one minute and multiplied by 60." But, of course, there was no guarantee that the minute selected by the reporter was representative of the traffic during the hour. After all, the number of newcomers probably diminished after the initial surge. Needless to say, the reporter's figures were not used.

In general, the desk should check any use of numbers. For example, a news release from a county office included this paragraph:

> According to population figures, Abington Township has taken over the top spot as the most populous municipality in Montgomery County, with a population of 58,624, some 4,200 less than in 1970, when the township was the second most populated municipality in the county, with 63,625.

The copy editor who automatically checks the arithmetic will find a discrepancy of 801. Even if someone must be called at home at night to clarify the arithmetic, the copy editor should not hesitate to do so. The county officer who made the mistake appreciates the backstopping, and the newspaper, by not printing the error, saves its credibility from another beating.

Verify Names

A radio news reporter who was terrible at remembering people's names would greet a familiar person whose name the reporter had forgotten with "Hi, how are you?" and then slyly add, "By the way, just how do you spell your last name?" The ploy fell apart one day when the person haughtily responded, "S-m-i-t-h." The news reporter, should not have been embarrassed, though, because some Smiths spell their names Smyth and others spell it Smythe, and all pronounce it the same way.

The failure to spell a person's name correctly, compounded with the failure to correctly identify the person by age and street address, could result in a court suit. The reporter who quoted a court official as saying, "Robin Shoemaker of Pilsdon was arrested on sodomy charges" has created a problem when it was not 22-year-old Robin Shoemaker at 136 Bath Ave. but 53-year-old Robin Shoonmaker at 211 S. 10th St.

Francis (a man's name) and Frances (a woman's name) sound the same. And is that person's name John R. Nichols or John S. Nichols? The telephone book, the newspaper's files or the city directory can provide the detail. The ultimate source, of course, is the person in the story, who can be queried by telephone. As a matter of policy, a copy editor should check every name in a story even if a reporter swears the check was already made.

Verify Dates

Some would argue that the best degree for a copy editor is a history degree. Although journalism tends to focus on current events, current events come with a history.

In writing the obituary of a local politician in 1987, a reporter talked about a meeting in 1944 between the local politician and Harry S Truman, then vice president of the United States. After recounting some dialogue between the local politician and Truman, the obituary writer said: "Two weeks later FDR was dead and Truman became president."

Nope. FDR died on April 12, 1945. Someone on the desk should have checked.

Use Foreign Words Correctly

Someone once complained that the English language does not follow the rules, especially when it comes to spelling. Well, that person is wrong. Anyone who knows the root of a particular English word should know how to spell it.

The plural of the Latin *alumnus* is *alumni*. Something done in memory of someone is *In memoriam,* not *In memorium.* The plural of *criterion* is not *criterions* but *criteria.*

Spanish causes problems for some copy editors. One copy editor headlined a story about Col. Sigifredo Ochoa Perez with "El Salvador shuts off rebel Perez." In Spanish, the surname is usually not the last name, which is the mother's name, but the middle name, which is the father's name. The correct second reference is *Ochoa.* And in editing this sentence, someone inserted the italicized article: "When they dominated the National League in the late 1960s, they were known as *the* El Birdos." In Spanish, *el* is *the.* Drop *the* in this use.

One foreign language that has changed in English is the Chinese language. Starting in 1979, the Chinese government changed the system it used to translate stories into English, converting from the Wade-Giles spelling system to Pinyin, meaning "transcription." Thus, Peking, the capital city, became Beijing, and Mao Tse-tung, the legendary leader of China, became Mao Zedong. Another conversion was Szechwan into Sichuan and Honan into Henan, although some American restaurants, when boasting of their regional Chinese cooking, advertise it as Szechuan and Hunan.

Spanish names are not the only ones that do not follow English style. Asian names are also different and not consistent from one country to another. In China, a person's name consists of a family name followed by a personal name. However, ethnic Chinese outside the People's Republic of China generally use the Wade-Giles system of spelling, which also uses hyphens. Korean names are similar to Chinese names, meaning that the correct second reference to former South Korean President Park Chung Hee is Park, not Hee.

In some Asian countries, married women adopt their husband's name but not in the People's Republic of China. The good reporter, when dealing with people of a non-Western culture, will ask what their preference is rather than imposing the Western preference.

The Overall Story

Exercise Doubt

It is to every copy editor's advantage to know the frailties of each reporter. One reporter overwrites every story because he sees a Pulitzer Prize at the end of the daily press run; another is too lazy to check names; so-and-so fancies herself an expert and knows more about the subject than her sources (she never makes mistakes; her sources do); another turns in sloppy copy; still another begins every story with a direct quotation despite the general injunction against that practice; finally, another is mischievous. He filed this story:

> City police estimate damage of $150 in an incident of criminal mischief at Memorial Park yesterday.
>
> Police said a 1,750-pound gravestone was reportedly moved from its place over a grave. Memorial Park attendant Caesar Romane said he was asleep at the time it occurred. When he went on his early morning rounds, he said, he noticed the incident in the "J" section of the cemetery.

A sleepy copy editor forgot the reporter's mischievous nature and didn't realize that the story was turned in on Good Friday. The next day's paper reported that the story was fictitious and had not been intended for publication. Neither the copy editor (who removed a direct quote: "Lo, the stone was rolled away.") nor the reporter was fired, but both should have been.

Less spectacular but just as much in error is the story about a man who donated 14 gallons of blood to a bloodmobile. Eventually the story reveals that the man began contributing blood in 1953, and then the reader realizes that the 14 gallons weren't given in one visit.

There's the story quoting an athletic director as saying he has devised a scheme for crowd control at the local football stadium, a scheme that will eliminate the panic and pressure at the stadium's "portholes." Unfortunately, the word appeared four times. The athletic director knew the difference between windows in a ship (portholes) and entranceways in a stadium (portals), but the reporter and copy editor didn't.

And a beer columnist reported one Sunday that once he had written a column about German beer, noting that German law permitted only four ingredients in beer—barley malt, hops, yeast and water. But a typist turned the ingredients into "barley, malt, hops, yeast and water" and the copy editor changed *four* to *five* rather than checking.

Despite the many examples in this section, future copy editors should not assume that reporters are all a bunch of error-prone, carefree, pompous egotists who care not one whit for quality. While all humans (copy editors included) have their shortcomings, many reporters are dedicated to their craft and become upset with themselves when they make mistakes and unhappy with copy editors who don't catch the errors. Rapport between reporters and copy editors makes for a better newspaper, and both would be remiss to view the relationship as "us vs. them." Reporters and copy editors are not separate camps; in fact, they cannot function as separate camps.

Don't Trust the Wires

The editors of wire services would agree with the advice that their work not go into any newspaper without being checked by a copy editor at that newspaper. The wire services make mistakes, sometimes attributable to humans working in haste but other times attributable to electronic machines malfunctioning.

The human errors show up in such examples as the story that starts out saying four women had themselves sterilized and then refers to one in an attribution tag as "one of the five women sterilized." Here is another human error that got into print:

> The victims, in addition to Mrs. Hopp, were identified as PGW customer relations specialist Edward Brown, 47; Henry Traynor, 38; Gerald Ladzenski, 26; Anthony Kasiewski, 54; Harry F. Smith, 50; and Alfred C. Kahrklinsch, about 62.
>
> The seventh body had not been identified, although PGW officials said customer relations specialist Edward Brown, who was at the scene when the explosion occurred, was missing.

The initial story listed the six names that could be confirmed and then published the speculative paragraph quoting PGW officials. Later, officials confirmed the seventh name and the wire service updated its story by sending a new paragraph listing all the dead. The instructions with the new paragraph said SUB (for substitute), but the wire service editor forgot to add a line advising copy editors to delete the speculative paragraph.

In a newspaper without a computer system, an editor might have sent the substitute paragraph to the shop and hoped someone would put it in the story. That would account for the confusing paragraph remaining in the story. But in a newspaper with a computer system, the copy editor could easily have retrieved the story from a holding file, fixed it and checked it, and caught the confusing paragraph about the seventh victim. The speed of the computer system makes it easy to reset entire stories in type.

Wirephoto captions tend to be more error-filled than wire copy. In part, that occurs because the person writing the caption is seldom the person who wrote the story. Information in captions can get superseded by additional information, making the initial caption wrong. Thus, it is the responsibility of the copy editor to check the wirephoto caption against the most recent story.

The machine errors show up only occasionally, when a computer allows part of one story to merge with another. People reading a story about a public utility commission meeting and suddenly coming across a paragraph about a terrorist group will certainly wonder what it all means to their electric bills. What it means to the newspaper is that some copy editor did not read through the entire wire service story. Thus, while all the errors noted here are wire service errors, they become the newspaper's once they appear in print.

A final note: A copy editor should immediately report to the responsible wire service bureau any error in a wire service story so the wire service can issue a correction.

Keep Style Consistent

"Style," a beginning copy editor once said, "is like a pica. Every editor works with it, but there's always an aura of mystery over the concept." The editor was complaining because she felt her co-workers did not appreciate the need for a consistent style. "You cannot have as many styles as you have reporters and copy editors," she said. "Style is not just a needless, antiquated detail, but a way of keeping the consistency and thus the credibility of the paper alive." Consistency, she might have added, establishes order, which aids clarity. The reader who sees a reference to "110 E. Foster Ave." in one story and to "110 East Foster Avenue" in another must wonder about the reliability of the people reporting the news. The reader affixes that doubt to the newspaper, whose credibility suffers not only on Page One but in every department. A newspaper that lacks credibility speaks with a muted editorial voice. Copy editors should not only keep the stylebook by their side, they should also refer to it frequently. The best copy editors, however, learn their paper's style to avoid spending too much time reading the stylebook when they should be editing copy.

Protect Against Libel

One restaurant reviewer said a restaurant offered "rock-hard Italian bread, pricey steaks and indifferent cooking" and cost his newspaper $23,000 in libel damages, while another reviewer at another paper said of a different restaurant: "My steak, listed as 10 ounces, seemed smaller. It appeared to have been cooked in a blast furnace, which may have accounted for its scrawny look." The reviewer also said that the prime rib his spouse ordered had "a strange, unpleasant flavor." The restaurant sued and lost. If you were an editor in Florida and you looked to those court decisions to figure out what is libelous and what is not, you'd have a hard time deciding. Both decisions were made in Florida.

No editor can be certain what a judge will find libelous and what a judge will say represents truth, qualified privilege, or fair comment and criticism—all defenses against libel. But a copy editor has to have a sense of what libel is. Generally, libel is anything published that besmirches a person's good name. It does not matter if the libel appears in a letter to the editor, an advertisement or a comic strip; the newspaper is responsible for it and can be sued, an expensive proposition even before a court hearing begins. (Radio and television stations are not responsible for libel committed in a live broadcast, but the person speaking the libel is.) In the heat of a good story, a copy editor should remember that waiting 24 hours before printing a charge against someone is better than damning a person to an onslaught of innuendo brought on by an erroneous newspaper story. When a person's reputation is being maligned, proceed cautiously.

Calling someone charged with a murder a "suspected murderer" means the person is a murderer suspected of having murdered again. The safest approach is to say the person has been "charged with murder." That's a fact. "Allegedly" won't save the newspaper. A sentence saying someone was "allegedly involved" in a check-forging scheme makes the scheme a fact before a court has found anyone guilty. Thus, even a person "allegedly involved" is tainted by association. To allege is to assert without proof. Say what the person has been charged with rather than alleging a criminal act.

Ascribing any criminal intent to someone invites libel lawyers by the dozens. In a strike, the president of a union was quoted in a newspaper as saying that one of his supervisors (and he was named) had sped through a picket line and hit a striker with his car. The story contained no confirmation from the police or the hospital, yet a crime had been claimed (it is illegal to hit someone with a car). Lacking some confirmation from authorities, the newspaper's best bet was to use the item without names and add a sentence saying the newspaper could not confirm the incident. The major point behind that example is that even though the newspaper quoted someone as making the charge, the newspaper can still be sued.

So can the person making the charge, of course, but the newspaper has more money. Quoting someone accurately does not absolve the newspaper of responsibility in a defamation action.

One day, for example, a college senior complained in his college newspaper that he had bitten into a nail in the pizza he was eating at a local (and he named it) restaurant. The senior went on to condemn the manager for not giving her a refund and then closed by saying her letter should serve as "a warning to unsuspecting pizza-eating college students. Beware of nails!" In this case, the newspaper got off with an angry complaint from the restaurant's owner. The newspaper was lucky.

Libel appears most frequently in crime news, sports stories, restaurant and art reviews (that go beyond the bounds of fair comment and criticism), cartoons (such as caricatures), local government reports, and editorials and commentaries (such as satire). Stories from the police beat need careful attention. More important, police reporters need to make sure they do follow-ups. In one instance, a newspaper reported that a teenager had been arrested in a rape investigation. Later, the police changed the direction of their investigation and the person was never charged. The newspaper, failing to do a follow-up story, missed this, and the man won a $1 million libel suit. The jury said the newspaper had published false information, even though it was correct at the time, and had failed to exercise reasonable care. In fact, the teenager waited a year before suing.

At the end of a court case, a judge sentenced a convicted woman to 60 days in jail for cruelty to her child. The newspaper ran an account of the trial and a photograph of the convicted woman, only it was a photograph of the official court reporter, not the convicted child abuser. The court reporter had a good case but graciously let the matter drop after the newspaper published a correction.

All stories, of course, are prone to providing material for a libel suit, and, as Florida restaurant reviewers can attest, a valid defense in one court may not work in another. Is the story balanced and fair? The test a copy editor should try: "How would I feel if this story were about me?"

Copy editors are not lawyers, and theirs should not be the last word when doubt exists about a potentially libelous story. Nevertheless, copy editors can do their best to protect the newspaper by ensuring that all sides of a story are given, that potentially libelous material is backed up by more than one source, that the person presented in a bad light has been given an opportunity to comment, that headline and story agree (in fact, headlines lack the qualified privilege some stories get), the identification of people in a photograph is accurate. Finally, in exceptional cases, copy editors should not be bashful about consulting a lawyer. Smart publishers keep one on retainer for just such a purpose.

Respect Privacy

When editors talk about respecting the privacy of individuals, they raise the issue beyond what a newspaper may legally publish and enter the realm of ethics: What should a newspaper properly publish? What is legal is not necessarily ethical, and what some people regard as an ethical issue, others do not.

One area where privacy issues arise frequently concerns rape victims. Some newspapers have been reluctant to publish the name of a rape victim, even when she testifies in open court. The assumption is that rape goes unreported because many victims cannot stand the perceived humiliation of being identified in public. In other words, they blame themselves for what clearly was a crime of aggression and violence against them.

In the mid-1980s, a 16-year-old girl in Mason County, Washington, was raped. She said later that she had been victimized three times—by the rapist, by testifying at the trial and by the local newspaper's account of the trial in which she was identified. (Curiously, *The New York Times* wrote about the controversy and published her name and photograph. Perhaps she was victimized a fourth time.) The publisher of the local newspaper argued that the newspaper published the victim's name out of a long-standing policy that seeks to get rape out of the closet and force society to confront it and to do more to help its victims.

Part of the argument focuses on treating rape just as the newspaper would treat any other crime. Others argue that rape is not like any other crime. Journalism professor Carol Oukrop says that "no other crime is so privately, personally devastating." Oukrop has come up with guidelines for handling rape stories, guidelines that copy editors would have to enforce. Among her suggestions:

• Publish a victim's name only in unusual circumstances (death of the victim or kidnapping).

- Don't specify the location of the crime, since this could help people identify the victim.
- Don't sensationalize or titillate.

Oukrop also advises reporters to check with police to make sure they believe a crime was committed. She suggests this because newspapers might not publish the name of the victim, but they will most likely publish the name of the accused. In fact, she urges that no story be published until formal charges are filed and then followed up throughout the process. When there's an acquittal, make sure the accused gets at least equal coverage.

Part of Oukrop's advice says don't sensationalize; avoid detail that merely titillates and appeals to prurient interests. That advice may be applicable to more than just rape stories. For example, Louis W. Hodges, a professor of religion at Washington and Lee University in Lexington, Va., tells of the newspaper story about an accident in which four of six people died. The two survived in the submerged car by finding an air pocket. One of the four friends was trapped below the air pocket, and one survivor later told of the friend's hand "reaching up toward him from below the water level." This survivor said he pulled on his friend's arm in an effort to save him, but he could not free him. The survivor said he knew his friend had drowned "when the air bubbled up."

Hodges described the story as a "splendid piece, the kind editors delight in, the kind readers devour. The details of the wreck, those things that preceded and perhaps caused it, were vividly told."

As Hodges noted, the mother of the boy who died last also learned about her son's final minutes. She told the newspaper that the scene would haunt her for the rest of her life. "God," she wrote, "hasn't anyone got a heart anymore?" Hodges pointed out that some tragedies come with what he calls "innocent victims." As he puts it, "Tragedy struck them; they did nothing to cause it, and they usually could not have anticipated and prevented the bad thing that happened. They feel that they have been victimized by hostile forces beyond their control. They hurt." In effect, the vivid newspaper story invaded the mother's life. It is something for copy editors to think about, because situations such as this one will arise again, and it will fall to some copy editor to at least ask questions about how vivid the writing should be.

Privacy issues arise elsewhere. Several years ago, a woman who worked at a day care center in the Bronx, New York, was accused of molesting young children. The Bronx district attorney brought charges against the woman, a 62-year-old grandmother, and she spent a night in a police station jail, where she was verbally abused by guards and prisoners. She was formerly charged the next day. She passed a lie detector test. A few days later a grand jury refused to indict her.

By the time the case reached the grand jury, it had been sensationalized in some newspapers. They had had a field day. The district attorney looked like a hero for a few days. But, in the end, the newspapers had been used. They jumped on the story without questioning the district attorney closely. If they had felt the competitive need to publish, they could have done it without naming the woman. After all, her name was in print before she was formally charged. Reporters need to realize that public officials, especially elected ones, are not necessarily the paragon of excellence, and their word is no better than anyone else's. Copy editors need to serve as the conscience for reporters. (Five years later, the New York Court of Appeals overturned the conviction of the only teacher charged, saying that the indictment had not been sufficiently specific.)

The reporter who interviews a child who just witnessed a fatal shooting has not only invaded the child's privacy but has offered the child a model of insensitivity. The reporter who rings the doorbell of someone whose only child has been missing and asks, "How do you feel about the disappearance of your only child?" deserves the contemptuous stare that serves as a response. If, however, the parents step from their home and conduct a news conference, the right to privacy recedes (although it doesn't go away completely).

A person's privacy seems invaded when that person, as an innocent third party, reports a crime, such as rape, and that person's name appears in print while the name of the victim does not because the newspaper has a policy of not publishing the names of rape victims. Fearful that innocent parties may suffer retaliation, some news media wisely refrain from reporting the names of third parties. After all, the person reporting the crime is not the news.

It is also not fair to visit the sins of adult children upon the parents, which is what happens in this story:

> The son of a Pilsdon police lieutenant was in court yesterday on several charges of theft, forgery and unlawful use of a credit card.
>
> Harrison K. Jones, 22, of Waverly, waived his preliminary hearing and was bound over for trial on charges filed by Pilsdon police. He is the son of Pilsdon police Lt. Percival Jones.
>
> The charges involved a credit card allegedly taken from a family member in May and about $1,500 in charges made on the card.
>
> Harrison Jones has been charged with burglary in the theft of two guns, which were later sold, and he was charged with several counts of theft and forgery involving stolen checks, which he later allegedly cashed.

No connection exists between the father's work and the adult son's crimes. The newspaper was wrong to make one and publicly apologized a few days later.

Other privacy invasions include eavesdropping and publishing or broadcasting stories that intrude on someone's seclusion or that present an excess of publicity about a person's private life. A transsexual who had had a sex-change operation from male to female won a $775,000 libel award after an *Oakland Tribune* columnist called her a male. The plaintiff said the column was a "callous invasion of privacy." A *Tribune* lawyer argued that the transsexual, then president of the student body at a small college, was a public figure, a questionable status at that level.

Publishing the criminal record of someone who has paid the debt and lived a crime-free life since may not legally invade that person's privacy but will certainly not win the newspaper any respect in the community. An exception most certainly would include anyone seeking a law enforcement position. The public has a right to know about such a candidate's past because it could have bearing on how the candidate will enforce the law.

Remember Your Audience's Tastes

Community standards sometimes more than the law dictate what a newspaper will publish. In many newspapers four-letter words are taboo simply because editors believe that children will read the newspaper and learn the words. That's not how children learn four-letter words, but seeing them in print can serve as reinforcement that such words are all right.

Sex is another area where community standards may determine what a newspaper publishes. Some mental health experts suggest that society has sexual hang-ups and that perhaps the news media that publish or broadcast stories on the subject have contributed to the hang-ups.

A newspaper should avoid such tastelessness as exhibited in the headline on a story about two composers dying two days apart: "Composers dropping like flies." Or the attempt at humor when Ray Kroc, then chairman of the board of McDonald's Corp., announced that he had entered an alcoholic treatment center and a columnist wrote: "I guess this means that Ray won't get Krocked anymore." Likewise, this headline on a story about Senator Edward M. Kennedy seems oblivious to the assassination of two of his brothers: "Kennedy comes to town to do or die." On a story about a blind person, an insensitive headline writer wrote: "Okay to be blind." Another headline writer, on a story about brain cancer among workers at a nuclear weapons plant, showed a lack of taste with "Brain cancer deaths spur thinking in weapons plant." A page editor, offered a feature photograph of a shrimp fisherman off the coast of Maine, declined to use the photograph because the fisherman was wearing a hat with this message on it: "Liquor in the front poker in the rear."

In the graphic writing category, a reporter, in a story about a high school teacher charged with 113 counts of corruption of minors, 18 counts of indecent assault and four counts of criminal solicitation to commit perjury, reported that the teacher sometimes touched the penises of the boys who posed for him. Some of the six telephone complaints the reporter received suggested that he had been too graphic. As an alternative, some newspapers would have changed *penis* to *private area* to avoid offending anyone but still conveying what had been alleged.

Copy editors need to be sensitive to their readers. That doesn't mean they should automatically remove something they perceive to be offensive. But they should not let something questionable by without a challenge.

Cool Off Copy

One of the jobs of a copy editor is to step back and take an objective look at a story. Just because a reporter turns in a story doesn't mean it should be published at all, or at least that day.

This sentence raises several questions and would be better without the italicized portion: "The only legal combatant defending the Illinois law is Eugene F. Diamond, a pediatrician who objects to abortion on moral grounds *and who has a daughter of child-bearing age.*" That phrase is unnecessary. It is inflammatory and suspect. One wonders, if Diamond had had sons, would the writer have included that information?

Here is a story that needs to be calmed down and cooled off.

> CORAL GABLES—A man police suspect may be a drug user is being held tonight for the vehicular deaths of two members of a Little Havana family.
>
> Orlando and Lourdes Alvarez were killed instantly when their car was sideswiped by another car whose driver police said may have been under the influence of drugs at the time of the accident.

Right there the red flags should rise to the top of the flagpole and start flapping loudly. As the story later says: "Charges of possession and use of a controlled substance are pending, following a blood test and lab report on approximately one ounce of white powder found wrapped in a plastic bag inside White's car." That sentence wasn't even attributed to anyone. The driver of the one car was charged with vehicular manslaughter. That's the story. If the tests show something else and the police file additional charges, then the newspaper has another story.

Less spectacular is the story about a fired government official showing up at a community Victorian-age Christmas celebration. This is the way the local newspaper covered his appearance:

> The two officers were joined by two others in modern dress. One of the officers said the added police presence was because of reports that the celebration might be disrupted by former Main Street Coordinator Thomas Williams. Williams was fired Oct. 6 by Historic Gibbsville Inc. for failing to follow directions.
>
> Police officials said that one other officer had been assigned to patrol the area because Williams had indicated that he might "take over the microphone to expand upon why he was fired."

> Williams showed up in top hat and cane at about 7:15 p.m. and mingled with those watching the carolers on the courthouse steps. The duty officers moved toward the steps as Williams moved closer to the steps. However, he departed as the singing finished. He could not be reached for comment.

The next day's paper devoted an entire story to explaining why the preceding information was wrong. The story included comments from several officials rightfully condemning the newspaper for poor reporting. It is the copy editor who challenges poor reporting and keeps the results from seeing print.

Test Sources

The reporter who swallowed her pride and wrote the follow-up correction to the last story in the preceding section informed readers that the only source for the fired official's planned disruption was "a citizen on the street," a citizen that police would not identify. The moral of the story: Test sources.

The line most frequently used in a discussion like this is, "If your mother says she loves you, check it out." Copy editors, of course, don't always have the time to check sources. One chief copy editor has a policy of quizzing reporters about their sources just to make sure the reporters have good sources. The policy paid off one night when a reporter turned in a story saying that a man about to go on trial in a rape case was a suspect in 20 other rapes. "How do you know that?" the reporter was asked. "The D.A. told me," he replied. "Can we quote him?" "Oh, no," the reporter said, "he won't say it for the record." Then neither should the newspaper.

One night a copy editor received a story saying that a woman accused in the mercy killing of her mother had apparently attempted suicide on the eve of her trial. The only source supporting that was someone in the district attorney's office. Curiously, the hospital would not confirm the nature of the woman's illness.

A day later, the newspaper reported the woman's illness: She had a blood clot on her brain. And that came from the hospital. The moral of the story: Figure out who the primary source is and then write the story according to the primary source. In a medical case, a medical person, not a legal person, seems to be the obvious source, and when the hospital refused comment, the reporter should have had doubts. She didn't, and neither did her backup, the copy desk.

Bad sources turn up in obituaries and weddings. People will submit false information to a newspaper to play a joke on a friend or on the newspaper. A Pennsylvania newspaper once published the wedding of a couple that included ushers named Hugh G. Wrection and Amos Behavin. The children of the groom were named Zachariah and Malachi, and the guests were entertained by "Shalome of the Middle East Dance Troupe, who performed a Syrian folk dance." Something there should have raised the eyebrows of a copy editor. The groom, by the way, was listed as the owner and operator of "Uncle Eyeball's Mountain Travelers' Emporium." He certainly pulled the wool over the copy editor's eyes.

It never hurts to ask.

Strive for Balance

Good journalists are fair. When a story contains information that is critical of someone, good journalists seek comment from the person criticized. Some stories virtually cry out for a balancing comment or fact, and when a reporter fails to provide one, the copy editor must flag the story.

Once, in a gubernatorial campaign, a story appeared saying the incumbent held a 2–1 lead over his challenger, according to information released by the incumbent's committee. The story contained the incumbent's opinions on why he was so far ahead. But it did not contain comment from the challenger nor did it explain how the poll was conducted. When a story is deficient, the copy editor raises questions.

A group of county prisoners once raised some issues with their local editor about balanced coverage of their plight. They advised the editor on how he could improve coverage of the criminal justice system (and, no, they didn't suggest that the newspaper stopped reporting criminal activity). The prisoners said:

1. Before a trial, avoid publishing what evidence the police have, because not all evidence is admissible in court.

2. Publish only the charges and avoid much of the background. One prisoner noted that even his parents' occupations were included in a story about him.
3. Go after the defense's version of events. Too much of the pretrial publicity comes from the prosecution's side. Seek out the defense attorney.
4. Aim for uniform coverage. Acquittals deserve as much display as the original story.
5. Explain the procedure better. For example, in some states, someone accused of a crime appears before a minor judiciary official. This represents the formal filing of the charge. Some newspapers report this part of the process—usually called arraignment—as though it is part of the trial when, in fact, the defense does not even make a case at this point.

Newspapers may have policies urging balance in reporting, but it is the copy editors who must make sure the policy is carried out.

Be Alert for Duplication

Some stories, especially those on the crime beat, can come from many different sources. One example suffices: A prison inmate is stabbed and his assailant is arraigned before a minor judge who refuses to name the injured prisoner. A story is written. The state police, on the other hand, provide the particulars of the crime and another story is written, although by a different reporter. One of the stories shows up on Page 2, the other on Page 16. Similar problems might arise at a newspaper with two wire services or a regular newswire and, say, a business wire. A story on the same event moves on both wires and appears on a news page and on the business page. The failure here is due to the lack of communication between two editors. In fact, the same wire service can file two accounts of the same event, especially if it is relying on local correspondents in two different communities near the event.

Duplication can also mean the copy distributor was not thinking and failed to exploit the VDT with its split-screen capability. Routinely, the desk should question some stories for duplication, and when a copy chief suspects duplication, he or she should check. VDTs with split-screen capabilities make the checking and comparison easier. They also offer the desk an opportunity to compare two wire services' versions of the same event.

Stamp Out Stereotypes

The news media should not reinforce stereotyped views of women, veterans, the United States, people over 60, African-Americans, Jews, Asians (not "Orientals") and any other group whose image is misleadingly preserved in a narrow wedge of description. This is a pitch against isms—sexism, ethnocentrism, ageism, racism—and phobias—homophobia and xenophobia.

The issue is how the news media portray the society they report on and the assumptions journalists make in their copy about, among other things, sex and race. And the issue is discussed in an editing text because copy editors are the ones who ultimately must change stereotypical writing.

First, consider the portrayal of women. Frequently, that portrayal suggests that they are not the equal of men, that they gain their status only by their relationship with men, that they are not individuals in their own right. This lead, for example: "A Center City lawyer and one of his female clients have been arrested on warrants charging them with a variety of sex offenses, including corrupting the morals of a minor." Or this caption showing siblings Marvin and Anna Gaye attending the funeral of their father, Marvin: "Marvin Gaye III and sister Anna attend the funeral services yesterday . . . ." In both instances, the woman gets her status from the man.

The preceding may be subtle to some, but the next example is blatantly sexist and racist. From a *New York Times* story: " 'I have an unlimited supply of wisdom,' said Mr. Holmes, who was accompanied on his rounds by a striking young woman of Asian appearance." In the first place, avoid references to a man or woman's physical attributes. Delete *striking young woman* and *muscular man;* focus on substance.

Second, avoid references to race. Racial references appear frequently in crime news. One college newspaper, in a roundup of police news, reported in one paragraph that a man had complained about "an African-

American male choking and punching him repeatedly in the face and back." Two paragraphs later, in an unrelated incident, an item said, "Williams said he became involved in an angry dispute with a man who left in a vehicle bearing a New Jersey license plate." Why is race mentioned in one but not in the other? Do we assume that African-Americans are violent but don't drive cars? Is a reference to race necessary in either item? Should race be used as a description at all?

To that last question, some people would respond yes. They argue that by publishing the race of a criminal suspect, the general populace can be on the alert and help police. So they would say that it is all right to publish a story about "an African-American male choking and punching him repeatedly in the face and back. The suspect was described as being 6 feet tall." Can you imagine the residents of a town out looking for all the 6-foot-tall African-American males? Realistically, how many suspects are captured because some alert newspaper reader saw them and turned them in? Besides, eyewitnesses are notoriously inaccurate with verbal descriptions. What police have found best for descriptions is to create a composite that the eyewitness endorses and to publish the composite.

One exception to the no-race rule occurs when crimes are committed against people because of their race. If a person of Chinese ancestry is beaten to death because his killers thought he was Japanese, then race is an important element in the story. When five white police officers shoot a man after a high-speed chase and the man was an African-American with no criminal record, race probably did have something to do with the shooting and thus becomes a factor in the story.

Sometimes writers, and their editors, assume the point of view of a white male. In a newspaper essay on alcohol-dependent authors comes this racist paragraph:

> "I have a feeling that most writers write for one of three reasons—pain, fear or anger," said the playwright, who is black. "For me, it's been anger. When I was drinking, I'd collect grievances. I had this pile of news clippings from *The New York Times* that made me say, 'Isn't this sickening? Isn't this awful?' Alcoholics love to collect grudges and grievances. And alcohol helps ease the pain."

The relevance of the playwright's race is unclear.

The essay, by the way, contains a sexist reference a couple of paragraphs later. This is the essayist telling how he found subjects for the essay: "So a friend in A.A. arranged an informal seminar with three writers who are recovered alcoholics—a veteran screenwriter, a middle-aged playwright and a woman who writes children's books and suspense novels." Any doubt about the color and sex of the "veteran screenwriter"? Spurn the mentality of the reporter who always identifies African-American criminal suspects as blacks but never whites as whites and who passes off his ignorance with the line, "If they're not black, they must be white."

Ignorance also produced this lead on the story of an African-American man found guilty of murder:

> Jimmy Lee goin' to the Big House.
> Killed a man.
> Now he's going to pay—37½ years to life is what
> District Attorney Paul Carbonaro will ask.

The writer is mocking a speech pattern attributed to African-Americans who grow up in poor neighborhoods. That's racist, and the copy desk should have red-flagged it.

Other forms of racism occur when an African-American might be described as well educated or a woman performing well in a job as capable. Such references suggest that these people are not the norm, which is another form of racism and sexism. The rule of thumb: If you wouldn't write it about a white male, don't write it at all.

African-Americans are not the only ones to suffer from stereotypical writing. Several years ago, a police department reported to the local news media that someone had committed a robbery at a local convenience store. The suspect was described as a Native American. Suspicious, the local radio station newscaster called the police chief. "How do you know this?" the newscaster asked. "Because he had long hair," the chief of police replied.

Native Americans are portrayed as backward savages in the cowboy-and-Indian mode. Little effort is made to tell the entire story of Native Americans, their problems with unemployment and alcoholism, unless a drunken Indian kills someone. As one Indian editor and publisher put it: "The mass media have not been kind to the American Indian. We are either the noble savage or the falling down drunk. They have left us little ground."

Asians suffer, particularly in editorial page cartoons in which Asians are shown as having slanted eyes. This leads to the racial slur "slant" or "slant-eye." Another stereotype is the image of the Asian woman as exotic and submissive. References to "China doll" and "dragon lady" reinforce that notion. Racial slurs that may not be self-evident include "Chinaman" and "Jap." Use "Chinese" and "Japanese."

One time a sports columnist was writing a story about foreign gymnasts on his local university's team. Among the foreign gymnasts, he said, was Mario Lopez, a native of Puerto Rico. Puerto Rico is a commonwealth of the United States, and people born in Puerto Rico have the same citizenship rights as people born in one of the 50 states. So the columnist corrected himself, explaining first what he had said, then adding, "Wrong. Puerto Ricans are accorded U.S. citizenship at birth." Wrong. Puerto Ricans are born citizens of the United States. Nobody does any according. Keep in mind, too, that *America* designates two continents (North America and South America) and several islands and that the word is not synonymous with *United States.* The wire service reporter who wrote that "Cuban president Fidel Castro came to America today . . ." probably flunked geography. After all, Cuba is part of America and, as the sentence concludes, Castro knew where he was—"I'm glad to be in the United States."

Be sensitive to ethnic origins, unlike the writer of a caption on a photograph of an anti-Israel speaker. The editor began the caption with "Shalom," which is Hebrew for peace. No anti-Israel speaker would use the word, and pro-Israel people would be offended by its use in this situation.

Here is another example of an ethnic slur:

> Ten years into the Madison Avenue era, only a few law firms, and only certain kinds, use the newspapers. One will never see Sullivan & Cromwell alongside the bartending schools or high school equivalency courses. Most are personal-injury firms whose names, like Lon-

ghi & Loscalzo or Gersowitz & Libo, seem lifted from
the log at Ellis Island rather than the pages of Martin-
dale-Hubbel.

In apologizing, *The New York Times* said:

> The passage was intended to contrast "old line" firms
> with those that commonly advertise. The contrast was
> accurate, but the Ellis Island reference suggested ethnic
> disparagement; it should not have appeared.

Consider senior citizens. They too are the subject of stereotypical
writing. This example, which also shows a dangling participle, will suf-
fice: "Munching on homemade lemon cake and sipping coffee or tea,
casual conversation is exchanged. By the loud laughter and jokes passed
back and forth, perhaps with unconscious alterations, no one would expect a bunch of senior citizens to be so full of energy." Beware of demeaning and patronizing stereotypes: cute, sweet, dear, little, frowning, feeble,
fragile, gray, doddering, eccentric, senile, fuddy-duddy, Geritol generation, golden agers. With life spans lengthening and the vitality of people
lasting into their eighth and ninth decades, do not use terms that suggest
people older than 60 are elderly or slow moving or senile.

Also suffering at the hands of insensitive writers is the handicapped
person. And there is an example, for the better description is "person with
a disability" and the better description for "disability" is "inconvenience,"
because it lacks a negative connotation. Journalists should not refer to a
person's disability unless it is relevant to the story. So what if a person sits
in a wheelchair while playing a violin; the action is playing the violin.
Don't turn the achievements of people with disabilities into superhuman
efforts, suggesting they normally lack talent. Treat people the same rather
than differently.

Also subjected to stereotypical portrayal are homosexuals. The out-
break of AIDS has stiffened public intolerance at a time when compassion
and concern are needed. The news media need to be sensitive to this. A
person's sexual orientation (not "preference") is that person's business.

Avoid the Vietnam war and World War II syndrome of providing a
criminal suspect's military background to the point of creating the im-

pression that a high number of veterans are involved in crimes. That happened after World War II and did not cease until veterans' groups complained. Post-Vietnam reporting created the stereotype of the half-crazed veteran who held people at bay with an arsenal of weapons. Television writers helped fan the image until virtually every Vietnam veteran was considered a dope addict about to shoot up a town.

Journalists should challenge racist, sexist, homophobic language in their news medium. In fact, journalists should challenge any language that demeans anyone in our society. Copy editors, as the last line of defense, have to be doubly on their guard to keep demeaning language and stereotypes out of news copy. Ask a question suggested earlier: How would I feel if this story were about me? Treat the subjects of stories as individuals rather than as members of a race, a sex or an age group, and stereotypes can be avoided.

Be a Self-Checker

Except on larger newspapers, a copy editor lacks a backstop, another copy editor to ensure that mistakes were not edited into a story or that a headline fits a story or that a caption is accurate. On the third read of a story, good copy editors check their work carefully and with prejudice. They do not say, "I did it, therefore it must be right." At all times they keep their limitations in mind. Did they make a change that creates another problem? A self-checker takes the time to do the job well and to check the job once it's completed.

Sources and Resources

Bailey, Tom. "Some Precautions That May Avoid or Defend Court Actions." *APME News* (August 1984): 2–7.

Burnam, Tom. *The Dictionary of Misinformation.* New York: Thomas Y. Crowell, 1975.

_____. *More Misinformation.* New York: Lippincott & Crowell, 1980.

Burstein, Daniel. "I Dreamed I Saw Pol Pot Last Night." *The Quill* (May 1982): 16–19.

Cranberg, Gilbert. "The Editor-Error Equation." *Columbia Journalism Review* (March/April 1987): 40–42.

deView, Lucille S. "Test Your Bias IQ." *ASNE Bulletin* (September 1984): 18–19.

Hodges, Louis W. "Vivid Writing Can Compound Tragedy for Victims." *Presstime* (October 1983): 25.

Johnson, Jim. "The Press Should Show More Sensitivity to Disabled People." *Editor & Publisher* (February 22, 1986): 64, 45.

Johnson, Kirk A. "Black and White in Boston." *Columbia Journalism Review* (May/June 1987): 50, 52.

Mawson, C. O. Sylvester. *Dictionary of Foreign Terms*. 2nd ed., rev., updated Charles Berlitz. New York: Thomas Y. Crowell, 1975.

Oukrop, Carol. "Is There a 'Right' Way to Cover Rape?" *ASNE Bulletin* (February 1983): 26–27.

Rich, Carole. "Don't Call Them 'Spry.' " *The Quill* (February 1989): 12–13.

Rivers, Caryl. "Mythogyny." *The Quill* (May 1985): 7–11.

Rush, William L., and the League of Human Dignity. *Write with Dignity: Reporting on People with Disabilities*. Pamphlet distributed by the Gilbert M. and Martha H. Hitchcock Center for Graduate Study and Professional Development, University of Nebraska School of Journalism. (Additional copies are available from the Hitchcock Center, 206 Avery Hall, Lincoln, NE 68588-0127.)

Sing, Bill, ed. *Asian Pacific Americans: A Handbook on How to Cover and Portray Our Nation's Fastest Growing Minority Group*. Los Angeles: National Conference of Christians and Jews, Southern California Region; Asian Pacific Media Image Task Force; Asian American Journalists Association; Association of Asian Pacific American Artists, 1989. (Additional copies are available from the National Conference of Christians and Jews, 635 S. Harvard Boulevard, Los Angeles, CA 90005-2596.)

Skaggs, Albert C. " 'Is This Libelous?' Simple Chart Helps Student Get Answer." *Journalism Educator* (Autumn 1982): 16–18.

Urdang, Lawrence, ed. *The New York Times Everyday Reader's Dictionary of Misunderstood, Misused, Mispronounced Words*. New York: New York Times Book Company, 1972.

Ward, Jean. "Check Out Your Sexism: A Quiz for Journalists." *Columbia Journalism Review* (May/June 1980): 38–39.

―――. "The War of Words." *The Quill* (October 1980): 10–12.

Chapter 4

The Written Word

The Need for Graceful Prose

Have you ever walked through a stream with a mucky bottom and your feet stuck with every step so that you had to jerk them to get them out of the mud and move on? Then you know how readers feel when they encounter sentences bogged down by wordiness or ambiguity, or when they trip on points unrelated to the main thought. Smooth writing, in other words, equals smooth reading, an essential ingredient in any printed medium competing with television and radio, the easy media to consume. The television viewer merely sits before a moving picture enhanced with sound; that requires no effort. But reading a newspaper or magazine requires some energy on the reader's part, which means the writer must use good writing to reduce the reader's expenditure of energy.

The bridge between the writer and the reader is the copy editor, who must carve—but not butcher—each story so that it runs smoothly through the reader's mind. The copy editor works hard for the reader to ensure easy reading by deleting cliches, extraneous words, jargon, ambiguities, nondescript adjectives and adverbs. How well the whole stands up, of course, is as important as its parts.

Does the story get right to the point? Is it accurate? Is the lead smooth or does it meander and puzzle? Does the second paragraph deliver on the promise made in the lead? Does the third paragraph continue the development implicit in the lead and second paragraph? Are the direct quotations worthwhile to the story? Are opinions attributed? Is the tone of the story appropriate for the subject matter? Do sentences flow? Has the writer drawn the most out of the language?

Those and other questions should confront copy editors every time they edit a story. The errors copy editors fix vary as much as the personalities of the writers, but the principles of good writing and good editing remain unchanged, and it behooves each copy editor to observe those principles time and time again with concern for the quality of the prose and the exactitude of the message.

The good copy editor does not suffer from itchy cursor, does not edit for the sake of editing, but instead carefully, yet quickly, studies the story to ensure that it performs, that it is the concert of words the writer intended for the reader to enjoy. A good copy editor does not automatically remove verbiage without reason. A mindless copy editor, intent on saving space, would have told President Lincoln to tighten the opening of the Gettysburg Address from "Four score and seven years ago . . ." to "Eighty-seven years ago . . . ," assuring brevity but destroying rhythm.

A good copy editor knows that subjects and verbs function best when close together. Search through this example for the impact neutralized by too great a distance between the actor and the action:

> The Barbell Club, which won't be able to use the facilities during the day even though it donated approximately $1,200 in equipment to the weight room last year, also had no say in the change.

Pity the reader who must wade through word after word after word, words that don't link directly to the subject. Recognizing the muck at the bottom of such a sentence, the copy editor inverts the order, putting the verb and subject up front and close together, the better to make the point:

> Also given no say was the Barbell Club. It won't be able to use the facilities during the day even though it donated about $1,200 in equipment to the weight room last year.

Comprehension advances a big step in the rewrite, and transition is aided because *also* leads off the sentence, thereby linking the previous thought to the new thought.

Points unrelated to the main thought of a sentence fall to the copy editor's cursor. A sentence should contain one thought, the copy editor knows, and when a sentence bulges with several, the unrelated points become nonsequiturs. "Born in Los Angeles," such a false sentence might begin, "the deceased was a member of the Barbell Club." The copy editor separates the nativity from the activity and places them in their own appropriate sentences.

Words get special treatment, almost a fondling, among copy editors eager to oust gracelessness and inelegance from a story. Times have changed since copy editors lost a week's pay for letting into print one misused word, but the punishment might be worth restoring for slovenly editing.

No copy editor sensitive to the difference between transitive and intransitive verbs would allow either of these headlines: "Girl in red bikini defects Russia" and "Scared Americans evacuate Iran." Russia and Iran can be objects of verbs but not of these intransitive verbs.

One wonders who the bigger fool is when sentences such as this see print: "Lubold was almost near perfect"—the anonymous copy editor, who was far from perfect, or Lubold, who might as well be "almost nearsighted" or "a little bit pregnant" or "virtually unique." For the reader, the error besmirches the newspaper's credibility, while at the newspaper, the desk, not the writer, bears the shame. The laughter aroused by "Former President Gerald Ford breakfasted on Capitol Hill today" is directed at the copy editor who failed to see the double meaning. As the copy editor's editor later asked, "Isn't Capitol Hill nutritionally deficient?" The copy editor wisely did not respond.

The News Story

In the news story, attention focuses on various related parts. Most obviously, the lead is the key to the story. But the copy editor must also examine the remaining parts of the story to see how they fit with the lead.

Even the ending of a news story bears examination. The copy editor must ensure that news style is followed and that the context of the story is clear. Does the story flow smoothly? And when the story is not the standard inverted pyramid, what should the copy editor be looking for? We begin with the lead.

Leads

Although the inverted pyramid formula for writing news has fewer and fewer adherents as newswriting styles change, its underlying concepts are still valid. No matter if the story begins with a who-what-why-when-where-how lead or with the subtlety of a novel, the principle remains the same: Does the lead work? The person who can best answer that is the copy editor, the first tester of any story. The copy editor, although required to read the entire story, must decide if the reader, lacking the compulsion of a job, will do the same. If the lead fails, the copy editor must determine why and then return the story to its writer or apply the polish at the desk. The lead is an implied promise to the reader. The body of the story delivers on the promise.

Leads come up short or fail outright for any number of reasons. One guarantee of failure is the imprecise lead that waffles for 40 words and never settles down to tell the story. Such leads attempt to say too much and are best repaired through excision. Cut the facts not required to tell the story's main point and blend them as needed in subsequent paragraphs. In some cases, the excised facts might provide the information for a new paragraph.

Leads can present so much information that the reader feels overwhelmed rather than informed. This lead, for example, says too much; the reader is left gasping:

> FBI investigators poked through debris in a marble hallway outside the Senate chamber this morning, searching for the remnants of a bomb that exploded in the heart of the Capitol shortly before midnight, heavily damaging a congressional cloakroom and destroying priceless works of art.

That lead can be dismissed out of hand on length alone; it is 44 words. But length aside, count the number of verbs. The lead contains five verbs, *poked, searching, exploded, damaging,* and *destroying,* which leaves the reader wondering what the action was. Verbs are the engines of sentences, and the good writer uses just enough power to pull the nouns along. In this particular example, a copy editor rewrote the lead into two paragraphs:

> FBI investigators poked through debris in a marble hallway outside the Senate chamber this morning, searching for the remnants of a bomb that exploded in the heart of the Capitol shortly before midnight.
> Although no one was hurt, a congressional cloakroom was heavily damaged and many priceless works of art were destroyed.

Leads badly written become parodies of themselves and sometimes sound like the summary of a soap opera. This lead suffers from that problem and from having too many verbs: "Relatives prayed at her bedside, and her mother, the victim of a mistaken injection, lay comatose, as a premature girl took a turn for the worse and lost a 24-day fight for her life, the family's lawyer said." Simply put, the baby died.

Another parody lead: "Emergencies have been declared in two northwest Washington counties hit hard by mudslides and flooding while a woman who was swept into a lake by a 4-foot wall of water escaped unharmed after a 20-minute swim." The writer is trying to convey too much in a sentence; the copy desk should rewrite the lead into two sentences.

Leads without news put readers to sleep. The story that begins "City Council convened last night to discuss next year's budget and last year's unresolved contract with union employees" only to later reveal that the City Council raised taxes and fired the unionized employees guarantees an unread story. With the news-eager reader in mind, the copy editor reorders the story, often by eliminating the discussion angle for one of precision: "City Council last night raised taxes an average of $20 to pay for hiring employees to replace those fired for not signing a contract."

Such a lead deserves its name, pocketbook, because that's where the reader is going to feel it. Now, the story will probably be read.

Cliché leads dampen reader interest because they display the writer's lack of concern for original prose and their lack of news. "I've read that before," the reader might think when the same old words appear. Consider the family-outing-ending-in-tragedy lead: "A family fishing outing ended in tragedy when a man and his 14-year-old son were swept off a breakwater by the highest surf in eight years yesterday." A copy editor could remove the cliché: "The highest surf in eight years swept a man and his 14-year-old son to their deaths from a breakwater where they had been fishing yesterday." Removing the cliché makes the lead direct, appealing and more original.

Leads lacking comparative data leave readers suspended in a "So what?" state where they refuse to hang on long enough to see what the second paragraph says. A lead that reports the number of deaths from heart disease without comparing that number to the total number of deaths in the population leaves the reader without a yardstick to measure the information: "Heart disease claimed 378 lives in Pilsdon last year, according to a recent report from a Heart Association official." Is 378 high? Low? How does it compare with total deaths? That information is probably hiding in the story's body, whence (not *from whence*) the copy editor should dislodge it and place it up front: "Heart disease claimed 378 lives in Pilsdon last year—more than any other cause of death, a Heart Association official says."

A lead piled high with statistics is likely to stupefy readers rather than enlighten them. A story beginning "Four Clive County residents ranging in ages from 17 to 75 died in three traffic accidents within a 12-hour period" suggests the clumsy hand of a sportswriter raised on stolen bases, runs batted in, walks, and, yes, strikeouts.

Leads containing lists, a superficial check-off of major actions taken at some meeting, make the reader yearn for the lead that puts the most important action up front. A lead of lists delays the news and keeps the reader from finding out what happened. Here is a list lead from London: "Suspicious vans stacked with cages, 800 paws found on a rubbish dump and thousands of missing felines point to catnapping on a massive scale in England and Wales, a pet charity says." It is not until the second half of the sentence that the reader learns what the list is all about.

Dependent clauses at the start usually put leads into the read-me-again category because the clauses appear ahead of the main part of the sentence, the part the clause depends on to make sense. For instance: "Armed with a bat that was heavier than any he's ever handled before, Tiger star 'Slugger' Strongarm tapped in the winning run . . . ." Another example: "Because of the high divorce rate, State Rep. Jonas A. Winston proposed yesterday that the state require engaged couples to wait six months before getting married." In both, the beginning clauses bewilder the reader because the clauses lack context. "Why am I reading this?" the puzzled reader asks. Rewritten, the second lead might say, "State Rep. Jonas A. Winston has proposed making engaged couples wait six months before marrying as a way of curbing the state's high divorce rate." (Dependent clauses at the start of non-lead sentences usually cause none of the same problems.)

Leads that come up short can usually be repaired with information from the second paragraph of the story, because that's where the news often lies if the writer has failed to report first the most current important detail. For example, a person has been arrested and taken before a judge, and the judge has set bail. The arrested person cannot post bail and has been jailed. A lead that misses the mark might report the arrest, but it should report the person being in jail in lieu of bail. The jailing of a person in lieu of bail usually subsumes the arrest, the appearance in court and the setting of bail, so provide that information in subsequent paragraphs in decreasing order of importance.

Direct quotation leads, especially in hard news (24 hours young or younger), should be paraphrased on the assumption that any writer can improve on the spoken word. To be allowed into print, a quotation lead must be compelling, must still meet the number one purpose of a lead—to engage the reader. Quotation leads are also flawed because they lack context. The reader first meets quotation marks, not an attribution tag, and thus does not know who is speaking. Such leads make a reader go by twice (if the writer's lucky enough to get a second chance) in order to make sense out of the direct quotation.

Copy editors should be alert for cute leads. Oh, they may raise a smile, but the smile soon will be replaced with a question: What is this about? Consider this lead: "It's Fall, they're falling, the leaves are appalling." The story is about a board of township supervisors setting the schedule for leaf collection, hardly the stuff of rhymes.

On the other hand, when the tax collector appeared at the board of supervisors meeting to ask that all houses get street addresses so that he could reach people through the mail the first time, a reporter missed an opportunity to be bright. He turned in this yawner: "The Ferguson Township Board of Supervisors last night authorized a system of numbers for street addresses for Ferguson Township residents." A copy editor converted it to "Ferguson Township supervisors want to make sure the taxman doesn't have to write twice." Even if you are not familiar with James M. Cain's *The Postman Always Rings Twice* and miss the literary allusion, you can still appreciate the sense of the story.

That does not happen with this lead: "Students wearing the single white glove and black-studded belt popularized by Michael Jackson told the school board that a high school rule barring them from honoring the superstar by mimicking his wardrobe is no thriller." Only if you know that Jackson had popularized a song titled "Thriller" would you get the allusion.

The good lead does more than recite a story; it advertises the story's best points. When a presidential candidate spoke in coal-laden Pennsylvania, one journalist wrote, "Republican presidential candidate John Connally last night said that coal could be the key to the solution of the country's energy problems." But Connally lived in Texas where oil, not coal, is an important fuel. A sprightly lead would can the ho-hum and make something of the contrast: "A presidential candidate from oil-rich Texas said last night coal could be the key to solving the country's energy problems." That lead points out the contrast between the candidate and the candidate's platform.

Again, the copy desk needs to be alert for ways of improving leads. This lead was spurned by the chief copy editor one night, who commanded one of his rim people to brighten it: "Many businesses around the country have been affected by the baseball strike, although the Gillette Co. of Boston, the country's leading razor company, may suffer more because it has tied a promotion to the baseball All-Star game next month." Given that the story was going on the business page, a copy editor could assume that the readers would know what the Gillette company is. He produced this lead: "The Gillette Co. of Boston could be in for a close shave if the baseball strike continues until the All-Star game in July."

A time element can dull an otherwise good lead when placed out front. Newspapers usually do not report hard news older than 24 hours, so no story needs a time element at the beginning. Given newspapers' trend toward feature leads on news, copy editors have to decide if the time element is necessary in the lead at all. Thus, an otherwise interesting lead should not be tampered with to fit in a time element not crucial to the major point of the story.

This Thursday afternoon lead on a Wednesday morning story by Paula Maynard of United Press International ignores the time element and stresses the human element of a tragedy.

> Six-year-old Travis Crook, stabbed and bleeding, walked with his dog the one block to school with a message for his principal: The boy's mother and younger brother had been slain.

Editors call the preceding a second-day lead, not because it necessarily appears on the second day after the event but because it is the second lead on the story, the first having been written for an earlier edition or by the competition. Faced with a competitive situation, Athelia Knight of the *Washington Post,* started a stabbing story this way:

> It was about 3 a.m. yesterday when D.C. City Councilman David A. Clarke left a sandwich shop at 18th Street and Columbia Road and began walking home. As he reached 16th and Harvard streets NW, he said he sensed someone behind and continued walking at a steady pace.
>
> Clarke said that when he reached the walkway to his home at 320 17th St. NW, three men jumped him from behind, punched him in the face and stabbed him twice in the back. Clarke suffered superficial wounds to his back and was in good condition late yesterday at the Washington Hospital Center.

Perhaps the example shows a case of having your hard news and featurizing it too, because the headline on Knight's story makes clear what the story is about: "City councilman is stabbed outside his Northwest home." That shouldn't detract from what Knight did; she told the story from the victim's point of view, and her approach makes for a more compelling beginning than this:

> A D.C. city councilman was in good condition late yesterday at the Washington Hospital Center, where he was taken after he was stabbed twice by three men near his home early yesterday morning.

That's what used to pass for a second-day lead at third-rate newspapers.

The Body of the Story

Once the lead has taken shape, the development of the story concerns the copy editor next. One of the single biggest story organization problems stems from reporters who fail to follow their leads, fail to keep their initial promise to the reader. They instead lapse into background in the second and third (and maybe fourth) paragraphs while the reader hangs around (and a writer should not assume that will happen) waiting for current information. A news story should play up the news, what happened within the past 24 hours, not what happened two days or three weeks ago. Save that for later in the story, or for history books. Here is a story in which history wrongly takes precedent over timeliness:

> WASHINGTON—John Newton Mitchell, the gruff former attorney general who went to prison for conspiring to cover up the Watergate scandal in his friend Richard Nixon's White House, is dead at 75 after collapsing on a Washington street.
>
> Mitchell was the highest ranking of the government officials who served time for the political scandal that brought about Nixon's resignation from the presidency in August 1974.
>
> "I considered John Mitchell to be one of my few closer personal friends," Nixon wrote in his memoirs. "I believed that I owed my election as president in 1968 largely to his strength as a counselor and his skill as a manager."

An ambulance crew, alerted by a 10-year-old boy who was skateboarding, found Mitchell unconscious on a street in the Georgetown section of Washington in early evening Wednesday. Mitchell had suffered a heart attack.

He stopped breathing as he was being taken to the hospital and died despite cardiopulmonary resuscitation.

Mitchell was convicted on Jan. 1, 1975, of conspiring . . .

The story should first focus on how the man died—that's what the lead promises—then provide background for people who need detail. This organization seems more suited to the facts:

WASHINGTON—John Newton Mitchell, the gruff former attorney general who went to prison for conspiring to cover up the Watergate scandal in his friend Richard Nixon's White House, is dead at 75 after collapsing on a Washington street.

An ambulance crew, alerted by a 10-year-old boy who was skateboarding, found Mitchell unconscious on a street in the Georgetown section of Washington in early evening Wednesday. Mitchell had suffered a heart attack.

He stopped breathing as he was being taken to the hospital and died despite cardiopulmonary resuscitation.

Mitchell was the highest ranking of the government officials who served time for the political scandal that brought about Nixon's resignation from the presidency in August 1974.

"I considered John Mitchell to be one of my few closer personal friends," Nixon wrote in his memoirs. "I believed that I owed my election as president in 1968 largely to his strength as a counselor and his skill as a manager."

Mitchell was convicted on Jan. 1, 1975, of conspiring . . .

Another organizational problem develops with the multitopic story, which begins on one issue, then abandons the issue in the second paragraph for another issue. For example:

Mayor William F. Shanahan says disciplinary action
will be taken against police sergeants and lieutenants
who, angry over unprecedented layoffs, called in sick or
generally ignored prostitutes, gamblers and traffic
violators.

Meanwhile, members of Firefighters Local 69, whose
ranks also are to be trimmed by job cuts, planned to set
up informational picket lines today outside the fire administration building.

Local President John Henry said on Wednesday that
members of the Fraternal Order of Police, which represents much of the city's 8,000-member force, would
join the firefighters and march to city hall for a joint
informational picket.

"We will do whatever is necessary to save the jobs of
our members," Henry said.

He noted that the membership had voted to authorize
a strike but said no walkout was planned. Henry said he
would meet today with Shanahan.

Shanahan's promise of disciplinary action followed a
day in which officers in some districts refused to write
tickets.

Four paragraphs intervene between the lead and the first paragraph
that fills out the lead. The copy editor should make the appropriate
changes by shifting paragraphs or creating a sidebar.

Endings

Not every story is written in the inverted pyramid style, that is, with the
facts diminishing in importance as the story goes on. Sometimes a story
can have a definite ending, something that neatly ties the information
together. The copy desk needs to be sensitive to the journalist who puts
an ending on a story. Does the ending work? What might be done to make
it better?

One word of advice: Don't end a story with an attribution tag. It is
the direct quotation that makes the ending, not the attribution tag. Compare these final paragraphs and see which one ends the story better:

"If I had to depend on men to buy romance books,
I'd be broke," she said.

> "If I had to depend on men to buy romance books,"
> she said, "I'd be broke."

The original ending on the story is the first paragraph. An alert copy editor improved it immensely merely by moving the attribution tag.

Another copy editor improved the ending of an analytical story written the day Indira Ghandi, the prime minister of India, was assassinated. The story focused on the political dynasty of Mrs. Ghandi's family, beginning with her grandfather, an early political leader in the Indian independence movement, and then mentioning her father, Jawaharlal Nehru, the first prime minister of India. The original story ended this way:

> The following year, her first-born, Rajiv, yielded to mounting pressure and quit as an Indian Airlines pilot to become a member of Parliament. He too moved full time into the prime minister's residence to learn politics and power.

The copy editor realized that the ending wasn't enough, that it failed to fully exploit the theme of the story, which was the political dynasty. So she deleted the last sentence and substituted this one:

> Today, Rajiv was sworn in to succeed his mother as prime minister of India.

That sentence, provided by an alert copy editor, ties the story together. Copy editors need to be alert to every story's potential.

News Style

Presenting news to readers who might want information quickly requires the news writer to avoid an episodic bent (and then . . . and then . . . and then . . .) and to condense information as tightly as possible. Don't allow two sentences in backward order when one in news style order will do:

>   Hockton proposed that the trustees add a surcharge
>   to the Spring Quarter bill instead of raising tuition. [No
>   news so far; the trustees' vote will be the news.] The
>   motion failed, 14–7. [The news.]

Regrettably, the reporter has forced the reader to hang on to learn
the news, which is then poorly presented in a limp sentence that seems
stuck onto the end of the paragraph as an afterthought. This rewrite
rejects the episodic structure and condenses the information for a quick
read:

>   The trustees rejected, 14–7, a motion by Hockton to
>   place a $35 surcharge on Spring Quarter bills instead of
>   raising tuition.

The issue here is not sentence length but priority, of letting the reader
know quickly what happened. The copy editor who turns episodic writing into news style serves the reader well.

Context

Context problems arise on different levels. At one level, a reporter fails to
provide the context for a direct quotation. Reading through a story, the
reader encounters, "We've asked for Timothy O'Hara's resignation." The
next paragraph reveals that O'Hara is the county planning director but
doesn't explain why his job is on the line. Three paragraphs later the
reader learns it was O'Hara who hired the consulting firm that approved
building a county park on chemical-polluted land, a problem that should
have been detected before the county purchased the land. But the reader
doesn't learn that at the right moment. The copy editor thus must rearrange or rewrite the story to give the direct quotation context.

The larger context problem occurs when a writer assumes the reader
knows the history of the story and fails to provide brief but appropriate
background. The focus of a breaking news story is what happened within
the past 12 to 24 hours. But many of these stories come with history,
history that needs to appear somewhere in the story. The caution is that it
not appear too soon and intrude on the current angle.

Viewpoint

Point of view problems occur when the reporter forgets how the reader will receive a story and writes it from the reporter's perspective rather than from the larger perspective of the reader. When such errors appear, they should be removed from copy. The reporter who writes about "our weather" might confuse the reader who thinks *our* refers to the newspaper. Change *our* to the appropriate name for the area. Similarly, a reporter could unintentionally become part of a story by using the personal pronoun *I* outside direct quotations. Usually, the reporter failed to provide quotation marks, but the copy editor should ensure that *I* doesn't refer to the reporter.

The writer of the headline "Spring cold snap sends snow to Pa." also has a point of view problem, since the headline writer works for a Pennsylvania newspaper. The headline would work well in Ohio, but to reflect a Pennsylvania point of view, it should say, "Spring cold snap *brings* snow to Pa."

Fairness must be maintained; the copy editor must check that the reporter is neither under-playing nor overplaying a story. Likewise, the copy editor must function as a goad when a reluctant reporter holds back because of the fear of offending some newspaper policy. Similarly, the copy editor should ensure that the reporter did not fashion the story to elicit undeserved display from a prejudiced editor. That often puts the copy editor in the middle, but if copy editors remember that they work for the reader, they'll maintain their balance.

Attribution

Attribution tag placement rates special attention from the copy editor, who should make sure that all tags appear as unobtrusively as possible. Bury attribution tags so they're not hanging off the ends of paragraphs or not starting paragraphs in such a way as to disrupt the flow of the story. Within paragraphs, the best place is between two sentences, such as:

> "We've come to the end of the road," Herlocher said. "Nothing can go beyond March 1. That's the absolute final date."

A similar situation occurs in compound sentences, where the attribution tag fits best between the two sentences joined by a conjunction or a semicolon.

> "Michael played a great game, but you shouldn't let one person beat you and that's what we did," Boston's Kevin McHale said.

Rearranged:

> "Michael played a great game," Boston's Kevin McHale said, "but you shouldn't let one person beat you and that's what we did."

Within a sentence the attribution tag fits best at a natural break, as in this example:

> Officials earlier reported only six deaths. Eight of the deaths, they said, went unreported for a time and three people reported dead were found safe.

The preceding sentence also demonstrates a method of emphasizing a phrase by breaking the sentence with an attribution tag. By placing the attribution tag after *Eight of the deaths,* the writer puts emphasis on that phrase. The tag could begin the sentence, but *they* might confuse the reader who momentarily links the plural pronoun to *deaths* rather than *officials.* Tucked inside the sentence, the tag remains out of the way yet still functions as intended.

An ill-placed attribution tag can disrupt the flow of a sentence:

> "We were very pleased," Mitinger said, "very happy and very lucky. To win any golf tournament, you have to have a little luck."

Such placement of the attribution tag breaks the rhythm of the direct quote. The sentence sounds better if the attribution tag appears between the sentences:

> "We were very pleased, very happy and very lucky," Mitinger said. "To win any golf tournament, you have to have a little luck."

It is also essential that an attribution tag not be torn asunder. Speaker and verb should be close together, if not next to each other. This is an example of how not to write it:

> "I have a sore back and a stiff neck," Sampson, who has played in all 72 of Houston's games this season, said.

The writer of that sentence blindly followed the dictum that attribution tags should always appear in a subject-verb sequence. And that is good advice, most of the time. But sometimes a long modifying clause comes with the subject and the dictum doesn't hold up. In this case, an inverted attribution tag is the lesser of two evils:

> "I have a sore back and a stiff neck," said Sampson, who has played in all 72 of Houston's games this season.

For transition purposes, attribution tags need to begin paragraphs or appear early in the first sentence of a paragraph when the story contains more than one speaker and the writer is shifting from one speaker to another.

Attribution tags are also sources of information for the reader. They must be placed correctly so that the reader knows the source of information. This sentence suggests the source of information for not releasing someone's name is some detectives; actually, the reporter is making the statement:

> The charges involved Platt's 11-year-old daughter,
> whose name was not released, detectives said.

The only way of making that clear is to begin the sentence with the attribution tag.

> Detectives said the charges involved Platt's 11-year-old daughter, whose name was not released.

Direct quotations provide another spot where a copy editor must maintain vigilance against error. The Iranian student who refers to the United States' acceptance of Iran's former shah as "an *insultation* to the Iranian revolution" doesn't know he has misused a word, but the copy editor does and should quietly fix the error. The issue, in that case, was political, not grammatical. Similar errors should be fixed rather than published to the embarrassment of the speaker and possibly of the newspaper. Intentional language errors should stand, especially when they are used by the speaker for effect or are typical of the speaker and are used by the writer for flavor.

However, the best way of fixing errors is not to clear up the mistake within quotation marks. That misleads the reader. One editor, for example, always shifts the word *only* in a direct quote because people usually place it incorrectly. But that is false, because spoken speech and written speech are not always the same. Thus, the editor who fixes direct quotations makes people sound stiff and formal. If the sentence contains a mistake, the editor should paraphrase the sentence. The virtue of a journalist is in telling an accurate story. Direct quotations can be ambiguous or presented out of context. The journalist's first obligation is to accuracy. There is no shame in paraphrasing.

When copy editors believe they can edit direct quotations, problems arise. One beginning copy editor, told to tighten sentences, deleted the italicized words from the following direct quotation:

> "He was an average student, an *average* wrestler on the freshman wrestling team and an *average* instrumentalist in the concert band," Hoose said.

Unfortunately, Hoose fell victim to a below-average copy editor. Hoose was making a point that the subject of the sentence was average. If the copy editor felt the quotation was wordy, paraphrasing it was the only recourse:

>Hoose said he was average in all areas.

Of course, that loses the flavor of the quotation.

Finally, copy editors should ensure that tags not only appear in the right place but that they appear. Unattributed sentences in news stories read like opinion, the opinion of the newspaper. But the newspaper wants only to cover the news as fairly as possible and to keep opinion out of the news columns. When anyone on the desk doubts the veracity of anything, senior editors should be consulted.

Tone

A copy editor should also oversee the tone and mood of a story. Keep irreverence from serious stories and confine flippancy to night club acts. Remove unintended slang and colloquialism. The following sentence from a caption on a photograph of people piling sandbags next to a threatening river strikes the wrong tone:

>Building sandcastles is fun but these Tijuana volunteers are not having a good time.

Combining a fun idea with life-saving efforts does not come off well. This headline, about the fatal crash of a jet owned by the Kellogg company, should not have seen print: "Kellogg jet takes dive." The copy editor may laugh when seeing such absurdities, and that should flash the warning light that something's wrong.

Sentences and Paragraphs

Rules about sentences and paragraphs in the news media are based on utilitarian notions, not literary concepts. Journalists lean toward short sentences (an average of 17 to 20 words) because readability experts say that such sentences convey information easily. Still, don't count words in a sentence but ask first how the sentence works. That's the test. It's a matter of quality, not quantity.

Here is a sentence that runs on and on because the writer tried to link too many facts:

> According to Jefferson, the latest fossils came from a site that was first discovered in 1972, when utility work crews accidentally cut into it, "but we hadn't expected it to be this size."

The most accursed sentences of the lot are the fragment and the run-on. The fragment usually lacks a subject or verb; the run-on, as the name implies, is a continuous gaggle of words that seem to never stop. Because so many thoughts make up a run-on sentence, clarity suffers; a run-on offers too much for the reader to digest.

The good copy editor, however, does not join a fragment to a whole, or halt a run-on sentence, without first ascertaining that the "error" impedes reading ease. Fragments can effectively make a point, especially in an editorial or a column. They are not as useful in straight news stories.

As for paragraphs, the rule used to be "Keep them short," say, two sentences, sometimes three, and then only if the sentences are short. An important reason for short paragraphs is the reader. Newspaper readers, the research shows, see long paragraphs as roadblocks, and their interest will flag if they sense a long paragraph ahead. Also behind that rule was a desire to make stories easier to cut (computer typesetting has negated that reason) and to put white space among the gray columns of type.

Newspaper utility. aside, one old paragraph rule retains its virtue— the one that says a paragraph is (at the least) a series of related sentences. It is this rule that some newspaper paragraphs wrongly violate or ignore. If a copy editor reads three consecutive one-sentence paragraphs, the copy editor should evaluate them to see if they are related. If they are, they should be yoked into one paragraph. Paragraphs of related sentences make the story easier to read than if each sentence is a paragraph unto itself. Paragraphs of related sentences establish relations and made the information more understandable.

By the same token, if a paragraph takes three sentences, then the first cannot be about oil in Iran if the second is about a rebellion in Afghanistan and the third is about Muslims in Pakistan, unless the writer makes the relation clear. If no relation exists, the copy editor should depress the paragraph key at the end of each sentence to create three paragraphs. If a relation exists, then the writer or the copy editor must show it through transition.

Transition

Transition is the lubricant of good writing. The lack of it makes the reader stumble and turn away from a story because it seems to have suddenly changed topics without warning. Abrupt shifts are avoidable, although a writer might slip when writing against deadline. Then the desk must provide transition, which can improve a story faster than rewriting because one word can make a lot of words make sense. In fact, journalistic writing avoids long or formal transitions because they delay the reader who is quickly seeking information. By the same token, a story should not come off as a disjointed gathering of paragraphs. The longer the story, the more formal the transition.

In the typical news story (10 to 15 inches), the most effective transitional devices are short. A copy editor can readily change a topic on the strength of one word: *but, however, and, meanwhile.* A change in time or location can also be signaled easily: *later, elsewhere.* Geographical references make effective transition. In a winter storm roundup written for a national audience, the change of location can be heralded with the name of a town. For example:

> A winter storm pounded the Middle West today, then headed toward the Atlantic Ocean . . .
>
> [two paragraphs later]
>
> In Des Moines, Iowa, schools closed as 10 inches of snow piled on top of 24 inches left by a storm last week.
>
> [four paragraphs later]
>
> Commuters in Chicago were kept home . . .
>
> [three paragraphs later]
>
> By the time the storm reached Cleveland . . .

Each stop along the way comes early enough to alert the reader to the change in location. The failure to provide transition can make for ambiguity beyond repair, as shown in this example:

> In Laramie, a 53-year-old man opened fire with a shotgun and killed a youth after the youth threw snow-balls at his house, according to police.
> Wyoming Gas Co. spokesperson William C. Freed . . .

At first the reader may believe that Freed pulled the trigger, but what happened was the writer failed to use transition to advise the reader that the story was shifting from a slaying to a statement on thermostats. The copy desk failed for not catching the shortcoming and fixing it, perhaps by starting the new paragraph with *elsewhere*.

Starting paragraphs with titles instead of names is also effective transition. Imagine a story on Pentagon spending that begins by quoting some members of Congress but eventually shifts to get the Pentagon's version of events. If the shifting paragraph begins with a person's name, the readers won't realize that a shift has occurred. But if the shifting sentence begins, "The Pentagon's chief spokesman, Fred Hoffman, disclosed . . . ," the reader knows a shift has occurred. That's good transition.

A good writer can also rely on topics to effect good transition. Here are two paragraphs from a story about a dangerous stretch of Interstate 24 in Tennessee. Note how the first paragraph ends and the second begins; note how the writer, Justin Catanoso of the *Knoxville Journal,* went from the general to the specific.

> In an effort to decrease the dangers of Monteagle, the state Public Service Commission is planning to pull over all trucks at the top of the mountain, inspect the vehicles and the drivers, and remind them that 35 mph is the downhill speed limit.

> Excessive speed was a contributing factor in more than 70 percent of the fatal accidents, according to records provided by the Tennessee Highway Patrol.

Repeating the word *speed* also aided transition. Repetition of key words is an effective transitional device. The journalist who won't use the same word twice but instead seeks out every synonym does not do justice to clarity. In such writing, *rainstorm* becomes a *torrent* becomes a *gusher* becomes *cloud emptier* and so on. A copy editor can effect good transition by repeating *rainstorm* rather than allowing the various synonyms to stand.

Avoid jarring the reader. Here are two paragraphs from a talk about suicide. After the speech, a student named Janet stood up and talked about the time she had attempted suicide. One journalist covering the talk used the story of Janet as his lead and then switched to remarks by the speaker. But he did it clumsily, as this example shows:

> Janet did not succeed in ending her life, but she did discover that her problems could be solved and that living was the answer.
> Dr. Renae Grant, a clinical psychologist at the University's Center for Psychological Services, told the same audience that if people are aware of the warning signs of suicide, more people like Janet may receive help.

The change from Janet to Grant can be done more smoothly by rewriting the second paragraph. This is what a copy editor did:

> More people like Janet may receive help if people are aware of the warning signs of suicide, according to Dr. Renae Grant, a clinical psychologist at the University's Center for Psychological Services.

With the rewritten paragraph, the story's focus shifts smoothly from Janet to Grant.

Transition bridges thoughts, sentences and paragraphs, and copy editors need to be good bridge builders.

Other Writing Styles

Not every article in a newspaper is written in the standard inverted pyramid style. A good newspaper also contains in-depth articles, feature stories, editorials, columns, entertainment and recreation news, reviews of books, theaters and restaurants, and profiles of people in the news. The writing style used for each can be different. That, however, should not detract from their value to the reader. The work is still journalism and should be produced under the highest standards possible. All copy in a newspaper should as accurate as hard news and deserves as much attention from the copy desk.

When dealing with other story types, copy editors must recognize that they are dealing with writing of a different form and probably of a different intent. Granted, all material in a newspaper (even advertisements) aims to communicate, but where hard news may provide timely, limited-use information, other news can cover a range from entertainment to persuasion.

Whatever writing style a reporter uses, a copy editor bears the ultimate responsibility for the success or failure of that style. The copy editor works carefully to avoid tramping on a writer's style while ensuring that the story is clear to the reader. Stories not produced against the tight deadline of hard news come in different forms and temperaments, which can cause problems in the hands of the unskilled. An inept writer, far from creating what some would loosely call a work of art, can instead produce a parody of literature. The copy editor must watch for such mistakes, beginning with the lead. Here is the beginning of an in-depth article:

> *Helen is a lady with a pleasant personality who always has the time, it seems, to take time out from her canasta games to speak with friends and visitors at the Polk Senior Citizens Center.

Although 84 years of life have taken away some of her hearing, they have not robbed her of the firmness in her voice as she fondly recalls earlier days growing up in Polk and watching the town grow with her.

As a senior citizen and a retiree, she lives on a fixed income but still manages a comfortable life as a tenant in a downtown high-rise apartment building.

By now the reader must imagine this story's focus is senior citizens. The writer has certainly given that impression. Here is the next paragraph:

In the midst of this picture of tranquility, however, a gray cloud hangs overhead, a harbinger of potential problems. Helen's apartment building is "going condo."

A couple of paragraphs later, this sentence appears: "This is not a scene from a soap opera."

But the writing is. For the writer has gotten off track, has been told to write a feature lead and thinks that such a lead is merely an introduction of one of the characters in the story. The writer has attempted to make drama where pathos exists, and has created a parody instead. The desk should send such a story back to the writer with advice on how to rewrite it.

What has happened has been the adaptation of literary techniques. Journalists strive for drama, for dialogue (rather than just direct quotes), for concrete images, for detail that puts the reader on the scene. Such pure intentions, however, are not without their flaws, for the writer bent on using literary techniques often uses them for their own sake rather than for the sake of telling the story. The result is a lot of irrelevancy. With apologies to the late novelist John O'Hara, this example:

His pin-striped tan vest nicely setting off his neatly cuffed light blue shirt and brown polka-dotted tie, Francis S. Novinski was not alone as he sat in his chair behind his desk in the expansive, windowless executive office of the Schuylkill-Carbon Agency for Manpower (SCAM) in Gibbsville the other morning.

But neither was he visibly apprehensive as he coolly eyed three Gibbsville Standard reporters who were quizzing him on the intent of his newest brainchild, the Schuylkill Comprehensive Management Corporation (SCMC).

The impression he wanted to convey was one of self-confidence. If there was the slightest sign of nervousness, it was in the crossing and recrossing of his legs.

His angry demeanor of the afternoon before, when he was first questioned on the less than easily comprehended SCMC fiscal management plan that he had submitted to the county as a possible remedy for its money woes, had disappeared.

Novinski leaned forward to answer some questions, swiveled or relaxed backward while responding to others. His "this is my turf" air was evident as he defended the SCMC concept, even though some of his comments appeared to be nebulous and contradictory.

All the story lacks is blue cigarette smoke wafting its way ceiling-ward and fedora-wearing tough guys Jimmy Cagney and George Raft in the roles of hard-hitting, inquisitive *Standard* reporters. Most of what the writer of the preceding has offered is not relevant to the main point of the story, which is an explanation of Novinski's proposal to solve the county's money problems. Any taxpayer would want to know more about solving money problems and less about Novinski's wardrobe and nervous habits. Again the copy editor sends the story back to the writer with suggestions for rewriting.

Detail in a story is fine, but it must have some bearing on the story. Why mention that the subject of a story chain smokes unless that person is a coal miner with black lung disease, which, like cigarette smoking, impairs breathing, or that person heads a fund-raising campaign to eradicate lung cancer? The details must say something germane about the people in the story. If they do not, the copy editor should remove them.

Here is a lead in which the writer did not let the detail speak for itself:

> TUCSON, Ariz.—In 1981, their lives were simple and quiet. Pennsylvania native John Fife was the preacher at a small barrio church on Tucson's dusty south side. Jim Corbett, a graying anti-war activist, was teaching desert goat ranchers how to improve milk production.

The copy editor looked at the lead and wondered if it was necessary to press the point, given that the detail said it all. So he removed most of the first sentence and linked the remainder to the second sentence. This was the result:

> TUCSON, Ariz.—In 1981, Pennsylvania native John Fife was the preacher at a small barrio church on Tucson's dusty south side. Jim Corbett, a graying anti-war activist, was teaching desert goat ranchers how to improve milk production.

The chief copy editor applauded the work, telling the copy editor that he had "removed the talkie, and left in the picture."

Another copy editor lacked that good judgment. Apparently suffering from an aversion to colors and mood, the editor removed the italicized words in the following:

> NEW YORK—As Dr. Seuss, he can converse in private with the Lifted Lorax, a roly-poly *brown* creature with a *yellow* walrus mustache, or drip a nasty *green* slime on Bartholomew Cubbins.
>
> As Theodor Geisel, he grumped *gently* about the hoopla over his special Pulitzer citation.

The copy editor must recognize when to let a story alone and when to help a story along. Here are the first three paragraphs of a front-page story from *The New York Times*.

WHY, Ariz.—It was the sweetest and gentlest of desert evenings, pitch black except for a sliver of new moon and the light from a hundred thousand stars. Nearby, a coyote scampered among the stately organ pipe cactuses, its occasional mournful howl slicing the silence like a jagged knife.

Presently the stillness was broken by a softer sound, a brief, two-toned whistle. For half a minute there was nothing, then an identical whistle was heard from beyond the rise, followed by a flash of light and an answering flash, the signal that the way was clear. Within seconds, shadowy figures emerged from the desert. Smiling and talking softly, they gathered in a circle near the little-used highway.

After a moment, Bernabe Garay stepped forward. A dignified, cheerful man with a fondness for battered hats, "Don Berna" had led the others here: by bus, third class, from their cloud-high, stone-poor village in the Sierra Madre; by pickup truck, at danger rates, from the border town of Sonoita to the gap in the barbed wire where, a few hours earlier, at nightfall, they had become illegal aliens; on foot, pressing hard, wary of rattlesnakes and border patrols, to a prearranged pickup point here in the Arizona desert. As it would prove, they had yet to face the greatest obstacle in their journey in search of work in the citrus groves around Phoenix.

The writer, John M. Crewdson, has definitely chosen a literary, but factual, start for his story, which a copy editor helped by simply headlining it, "The Illegal Odyssey of Don Bernabe Garay." The package comes off as a short story.

Here is another lead, this one on a sidebar about the funeral of an undercover narcotics investigator. The story, written by Doris Wolf, appeared in the *Finger Lakes Times* of Geneva, N.Y.

BUFFALO—It was a day the brave men cried. They came, almost 3,000 of them, to salute a fallen comrade, a man some had worked or trained with, but most never knew.

It was enough that he wore the uniform. They came to bear witness to undercover narcotics investigator

Robert Van Hall, a former Waterloo and Geneva area resident who was killed in a shotgun blast while on a drug investigation in Corning Friday night.

The men wore the somber gray uniforms of the New York State Police, the blue of the Massachusetts State Police, the high brown leather laced up boots of the Rhode Island troopers, the crimson red jackets of the Royal Canadian Mounted Police, the earthy brown of the N.Y. State Department of Environmental Conservation. They wore shoulder patches that read California, Illinois, Toronto, and Border Patrol.

Their badges, silver or gold shields or stars, were bisected with strips of black tape in official mourning.

The uniformed police stood in sharp contrast to Van Hall's fellow plainclothesmen, who wore beards, mustaches and trench coats.

A copy editor must also know when to ignore a rule, such as the one that requires identification right after a person is named. In the following story from the late *Philadelphia Bulletin,* identifying the person when his name first appears would not only make Warren Froelich's lead clumsy but would get in the way of the story:

John A. Carr was virtually speechless.

A web of scar tissue, created by massive doses of radiation used to treat his cancerous larynx, tied his two vocal cords together so he could barely speak above a whisper.

What's worse, the web covered almost half his voice box, making it difficult for him to breathe.

Doctors told him his only option was complicated surgery, in which his throat would have to be slit, the web cut away, and a plastic triangle bolted in place between his two vocal cords until they healed.

The procedure would have involved a two-week hospital stay and cost more than $14,000.

But then Carr was told about laser surgery. Soon, his web was literally vaporized through his mouth during a half-hour procedure at Montgomery Hospital in Norristown, Montgomery County.

> That night he felt no discomfort, no swelling and saw no blood. His throat—which remained uncut—felt so good, he ordered doughnuts, crackers and a cola, which he ate with no ill effects. He checked out of the hospital the following day.
>
> Three weeks later, Carr, president of the Suburban Bank North in nearby East Norriston Township, was anything but speechless. His voice had returned.

As it turns out, the subject of the story is a banker, but his job has nothing to do with the main point of the story—laser surgery. The copy editor who read the story followed a higher rule—common sense.

One effective writing technique tells the story from the subject's point of view. That requires extensive research on the reporter's part, but the result can be very compelling. Sometimes reporters obtain the information, but fail to exploit it. An anecdote deep in a story may be just the thing to begin the story; the copy editor should look for an appropriate anecdote and in consultation with the writer move it forward. (See Chapter 7, "Consultative Editing.")

The subject matter frequently lends itself to an above-average telling of a story. Testimony in a trial reads better when presented in the way it was given in court rather than in the inverted pyramid form that upsets the suspense. Knowing where to begin the story is also important; the writer must pick up on the story just as it is ready to explode. Anita DiBartolomeo of the *Bucks County* (Pa.) *Courier Times* wrote this story against a very tight deadline one morning:

> In bone-chilling detail, a sobbing Loretta Todt yesterday described to a Bucks County Court jury how she had dozed off watching television last March 19 and awoke as a man crept onto her bed, grabbed her by her nightgown and shot her in the eye.
>
> Mrs. Todt, speaking softly in a cracking voice as tears streamed down her face, said she saw another person standing in the darkened bedroom as her assailant grabbed her.
>
> Mrs. Todt said she was lying in bed, enjoying the television program "Vegas" the night she was shot.

"The next thing I know is that I'm on the bed and there's somebody that's on the bed with me," she said. "The person was sitting on my right side there with me. The man was holding me like this (grabbing at her blouse).

"I heard a thumping sound in which my head went like this," she said, throwing her head to the side. "The last thing I remember is getting up. My head was really hurting . . . I saw the blood all over my pillow, all over the sheets of my bed and just kept thinking 'My head, it hurts.'

"I was looking in the (bathroom) mirror and I just kept seeing my head and the blood and it was all down the front of me. It was on my night gown," she said as she sobbed. "I came downstairs . . . I looked, my car was gone. I remember coming into the kitchen area to see what time, what night, where Bob was . . . The clock said 11:15 (p.m.) . . . Then it dawned on me. I knew it was Wednesday night, I knew Bob wasn't there."

Mrs. Todt said her 5-year-old son Anthony came downstairs after she had called her neighbors for help. "He was totally wide awake," she said as her 83-pound frame was wracked with sobs.

The frail, petite woman testified in defense of her husband, Bensalem special education teacher Robert Todt, 27, who is charged with plotting the murder attempt by hiring John Chairmonte, an admitted drug addict and former learning disabled student, to kill her. Mrs. Todt, 26, lost her left eye in the shooting.

When asked if she thought her husband was involved in the crime, Mrs. Todt replied, "What I believe is what I believe and I know my husband did not do this."

Not only should the reporter be commended for knowing how to write this story but the copy desk deserves a pat on the back for not insisting that the reporter rewrite it in the standard inverted pyramid.

In editorials, copy editors should ensure that the writer's main point is clear, that the point is made without stridency, and that erudition in the writer's style does not come off as condescension in the reader's mind.

In columns, copy editors should remove the personal pronoun *I* whenever it intrudes on the main point. For example, a columnist can say

"War is immoral." Since the columnist's name appears on the column, readers know they are reading the columnist's opinion. Columns, especially those written by local people for small dailies or weeklies, are sometimes folksy to the point of parody, and the desk should warn the columnist when that is happening. Some columnists need to be steered away from some subject matter (their personal lives) and toward more interesting subjects (other members of the community).

Profiles should not be just biography. If a reporter turns in such a profile, the desk should send it back with advice on how to improve it. Most likely, a copy editor can tell the writer to talk to some of the subject's friends (and enemies) in order to learn more about the subject. Direct the reporter to people who know the subject well.

The sports page represents the greatest potential for good writing and the greatest reality of bad writing. Sportswriters have long had more freedom than most writers in other sections of the newspaper, yet some sportswriters have spurned their journalistic mission and produced cliché-filled cheerleading articles. If boosterism and clichés don't do for some sportswriters, synonyms do, for the sports hack does not like to use the same word twice and will go to any length to avoid repeating a word. Some people believe that calling a left-handed pitcher a southpaw is good style; infrequent readers, though, must scratch their heads when facing sports page synonyms. The desk must clean up the copy. In all this, the copy editor and the reporter should remember that stories are written for readers, not for writers. In a contest between the reader's enjoyment and the writer's ego, the writer's ego should take second place from the beginning.

No Story Is a Formula

Unfortunately, some people have developed the attitude that a story for a newspaper or a broadcast can be written or edited only one way. Editors addicted to formulas count not only the number of words in sentences but the number of syllables in words. Four syllables or more and a word is out. No lead can be longer than 15 words. A 16-word lead? Rewrite it.

Those same editors insist that the inverted pyramid style of newswriting be followed to the point of absurdity, absurdity being the turning of an interesting story into a dull one. The inverted pyramid is functional and utilitarian, but editors should regard it as the basis for newswriting, not as the form all newswriting must take. The narrative approach to newswriting, especially with stories not of a breaking nature, may be the salvation of a print medium facing competition with television, Home Box Office, Teletext, specialty magazines and home computer terminals. Not only will some rules be broken; survival may dictate that they be discarded.

Similarly, the advice given in this chapter, in fact, throughout this book, should be measured against common sense. Function should dictate form. If the inverted pyramid works best in a story, use it. By the same token, the narrative approach to story telling may not work if the result is too long to engage the reader on the run. All rules require the copy editor to blend the practical and the theoretical with experience to learn what works best.

Sources and Resources

Babb, Laura Longley, ed. *Writing in Style.* Boston: Houghton Mifflin, 1975.

Berner, R. Thomas. *Writing Literary Features.* Hillsdale, N.J.: Lawrence Erlbaum Associates, 1988.

Clark, Roy Peter. "A New Shape for the News." *Washington Journalism Review* (March 1984): 46–47.

Clark, Roy Peter, ed. *Best Newspaper Writing.* St. Petersburg, Fla.: Modern Media Institute, annually 1979–1984.

Clark, Roy Peter, and Donald Fry, eds. *Best Newspaper Writing.* St. Petersburg, Fla.: Modern Media Institute, 1985.

Currie, Phil. "Greater Effort in Features Sections Can Awaken These Sleeping Giants." *Editorially Speaking* 40, no. 8 (September 1986).

Fry, Don, ed. *Best Newspaper Writing.* St. Petersburg, Fla.: Poynter Institute for Media Studies, 1986, 1987, 1988.

Ghiglione, Loren, ed. *Improving Newswriting.* Washington, D.C.: American Society of Newspaper Editors, 1982.

Ginn, John. "Poor Headlines, Cutlines and Leads Can Spook Fickle Readers." *Presstime* (October 1987): 34–35.

Lanson, Gerald, and Mitchell Stephens. "Jell-o Journalism: Why Reporters Have Gone Soft in Their Leads." *Washington Journalism Review* (April 1982): 21–23.

Chapter 5

Tightening Copy

Spare the Reader

Nobody enjoys listening to someone at a party tell a story in 10,000 words when the storyteller could have made the point in 250 words. Newspaper readers, like everyone else, don't like their time taken up with word-inflated stories. A journalist must compress the most information into the least space and time and do it clearly. Every story, whatever its news medium, should be written as tightly as possible. The goal should be: Leave not one extra word for the desk to remove.

The copy editor should prune any word, detail or bulky phrase that would slow the reader or listener. The process of carefully removing extra words and reshaping sentences to condense the message is called bleeding. It is a challenging job. But extra words mean fewer stories; fewer stories make the news package less interesting. The copy editor aims to produce the tightest, fullest package possible, whether it's a weekly newspaper or network news.

Here's a 39-word sentence that can be reduced by almost 50 percent:

> The bomb squad went to the scene and removed the grenades, placing them inside a bomb container and hauling them to the Philadelphia Police Academy in Northeast Philadelphia, where they were temporarily put in a bomb pit, police said.

Let's make one pass with the cursor:

> The bomb squad removed the grenades, hauling them in a bomb container to the Philadelphia Police Academy in Northeast Philadelphia, where they were temporarily put in a bomb pit, police said.

That pass reduced the sentence to 31 words. Another pass will get it down to 25:

> The bomb squad removed the grenades to the Philadelphia Police Academy in Northeast Philadelphia, where they were temporarily put in a bomb pit, police said.

The final pass will reduce the sentence to 21 words:

> The bomb squad put the grenades temporarily in a bomb pit at the Philadelphia Police Academy in Northeast Philadelphia, police said.

The principle behind the editing of that sentence can help a copy editor in any situation. Simply put, the copy editor needs to ask what action (verb) subsumes all other actions. That verb then carries the sentence. Is it necessary to say that the bomb squad went to the scene? that the squad placed the grenades into a container? that the squad hauled the container to a pit and dumped the grenades into the pit? All the reporter needs to say is that the bomb squad put the grenades in a pit.

Here is another example:

> A college graduate, he went to Boston College, where he earned a bachelor's degree in economics.

So much of that sentence is unnecessary. Here is a rewrite:

> He earned a bachelor's degree in economics from
> Boston College.

Subsumption is but one of many principles behind the tightening of copy. The remainder of this chapter explains how to identify and excise wordiness, make sentences direct, strengthen weak verbs, remove the passive voice where appropriate, eliminate redundancies, omit the obvious and reduce prepositional pile-up.

Remove Verbosity

Unnecessary wordage plagues all members of the news team, from the political columnist to the sportswriter. It is even more evident in the broadcast media when anchors and commentators work without scripts and lack an opportunity to edit their speech. The best, though, are skillful enough to speak tightly without a script.

Examples of verbosity include *on the grounds that* for *because* and *in the intervening time* for *since*. Related errors include verbs with unnecessary particles appended to them, such as *continue on, follow after, miss out, ponder over, slow down, slow up, cancel out, revert back, raise up, slim down, head up, check out*. They are better reduced to one word. Similarly, *take into consideration* equals *consider*. The problem also arises with modifiers. *Game-winning run* equals *winning run* and *three separate buildings* equals *three buildings*.

Make Sentences Direct

Indirect writing manifests itself in sentences containing *it is, there is, there are*. Those phrases can't always go, but not cutting them is the exception. In addition to reducing sentence length, the copy editor who cuts such phrases also strengthens the sentences.

Compare the following sentence pairs; the second of each pair is shorter and stronger:

There are 42 gallons per barrel.
A barrel contains 42 gallons.

As of this morning, there had been only one artist who canceled the trip.
As of this morning, only one artist had canceled the trip.

There is no tangible evidence to back up the account.
No tangible evidence backs up the account.

There is a possibility that the U.S. Customs Service may charge Harrison with smuggling.
The U.S. Customs Service may charge Harrison with smuggling.

It was the second such shooting incident in a little over a month.
The shooting was the second in little over a month.

There is no death penalty in Panama.
Panama has no death penalty.

Copy editors will find plenty of indirectness because such sentences come easily under the pressure of writing against deadline. However, such sentences are easy to repair, and copy editors should do so whenever possible.

Eliminate Conventional Information

Information that readers know simply because it is part of their culture can be deleted. Typically in accident and fire stories, reporters will write or say, "City police, *who investigated the accident,* said the driver fell asleep at the wheel" and "Ladder Company No. 6, *which responded to the alarm,* helped contain the blaze within a half-hour." If the police made the statement and if the firefighters fought the blaze, they had to have investigated or responded. It should go without saying.

Similarly, "The dentist cleaned out the cavity *with a drill*" and "Firefighters fought the blaze *with water*" contain unnecessary details. When a dentist doesn't use a drill or firefighters don't use water (which can happen), then it might be newsworthy. Otherwise, the tools of most trades are fodder for the editor's cursor.

Strengthen Weak Verbs

Any time actionless verbs appear, a copy editor should see if they can be replaced with strong verbs. The lead that begins "Four people *are* dead as the result of automobile accidents . . ." gains strength when changed to "Four people *died* in automobile accidents. . . ." To say "The city *has* no good water supplies" means "The city *lacks* good water supplies." "He said he *had* a poor start this year" means "He said he *started poorly* this year." With a strong verb, the preceding sentences shed their mealy-mouthed image.

Oust the Passive Voice

The passive voice (any form of *to be* plus a verb's past participle) is one of the most unsuitable constructions for newswriting in the English language because it hides the subject of a verb, that is, the newsmaker. Consider this lead:

> The awarding of contracts to two firms for supplying furnishings for county-contracted services *was delayed* by the country administration Thursday until *it is determined* who will own the equipment.

In the first case, the passive voice buries the identification of the delayer, and in the second, the passive voice enables the lazy journalist to avoid telling who will make the determination. Journalists should report the news, not hide it. The active voice rewrite adds a fact and is still tighter than the original:

> The county administration Thursday delayed awarding contracts to two firms for supplying furnishings for county-contracted services until the county controller determines who will own the equipment.

In the original, the controller's role hadn't surfaced until the fourth paragraph of the story.

Cut Weak Phrases

The flexibility of the English language allows its users to say the same thing in different forms. The copy editor must decide if the form chosen best suits the pace. Often weak phrases can be converted into nouns: "Seven people *who were at the party* were treated at the hospital" becomes direct when recast as "Seven party-goers were treated at the hospital."

Get the Right Word

Journalists can't survive without words. And when they use the wrong words, they threaten their own survival and cheapen the coin of the realm. One wire service reporter wrote:

> The regime admits that 5,000 have been interred since martial law was imposed, but reports reaching the West say 10 times that number have been seized.

As the closing verb should reveal, the regime had not buried 5,000 but had interned them, that is, put them in jail.

Putting quotation marks around a misuse of a word does not excuse the misuse:

> University police told the department that judging the degree of lighting depends on a person's frame of reference.
> "It's objective," said Bob McNichols, crime prevention supervisor.

Sorry, Bob; if you accept an individual's frame of reference, it's subjective.

Then there's the reporter who wrote about "the 'vanishing art' of telegraphy—sending messages over wires in Morse code." Unsure of herself, she even put *vanishing art* in quotation marks. This old Navy radio-man says telegraphy is a skill, not an art.

In a newspaper strike story, a journalist wrote:

> Teamsters drivers, topographers, the Newspaper Guild and the mailers who rejected the four-year pact last Friday plan to reconsider the contract today.

But let us hope they invite the typographers, the people who set type, rather than the people who specialize in the surface of a region.

Writing from Orlando, Florida, a sportswriter said:

> Johnston, marred in a recent slump which saw his average dip into the .230s, slapped four singles and knocked in three runs Wednesday as the Knoxville Blue Jays defeated the Orlando Twins, 9–3, in Southern League Baseball.

It must have been the Southern accent spoken into a Yankee ear, my correspondent suggests, that turned *mired* into *marred*. But an accent can't be blamed for a reporter's error when Joe Namath did his first broadcast for ABC: "Ironically," the reporter wrote, "Namath's first telecast for ABC was last summer on the day he was inducted into the Hall of Fame." Sorry. The events were coincidental but hardly ironic.

Journalists fracture words more than they should, and the copy desk needs to pay attention. One journalist wrote about *imminent domain* for *eminent domain;* another used *bacon soda* for *baking soda;* another decided that *duplicitous* meant *duplicative;* another described a *non-denominational* meeting as *non-dimensional;* and still another decided that *cocking* was the word to use for *caulking.* An obituary writer at the same newspaper listed a dead person's final resting place as the "Sylvan Heights *moslem*" instead of *mausoleum.* Some writers confuse *either* (one or the other) with *each* (both). And finally there is confusion between *eager* and *anxious:* some journalists don't understand that *eager* conveys a certain fever pitch, a desire, if you will, while *anxious*—think of *anxiety*—suggests concern. The easiest way to remember the difference is to memorize Berner's lament for middle-aged couples: "When you're no longer eager, it's time to get anxious."

In the meantime, get the right word.

Watch for Redundancies

Reading a story written as follows would be tiring: "The *fiery* flames burned the center *core* of the building where vandals earlier this month had *intentionally* destroyed some offices." The italicized words are redundant because their meanings are inherent in other words—all flames are fiery, the center is the core, vandals act intentionally.

If a person has *sufficient enough time,* that person can just as easily have *sufficient time* or *enough time.* Watch for the reporter who writes that a judge will "hear oral arguments" when the reporter could have written, "The judge scheduled oral arguments." Obviously oral arguments are heard. Pay attention for sportswriters who say a football player *quickly sprints.* Until coaches develop slow sprinters, quick sprinters are all they have, and all they really want. And be careful of the bank that offers *free gifts* for a large deposit; after all, if it isn't free, it isn't a gift. And if your editor offers you an *added bonus,* note that a bonus *is* something added. But remember to collect it first.

Journalists, writing on deadline, don't always look at the finer edges of their work. That's where the desk comes in. When someone wrote, "Previously, she has been a teacher, administrator and volunteer," the desk should have realized that the verb *has been* makes *previously* unnecessary. Likewise, this wire service sentence raises some questions:

> The report of a cease-fire agreement was leaked from a closed session of Lebanon's national reconciliation conference today.

Maybe *closed* provides emphasis, but one still wonders how a story would be leaked from a public meeting.

Of course, deskpersons can make mistakes too. A caption writer once declared that a football player had been named to an All-American team for "the second straight year in a row." Either it's "second year in a row" or "second straight year" but not both.

Finally, stay awake for those times when a seeming redundancy is needed. Referring to "a thousand square feet in size" is redundant, but the same phrase can't be cut from this: "She's small in size but big in stature." In that sentence, *in size* balances *in stature*.

Compress Wordy Phrases

Provided with a bountiful supply of nouns and verbs, some reporters will use a verb–noun construction in place of a verb. Stronger writing results when such constructions are turned into verbs. For example:

gave approval	approved
make a visit	visit
hold a meeting	meet
get in contact with	contact
get under way	begin, start
express different views	differ
made two attacks	attacked twice
caught many by surprise	surprised many
held a rally	rallied

These phrases and countless more like them should be compressed.

Evaluate Detail with a Cutting Eye

Detail serves an invaluable purpose in newswriting, especially when people can choose between the words of their newspaper and radio station and the pictures and words of their television station. Details enable print and radio journalists to compete against a television journalist who offers detail merely by focusing a camera. Despite the competition, however, print and radio journalists should recognize some detail for what it really is—filler—and delete it accordingly. For example: "The defendant stood before the judge and read the seven-page typewritten statement." That sentence can be pared several ways, depending on the circumstances. At the least, *typewritten* adds nothing. It doesn't matter if the statement is typed; in fact, given the increasing number of people who use typewriters and computers, reading from a handwritten statement would be more unusual. *Stood before the judge.* In court that's usually the way judges are addressed, so four more words of unnecessary detail can go. The kind of detail worth keeping would describe the defendant's mannerisms, delivery style, the judge, and so on.

Omit the Obvious

A 3-year-old boy climbs into a washing machine and his sister closes the door, thereby activating the machine. The reporter wants to make sure the reader understands the sister's presence and bogs down the story this way: "According to Todd's 7-year-old sister, Amy, *who was with the boy,* the washing machine started when she shut the door." Since she could not have done it by remote control, the italicized phrase adds nothing. Cut it.

Similarly: "The biology of sex, Biology 341, has been offered every winter for the past nine years and is continually filled *with students.*" Who else would fill a class?

Finally: "The cavern was flooded when a sudden rainstorm caused a stream to rise and seal the *only* exit." *The* exit is equivalent to the *only* exit, so *only* can go.

Unpile Prepositional Phrases

Under "Oust the Passive Voice," you saw a lead containing four prepositional phrases. Here is the active voice rewrite with the prepositions in italics:

> The county administration Thursday delayed the awarding *of* contracts *to* two firms *for* supplying furnishings *for* country-contracted services until the county controller determines who will own the equipment.

Notice how the phrases pile on top of one other until it becomes difficult to figure out which phrase modifies what. Carefully edit such writing to clarify. In this instance, two sentences would work better than one.

> The county administration Thursday delayed award-
> ing contracts until the county controller determines
> who will own the equipment provided *under* the
> contract's terms. The contract would have two firms
> supplying furnishings *for* county-contracted services.

Converting prepositional phrases into possessive or modifier forms usually removes the problem, although the editor should be careful not to use too many possessives or modifiers in a row lest one problem be replaced with another. Each sentence in the following represents a good conversion:

> The battle appeared to be the most significant issue
> of the decade.
> The battle appeared to be the decade's most signifi-
> cant issue.

> Requirements for the certification of paramedics will
> be upgraded.
> Paramedic certification requirements will be up-
> graded.

Knock Down Stone Walls

A stone wall in any form of news reporting is a sentence or paragraph that does not advance the story by offering news. In this example, the second paragraph is the stone wall:

> Pilsdon City Council last night raised real estate taxes
> 1 mill in order to pay for a new street sweeper.
> The council met in its chambers at 8 p.m. and was
> called to order by Mayor Joseph Picciano.
> The city needs the sweeper, City Manager James T.
> Owens said, because an unusually high number of
> storms have left streets dirtier than in past years.

When stone walls are as clear-cut as that one, the paragraph-delete command on the editing terminal removes the blockade. In some cases, rewriting may be necessary to blend some of the information in the second paragraph with news in the third.

Edit Elliptically

Sometimes the repetition of a word between sentences is unnecessary: its unwritten or unspoken repetition is understood by the reader or listener:

> The grant program receives the most federal funding;
> institutional programs receive the least.

Even though the second *receive* differs slightly from the first one, an editor can still safely delete it because the reader will supply the correct verb:

> The grant program receives the most federal funding;
> institutional programs the least.

The elliptical approach works well in lists:

> Guiser said strokes caused 67 deaths; hardening of the
> arteries, 17; rheumatic heart, 10; high blood pressure, 6.

Imagine how boring the sentence would be if *caused* and *deaths* were repeated for each new illness.

Faulty elliptical usage causes problems. For example, consider this extract from a caption:

> Two youngsters passing a gasoline station are uncon-
> cerned with the near $2 price of premium. You can bet
> motorists are.

The caption writer meant, "You can bet the motorists are concerned." But because the reader supplies the missing word from the previous sentence, the caption really says, "You can bet motorists are unconcerned." The caption could have said,

> Two youngsters passing a gasoline station are not concerned with the near $2 price of premium. You can bet motorists are.

Related complications arise with names in the possessive form when the writer believes that the name will carry over to the second thought. For example: "Simeon's conviction upheld; will reappeal." That says the conviction will reappeal, although the headline writer thought it said Simeon will. In that case, this rewrite would be better: "Simeon's conviction upheld; he'll reappeal."

Drop Unnecessary Pronouns

Part of elliptical editing is omitting some pronouns at the beginning of clauses:

> The editor who is highest in my esteem edits all copy carefully.

can be tightened to

> The editor highest in my esteem edits all copy carefully.

Similarly, *that, which* and *where* sometimes can be deleted, provided their omission does not create confusion:

> The fire chief said when the fire company arrived flames were spilling from all sides of the building.

Does *when the fire company arrived* modify *said* or *flames were spilling?* Insert *that* for clarity:

> The fire chief said that when the fire company arrived flames were spilling from all sides of the building.

A Closing Note

Every time someone puts words on paper, a copy editor needs to examine the writing for extraneous words. Remove them. Make copy as tight as possible without destroying meaning or rhythm.

Chapter 6

Language Skills for the Desk

The Function of Our Tongue

Nationally syndicated columnist James J. Kilpatrick once told a group of journalists that one of their holy duties is preserving the English language against decay through misuse. The columnist did not suggest that the journalists lock in to a set of rules and never bend them; instead, he said that journalists should preserve the language by using it correctly. Meeting that challenge lies with the copy editor more than any other person in journalism, for while the reporter may experiment with words, the copy editor must judge if the experiment succeeds or fails.

The people who work on the copy desk may not know how to parse or diagram sentences, but they do know that the English language is alive and changing and that they must consider that fact when editing. They appreciate the language's flexibility: how it allows, even encourages, nouns to become verbs, and verbs to become adjectives, even if for only one unheralded use. That doesn't mean copy editors tolerate linguistic experimentation that baffles or that they allow free-form writing, which means no form at all. Allowing totally idiosyncratic writing, in fact, could result in a modern Tower of Babel.

The copy editor knows that the first function of language is to communicate. The writer/speaker and the reader/listener must understand each other. Carefully crafted prose that the reader cannot understand serves no one.

Words mean different things to different people at different times. Thus, rather than merely consulting a dictionary for a word's definition, copy editors ensure that the context in which the word appears makes the intended meaning clear. Words mean what a society wants them to mean, and even within that society, subgroups can apply words to mean the opposite of what society at large considers them to mean. Just one example: In legal circles a *sanction* is a penalty; society in general uses *sanction* to mean approval.

Quibbling? Of course! That's what good copy editors do. They challenge. They doubt. They split hairs and then split them again. They don't let go of a precise meaning, a needed meaning, just because a dictionary lists as one of the word's 17 meanings some faddish dilution. Good copy editors are always fighting a rearguard action against changing semantics, not because they are fuddy-duddies but because they sense the need to preserve distinctions that society might blur through ignorant misuse.

A necessary difference exists between *convince* and *persuade; disinterested* and *uninterested; oral* and *verbal; hopefully* and *it is hoped; affect* and *effect; among* and *between; currently* and *presently; new* and *recent; compose* and *comprise; refute* and *rebut; damage* and *damages; farther* and *further; allude* and *elude.* Some purists have reluctantly given up on *presently* and *hopefully,* conceding that they are overwhelmed by the wave of imprecision that seems to be sweeping the country. (Every generation has been flooded by such a wave.)

Nevertheless, the journalist who searches for the exact word is probably the same one who seeks out the minute details of a behind-doors session held by a city council. It is a matter of doing a job well.

Here are five examples of writing not done well. The first shows an idiom common to the country at large:

> Testifying before the committee on drug abuse, Joe Bernard, who has had four of his 11 children addicted to drugs, told the committee to push for more money to fight drug abuse.

That father sounds as though he made his children take drugs, which, as the reader can infer from the remainder of the sentence, is not the case.

Less common is this example, which shows that some writers believe all words about death are synonymous with the word *death:*

> The spokesperson said cardiovascular diseases caused 378 fatalities last year.

But a fatality is a death resulting from an unanticipated disaster, such as a highway accident, whereas people with cardiovascular diseases are expected to die sooner than the population at large.

With polls so popular, copy editors must be alert for stories that overstate what polls do:

> The results of a poll issued today by Republican Harrison T. Heartbreaker prove he can beat Democrat Robin Earache in the U.S. Senate race in November.

Poll results don't prove anything; they indicate, or suggest, a conclusion. Language aside, copy editors should verify the validity of any poll before publishing a story about it.

Within political systems people sometimes form a dissenting group within the larger group of which they are a part. The dissenters represent a faction. Knowing that, ponder this misuse of the word:

> Various factions in the community met to discuss vandalism problems in the North Side.

Some of the people represented the schools, others the local Chamber of Commerce. Still others were residents. They didn't disagree with a larger group on anything; they did agree to do more to fight vandalism. No factions there.

Finally, a greatly overused word:

> The senator *formulated* his re-election plans.

Formulated sounds like so much artificial mother's milk; that is reason enough not to use it. Besides, it is of more use to chemists than to journalists. Try *formed, made, developed,* or *devised.*

Unlike the earlier examples of misused pairs, the preceding five examples won't show up in a usage book. That's fine. The point is not that copy editors should have at their fingertips a dozen usage books but that they should have in their brains a sense of the language, of how the meaning of words changes. Such a sense comes from reading a lot, including those usage books, but also books from different periods, by different authors, from different cultures and generations. Copy editors must be as aware of the language of Elizabethan England as they are of current teenage slang or Wall Street jargon.

Modern Conventions

Because copy editors are in the language business, they have to know the rules of grammar. In fact, they are expected to know more about those rules than reporters, who often write and punctuate by instinct. Copy editors need more than instinct to do even an average job.

Many who read newspapers or listen to radio and television cannot recite the rules of grammar nor could they fix an incorrect sentence. But publish or broadcast a mistake, and news consumers will react, not necessarily with the correct answer but with discomfort. They sense something is wrong although they're not sure what or why. Readers and listeners expect good language from their news media. They do not want sloppy usage; they look up to the usage in the news media and are critical when the usage is shoddy.

What follows is an abbreviated set of guidelines on the conventions of modern English. Many books have been written to explain grammar, so what follows should be taken as nothing more than capsule coverage of the volumes of insights, guidelines and rules. For the most part, what follows covers the more unusual errors that copy editors see. It assumes a basic knowledge of the rules.

Subject-Verb Agreement

Anyone who cares about language knows that subjects and verbs agree in person and number, that a singular subject takes a singular verb and so on. The same people also know that the only time a present tense regular verb changes form is in the third person singular, where most verbs add *s* to the first person form. Thus, in conjugating the verb *to know,* a user needs only two forms, *know* and *knows.* The conjugation: I know, you know, he/she/it knows, we know, you know, they know.

Copy editors should be alert to the sentence structure that separates the subject from the verb and misleads the writer in selecting the verb form. Here are some examples.

> "The American journalists' *interference* in the internal affairs of Bolivia and their biased *reporting*" was the cause of the expulsion, the foreign minister said.

The preceding compound subject (italicized) in a direct quotation is followed by a linking verb (*was*) and a singular predicate nominative (*cause*), which logic says agrees with the subject. Since *cause* is singular, the subject must be singular, thus the verb is singular. But verbs agree with subjects, not predicate nominatives, so the verb for this example must be *were.* (As you know from "Strengthen Weak Verbs" in Chapter 5, however, you can make a better sentence by discarding *were the cause of* and substituting *caused.*)

The same problem in a different form:

> A spokesperson said 3,200 gallons less propane were used this January.

This time the subject (*gallons*) appears plural, is usually plural, but is being considered here as a single unit and thus gets a singular verb. Monetary figures also are frequently treated as single units:

The kidnapping victim's father told the caller that $500,000 is a lot of ransom to pay for a journalist.

The next example:

A total of 47 persons were placed in local employment through the efforts of the State Job Security Bureau last month, the bureau's director announced.

The sentence shows the intruding plural prepositional phrase (*of 47 persons*) that has led the writer to use a plural verb. Writers' fingers move faster than their recall of subject-verb agreement, so it behooves the copy desk to watch for such problems. The writer was trying to avoid breaking the newspaper style rule that forbids figures at the start of sentences. The rule does not forbid spelled-out numbers, but many misinterpret it that way. Thus, rather than start a sentence with a spelled-out number, some writers insert flabby phrases such as *a total of*. Flab becomes the lesser of two evils, however, when the spelled-out number would twist the best of tongues. This is OK:

Forty-seven persons were placed . . .

But this isn't:

One thousand two hundred sixty-five local turkeys will not see the light of day tomorrow.

Here is a similar error:

A *quantity* of moon rocks are missing.

The subject (italicized) is singular, so it takes a singular verb:

A quantity of moon rocks is missing.

The easiest way to deal with this particular problem and many others that come under the rubric of language skills is to adopt a red flag approach to editing. In this instance, when you see a subject followed by a prepositional phrase, run up the red flag to remind yourself to check the verb against the subject. Make sure they agree. The same approach holds true for pronouns.

Problems with Pronouns

To avoid linking a pronoun to an unintended antecedent or creating a comical sentence because the wrong pronoun gets used, copy editors should triple their guard every time they see a pronoun. The question ought to be, What does that pronoun refer to? For example:

> Reports on what triggered Sunday's violence differed. *It* appeared, however, that *it* began when snipers opened fire with automatic rifles.

Those two italicized pronouns do not refer to the same antecedent. The first *it* represents an indefinite use, which is OK in weather reports ("It will be warm tomorrow.") but not very useful in clear writing. The second *it* refers to *violence* in the preceding sentence, but because *it* appears twice, the reader may be confused. The solution is to repeat the antecedent rather than using a pronoun.

> It appeared, however, that the violence began . . .

Although some editors frown on repetition, it proffers a path of clarity when the only other choice is a swamp of ambiguity.

Watch for pronouns doing double duty, that is, referring to different antecedents in another sentence or paragraph:

> Randy Sampson, who served as Thompson's man-
> aging editor, said the late editor showed his ability to
> lead shortly after assuming the editor's post.
>   "Newsrooms are often the battlegrounds of immense
> egos and *he* managed to pull us all together when the
> egos clashed," *he* said.

One pronoun used twice, two antecedents, an unknown number of confused readers. Since changing the *he* in the direct quotation would have
been tampering with a direct quote, the copy editor should have changed
the second *he* to the name of the speaker.

Doubling up can occur within a single sentence:

> The press has to make the public understand that
> First Amendment issues affect *them* as much as *they* af-
> fect the press.

Pronouns tend to affix themselves to the closest noun that agrees, so in
the preceding example the first pronoun must refer to *issues*. That means
the second also refers to *issues,* there being no other noun nearby.

> The press has to make the public understand that
> First Amendment issues affect the *issues* as much as the
> *issues* affect the press.

Imagine the puzzlement of the reader who just made that substitution!
Clarity can be achieved through the repetition of the correct nouns:

> The press has to make the public understand that
> First Amendment issues affect the public as much as the
> issues affect the press.

In the following example the problem may be with an idiom, not a
pronoun:

> The pilot told investigators *he* was not at first aware
> *he* was dangerously low on fuel.

The sense of the sentence comes through, but a copy editor wanting to avoid listening to someone's dumb jokes about the pilot's fuel tank would change the sentence:

> The pilot told investigators he was not at first aware
> the plane was dangerously low on fuel.

Pronouns and antecedents, like subjects and verbs, agree in person and number. Thus, a reference to *senators* requires the pronoun *they,* while *doctor* takes the pronoun *she* or *he.* But in some sentences the correct pronoun is not clear-cut:

> The first indication of trouble came when Arizona State University officials questioned $500 worth of telephone calls on _____ July bill.

In the original, the writer chose *their,* feeling that the antecedent was *officials.* The copy editor, feeling that the real antecedent was *Arizona State University,* changed *their* to *its.* The copy editor's editor, wanting to leave no doubt, changed *its* to *Arizona State University.* That's the lesson of pronouns: Use them cautiously so there is no doubt.

Some writers are bothered by using *its* to refer to a singular noun that has human qualities. Unthinkingly, they use *their* when they should use *its.* That happened in this sentence:

> The *rescue team,* clad in diving suits and equipped with air tanks, made *their* way into the cave after one of the rescuers made an exploratory pass through the entrance, Staubitz said.

An editor could change *their* to *its,* but a better way might be to change the antecedent:

> Members of the rescue team . . . made their way . . .

Writers concerned about avoiding sexist language try to write around the use of the pronoun *he.* The usual approach is to use plural nouns wherever possible (which is the approach in this book). But what happens when the sentence calls for a singular pronoun and one of the people referred to is a woman, the other a man? This is what happened in a story about a political campaign:

> The two major party candidates for state treasurer *each* attacked *their* opponent's record Tuesday in the first face-to-face meeting of the campaign.

Since *each* has no gender, rewrite the sentence and lean more heavily on that pronoun:

> The two major party candidates for state treasurer attacked each other's record Tuesday in the first face-to-face meeting of the campaign.

Verbs, Deadlines and Tense

The verb tense that appears most frequently in hard news stories is the past tense, which says the action in the story happened once and is now over. The city council meeting, the congressional hearing, the collision of two automobiles, the bankruptcy of a store, the death of someone in the community—all are told about in the past tense. For example:

> Joan M. Beasley, who is credited with reviving Pilsdon after the Great Depression, *died* last night in her sleep at the age of 92.

But when journalists are seeking to put immediacy or timelessness into their stories, they turn to the present and present perfect tenses. Those tenses offer the reader the sense that the story is now, not yesterday. The writer of a feature story about a man who raises prize-winning gladioli realizes that the story does not take place in one discrete period but encompasses many hours or days, even years, in the subject's life. That calls for present tense treatment, which engages readers at the moment they begin the story and makes them feel a part of it, as though they are watching it take place.

> Ralph Baker *does* not putter around his garden in the popular image of someone who *fusses* over every bloom and bug around. Instead, Baker, who *raises* prize-winning gladioli, *commands* his garden.
> "Turn more toward the sun," he *says* sternly to one budding plant, "and you'll find the warmth to grow."
> "Get out!" he *shouts* sharply to a bug sneaking up on a bud just peering above the mounds of earth that *separate* the rows of gladioli.
> The bug, enemy that it is, is given a gentle heave-ho from the garden on Baker's finger rather than a puff of bug spray from the can of insecticide he *carries* with him but never *seems* to use.
> "God made the bugs, too, you know," Baker *says,* explaining why he *evicts* bugs rather than killing them.

Even though the reporter may have written the feature story based on one morning's interview, the reporter still treats it as timeless by using the present tense. The reporter is suggesting to the reader that Baker acts like that all the time, not just during an interview.

The present perfect tense provides journalists with the proper vehicle for writing a timeless lead on a timely event. The reporter who wants to stress the action or even the implications of the action spurns past tense (and its attendant and sometimes intrusive time element) for the present perfect.

> A group of citizens unhappy with unchecked growth near their homes *has formed* an organization to lobby the City Council for strict zoning laws.

> Called Happy Acres Homeowners, the group orga-
> nized last night at the Jefferson Elementary School,
> which serves Happy Acres.

In the lead, the perfect tense removes the obligation of using past tense and allows the reporter to focus on the issue, the formation of the group. When the reporter uses the past tense in the second paragraph, he or she affixes the time element. That type of organization makes a great deal of sense in a newspaper, a medium in which the reader expects to find information of a timely nature. The logic is: Why give the reader the time element in the lead when the reader already has some idea of it? The time element is not the news; hide it. If the writer does not do the hiding, the copy desk should. The copy editor, after all, is the fine tuner of all writing.

Present tense overuse shows up in future tense situations, such as a Wednesday story containing this phrase: "The president speaks on Thursday to . . . . The use occurs frequently in all the news media. What is wrong with "The president will speak on Thursday to . . ."?

For some future events, of course, the future tense cannot be used. For example, it's 8 a.m. and the afternoon newspaper plans to publish a story about an event scheduled to occur at 2 p.m. that day. The reporter writes, "Striking teachers will vote on the proposal today." The problem is, by the time the newspaper reaches subscribers and is read, the evening will be over. In fact, readers who watch the 6 o'clock news on television while they read the newspaper will be confused when the newscaster gives the results of a vote that the newspaper said was going to happen. In such cases, the writer should hedge: "Striking teachers *were ready* to vote on the proposal today." The hedge gets the newspaper off the hook; if the event does not take place, the newspaper did not promise it would but merely said the event was scheduled. The reader understands that the newspaper does not control events.

Given the immediate nature of broadcasting, radio and television journalists don't usually face this problem unless they sense that something planned may never take place. A good example is a threatened strike that could be cooled by a last-minute agreement. The 6 o'clock news treats such a prospect this way:

> Members of the Paper Clip Assemblers Union are set to strike at midnight tonight, but last-minute negotiations might resolve the differences and head off the strike.

Note the present tense. A newspaper reporter would have to use the past tense (*were set*) for the reason cited earlier.

Also watch out for a shift in tense. In the following, the writer went from past tense to present tense without good reason. The correct tense for this sentence's verbs is past:

> Critics *faulted* short-sellers for making money on other people's misfortunes and *complain* they contribute little of economic value.

The second verb should be *complained.*

Parallel Construction

Items joined by a conjunction (*and, but, or*) should be parallel; that is, each item should appear in the same form as the others. Consistency of form makes for easier reading and clarity. Here is a sentence with a non–parallel construction:

> A doctor makes a diagnosis after *examining* a patient and after she *studies* the results of tests.

The verbs connected by *and* should be in the same form, either participle or third person:

> A doctor makes a diagnosis after *examining* a patient and *studying* the results of tests.

> A doctor makes a diagnosis after she *examines* a patient and *studies* the results of tests.

The following parallel construction problem shows up not in the tense of the verbs but in the voice and placement:

> Hinckley closed his eyes, his elbows rested on the defense table, his hands were clasped and his mouth rested on his thumbs.

Corrected, it flows better:

> Hinckley closed his eyes, rested his elbows on the defense table, clasped his hands and rested his mouth on his thumbs.

A less clear violation appears in the following:

> The old bonds will remain available until June 30 at financial institutions and through payroll savings plans until Dec. 31.

The affront here is not to the rules of grammar but to the logic of the reader who when reading the first two prepositional phrases (*until . . . institutions*) expects the next two to follow in the same date-place order. At first glance the sentence suggests that the bonds will be available until June 30 at financial institutions and through payroll savings plans [no time limit]. To ensure clarity, a copy editor would make the halves of the sentence parallel, one way or another:

> The old bonds will remain available until June 30 at financial institutions and until Dec. 31 through payroll savings plans.

> The old bonds will remain available at financial institutions until June 30 and through payroll savings plans until Dec. 31.

False Series

The absence of a necessary conjunction or the inclusion of a surplus verb creates a false series. In the following the series appears to contain four items:

> The premier today pledged to [1] disband the secret police, [2] cut off oil to Christian nations, [3] release all prisoners not accused of murder or theft and [4] introduced a new minister of state.

The absence of *and* between items 2 and 3 creates a false series that leads readers to expect all four items to begin with infinitives. But the fourth item is not really part of the series and should be severed:

> The premier today pledged to disband the secret police, cut off oil to Christian nations and release all prisoners not accused of murder or theft. The premier also introduced a new minister of state.

Principles Behind Modification

Words and phrases intended to modify other words and phrases function best when they are next to or as close as possible to what they modify. A copy editor should always check that modifiers follow this principle. The following contains a misplaced modifying phrase:

> Fourteen people were injured in the five-alarm fire, *including four firefighters.*

The italicized phrase modifies *Fourteen people* and should appear immediately after it:

> Fourteen people, including four firefighters, were injured in the five-alarm fire.

The following sentence sounds as though the city council is going to let any business that wants to erect groundpole signs on two streets:

> In other business, the council also discussed amendments to the sign ordinance that would permit businesses to place an additional groundpole sign *on Atherton Street and University Drive*.

To make it clear that not every business so inclined may erect signs, the italicized modifying phrase needs to be next to the noun it modifies:

> In other business, the council also discussed amendments to the sign ordinance that would permit businesses on Atherton Street and University Drive to place an additional groundpole sign.

Another example, this one a headline: "Talks are slow with striking teachers." The failure here is to make clear what the talks are about; the modifying phrase is misplaced. Put correctly: "Talks with striking teachers are slow." But adhering to the as-close-as-possible rule can create problems, as in this headline: "Women included in resumption of draft possible." The writer followed one rule at the expense of another—always be clear. A rewrite: "Women may be included in draft resumption."

Relative clauses also need to be next to the noun or phrase modified, as in this photo caption:

> Rescue workers lower the body of an unidentified teenager in Long Beach, Calif., *who was electrocuted after*

he climbed a power pole to retrieve a model glider. Efforts to revive him on the ground were unsuccessful.

The rewrite actually moves a different modifier in order to get the relative clause next to *teenager:*

> Rescue workers lower the body of an unidentified Long Beach, Calif., teenager who was electrocuted after he climbed a power pole to retrieve a model glider. Efforts to revive him on the ground were unsuccessful.

Another modifier typically out of place is the infamous dangling participle, commonly used by careless writers to begin a sentence when they haven't thought through what they're going to put in the middle or at the end of the sentence. For example:

> *Once a leading hostess in Newport's wealthy summer colony,* her estate is estimated at $35 million or more.

The modifying phrase obviously does not refer to *estate,* but lacking additional information on whom the sentence is about, the sentence defies repair. This one does not:

> *To investigate the suspected scheme,* two commercial companies were established in 1982 in Emeryville and Alameda by the Federal Bureau of Investigation and the Navy Investigative Service.

In that sentence, the investigators are clear, and rewriting the sentence in the active voice repairs the problem:

> To investigate the suspected scheme, the Federal Bureau of Investigation and the Navy Investigative

Service established two commercial companies in 1982 in Emeryville and Alameda.

And finally, for the dangler category, this gem from a police report:

> While on patrol in the 200 block of Calder Way, an intoxicated male pounded on the roof of police unit 6-15. No damage was sustained, so the actor was cited and released.

Adverbs are modifiers seldom used in newswriting, although some of them, such as *only,* serve to clarify information for uninformed readers. A person who is not a sports fan, for example, would need a signal that a basketball team that scores 35 points is not very productive. The sentence might say, "The Maple Syrups scored only 35 points." But in circumstances where the facts speak for themselves, a copy editor should remove *only.* For example: "The president of the union said the vote was 20,212 in favor of a strike to only 1,210 against." The reader needs no adverbial assistance to figure out the one-sidedness of that vote.

Another frequent *only* problem is placement. In speech, people say, "I only have three dollars to my name." On paper, though, *only* should appear as near as possible to what it modifies: "I have only three dollars to my name." (A note of caution: If the sentence had appeared as a direct quote, the copy editor would not change it. Again, quoted speech is treated differently.)

Specific references to facts not yet introduced in a story represent still another modification problem. A lead that says a city council raised taxes "at last night's meeting" is not only wordy ("last night" will do) but also assumes the reader knew before reading the story that the council met. The reader has to be told of the meeting before the writer can call it "last night's meeting."

Likewise, the story could not later turn to another topic and begin like this: "In other business, *the* proposal to require the curbing of dogs was presented to the council for the first time." The fault lies with *the,* referring to something the reader hasn't yet been told about. Change *the* to *a* and the introduction is accomplished. Then the next reference can be to *the* proposal because the reader knows about it.

Punctuation

Myths about punctuation marks are as numerous as stories about gruff copy editors. In trying to explain some punctuation marks, teachers have linked them to breathing—a period is a full stop (inhale and exhale), a comma means a short pause (inhale and exhale faster) and so on. Actually, punctuation marks define the relation of words in print. They represent tools for writers to show the end of a sentence, compound sentences not joined by a conjunction, a question, a phrase in apposition, a compound modifier, the beginning of a list or summary, the insertion of explanatory matter, possession and who is speaking. No huffing or puffing is required.

THE PERIOD. The end of a sentence is marked with a period. Most writers use it correctly without thinking. Period abuse, in fact, arises not at the end of sentences but within them, and with abbreviations, especially those created locally. The wire services' stylebooks list the abbreviations and punctuation of several national groups and give clear advice for local creations: If the abbreviation creates an unrelated word, insert periods between each letter. Thus, to guide the reader away from pronouncing its abbreviation, the group Youth Entertaining Common Hopes would use periods—Y.E.C.H.—or more wisely, change its name.

Do not place spaces within such abbreviations or between initials because a typesetting machine keys on space codes to justify lines and a space would make it split the abbreviation or initials between lines:

> One writer I admire is C. D.
> B. Bryan, author of *Friendly Fire*.

The author's name is C.D.B. Bryan.

Periods, by the way, always go inside quotation marks.

THE SEMICOLON. The semicolon is not half a colon, as its name might indicate, but rather functions like three-fourths of a period. It most commonly separates compound sentences not joined by a conjunction:

> The president chose to take the weekend off; Congress, on the other hand, uncharacteristically convened both days.

The biggest mistake writers make in such a case is using a comma for a semicolon.

The semicolon does have a comma-related function in separating complex items in a list:

> Police identified the dead as Kenneth R. Sweeney, who was driving the car; Jonathan A. Swanson, owner of the car; Julian Anglais, a Gibbsville automobile dealer; and Ellen T. Macungie, owner of a shoe store in Clive.

Generally, place semicolons outside quotation marks.

THE QUESTION MARK. Few copy editors have to ask when to employ the question mark; with one exception, it always appears at the end of a question. The exception is the paraphrased question: "The mayor asked if she could yield the gavel so she could speak to the assembly." No question mark.

Depending on circumstances, question marks can go inside or outside direct quotes. Inside:

> "What does this tax measure mean to the oil companies?" the senator asked.

Outside:

> Which word don't you understand: "philanthropist"?

THE COMMA. Writers usually don't have to be told when to use a comma; sometimes they have to be told when not to. Inappropriately (as already noted) some writers use the comma for a semicolon. If they would remember that commas define relations within a sentence and that semicolons usually appear between sentences, they would probably stop making the error.

Apparently afraid a collision might occur when two modifiers appear side by side, some writers separate the modifiers with a comma. That can be done only when the modifiers are of equal rank. "The bright, red fire truck gleamed in the sunlight." To test the comma, replace it with *and:* "The bright and red fire truck gleamed in the sunlight." Obviously the modifiers *bright* and *red* are not equal; *bright* modifies *red.* No comma. Equality exists in the following, so the comma is correct: "The glassy-eyed, limping man said nothing when a police officer approached."

The comma creates a series where none exists when a writer puts in commas where dashes belong: "Other sources for heating homes, natural gas and electricity, have also experienced at least small declines." The writer, aware of the use of the comma to set off a phrase in apposition, thought no further in punctuating that example and created sources that heat homes, that heat natural gas and that heat electricity. What the writer meant was that natural gas and electricity are sources for heating homes: "Other sources for heating homes—natural gas and electricity—have also experienced at least small declines."

Another comma error appears when a phrase calls for two commas yet the writer uses only one. Such a situation can arise with apposition or clauses; the problem is that the writer (usually) forgets the second comma, yielding, for example, "J. Edgar Hoover, the long-time director of the FBI is no longer the revered man he was at his death." The missing comma should appear after *FBI.* Some comma droppers omit the mark at the beginning of a clause: "Oakwood Manor which until last year had no paved roads, now has paved roads and a community swimming pool." Place a comma between *Manor* and *which.*

Commas always go inside quotation marks.

THE HYPHEN. The copy editor who remembers that a hyphen connects words and that a dash separates will correct many of the errors associated with those two punctuation marks. The hyphen's primary use is linking compound modifiers. This is especially important when the unlinked modifiers might engender another meaning. Compare these headlines:

> Race fixing trial begins

> Race-fixing trial begins

The first suggests a trial that has something to do with race; the second says clearly that the story concerns a trial about someone who tried to fix a race. The hyphen makes the difference.

Hyphens occasionally appear where commas function better.

> Heart attacks were the leading cause of death—at 257 last year, followed by strokes-67, hardening of the arteries-17, rheumatic heart-10, and high blood pressure-6.

Convert the hyphens to commas, and remember the function of semicolons in some series:

> Heart attacks were the leading cause of death at 257, followed by strokes, 67; hardening of the arteries, 17; rheumatic heart, 10; and high blood pressure, 6.

THE DASH. Copy editors have to ensure that reporters not only use the dash correctly in their stories but also type it correctly. On personal computers, which are designed to mimic typewriters, the dash does not exist but can be created by typing two hyphens. On a VDT, that won't work because VDT keyboards contain a dash, usually typed by shifting the keyboard and striking the hyphen key. The copy desk must be particularly careful to see that hyphens are hyphens and dashes are dashes.

Primarily, a dash sets off a phrase a writer wants stressed or signals a summing up in much the same manner as a colon does. An example first used under "The Comma" shows the setting-off use: "Other sources for heating homes—natural gas and electricity—have also experienced at least small declines." A dash can be used for a summing up: "The batter struck out, ending the game with two men on base—that's what his entire season was like." A similar use appears in the introductory paragraph of "Verbs, Deadlines and Tense."

The dash and colon are sometimes interchangeable when used to signal the beginning of a list. The dash offers more stress because it is a bolder mark; the colon, on the other hand, does its work quietly: "The president told members of Congress they must accomplish three things—help balance the budget within two years, reduce congressional spending, provide for a tax cut.

THE COLON. The interchangeability of the dash and colon does not extend to all functions of the colon. For example, the colon can be used, seems almost required, between long introductory phrases and direct quotations.

> The editor, who stood before the members of her staff to tell them about the closing of the paper, said: "I regret to tell you I have been able to confirm a rumor we have all been hearing—we are closing."

Colons sometimes cause problems when a writer or editor is unsure whether to capitalize the first letter of the first word following the colon. The rule is this: If what follows is a complete sentence, capitalize. The other half of the rule: lower-case for words or phrases.

PARENTHESES. The punctuation marks that set off secondary information in a sentence are seldom used in newspapers because of their disruptive nature. Sometimes a reporter uses a direct quotation that is not complete enough to be clear and the reporter parenthetically provides the clarifiers:

> "Now you know that (Harry) Hinder (last year's champion) played the most stupendous game (of racquetball) he's ever played (in singles competition), but wait till you see him next (in doubles play)," the director of the racquetball tournament said.

Because such insertions make a sentence jerk along instead of flow smoothly, they should be avoided. The desk should flag such sentences and require the reporter to rewrite them. In general, parenthetical inserts should be discarded through paraphrasing.

Because parentheses mean that what is contained within is secondary to the main point of a sentence, they should not be used in a circumstance like this:

> Strokes caused 67 deaths. Other noted killers were hardening of the arteries (17), rheumatic heart (10) and high blood pressure (6).

The figures in parentheses are part of the news and should not be subordinated.

THE APOSTROPHE. A writer shows possession usually by adding *'s* to a singular word and just the apostrophe to a plural word ending in *s*. The desk must be alert for those writers who add *s'* to non-standard plurals, such as *people*. It is "the people's right to know," not "the peoples' right to know."

The apostrophe also appears in contractions, such as *couldn't* for *could not*. One of the more vexing apostrophe abuses occurs when a writer wants the possessive form of *it*. The possessive form of *it* is *its*. No apostrophe. When a writer intends the contraction of *it is,* the correct form is *it's*.

QUOTATION MARKS. The exact words spoken by a person are enclosed within quotation marks. Words quoted within a direct quotation are placed in single quotation marks:

> "I called you 'lazy,' among other things," the mayor screamed at the police chief.

When a VDT does not contain double quotation marks, the user must strike the single quotation mark twice to create a double mark. Furthermore, some VDTs contain opening and closing quotation marks (called "left" and "right") for the (respective) beginning and ending of direct quotation. The desk must watch for closing quotation marks erroneously used at the beginning of a direct quotation, and vice versa.

Some Facts on Spelling

One of the myths of the electronic age is that computers always spell correctly. It matters not how many misspelled words a writer types in, a properly programmed computer will correct all except homonyms before they see print.

At last, the story goes, people who cannot spell can still work for newspapers; the computer will take care of their mistakes. Any salesperson peddling such nonsense deserves not to get the contract because the pitch is deceptive. The computer is not the cure-all for bad spelling. A good analogy is the pocket calculator that provides the wrong answer because a piece of dust is making a microprocessor malfunction. Only someone aware of the mathematical principles involved would spot the error, because such a person would have an idea what the answer should be. The spelling computer needs the same backstop.

Some spelling software suffers from a serious flaw: It flags misspelled words only if the misspelling has not become another word, such as *effect* for *affect*. The reporter who writes about a *board of trusties* should have been assigned to the prison beat. But the computer wouldn't know, and thus wouldn't be able to fix, the misspelling. That leaves the correction to the copy editor, a human programmed to know the difference between *trusties* and *trustees* and countless other possibilities. In addition, the good copy editor knows the so-called rules of spelling and the exceptions (the noun is *fire* but the adjective is *fiery*) and the exceptions to the exceptions.

Running through a list of rules here would consume much time for a marginal yield. Entire books have been devoted to spelling rules, and copy editors still find the best book of all to be a good dictionary. In brief, however, here are some useful spelling rules:

- When seeing a word for the first time, a copy editor should look it up.
- When absolutely certain of the spelling of a word, a copy editor should look it up.
- When in doubt about the spelling of a word, a copy editor should look it up.

- A copy editor should compile a list of words he or she has particular difficulty recognizing as misspelled. Such a list spares that editor the need to search through a dictionary each time.
- Devise mnemonics, memory aids, for tricky words. For example, *every time* and *any time* are two words *all the time*. (Although it is itself three words, *all the time* reminds me not to write *everytime* and *anytime*.)

The importance of spelling names correctly cannot be overstated. Several years ago an emotionally disturbed boy ran away from a center where he lived. His body was found three days later and sent to the morgue. The boy's surname was Fichtner. It was stenciled inside his pants. But after the medical examiner completed an autopsy, he wrote *Fitchner*, and the body went unclaimed for more than three months. Had the medical examiner checked, the grieving parents would have been notified and thus spared months of suffering.

Copy editors check. Making sure words are spelled correctly is only one of a copy editor's many duties, and the harried editor might consider it last among equals and therefore not worth as much attention as checking facts. A spelling error is a major fact error. It reflects harshly on the credibility of the newspaper. It makes the reader wonder, If a newspaper cannot spell correctly, how accurate can its reporting be? The few moments spent checking the spelling of a word are worth it.

Sources and Resources

Berner, R. Thomas, *Language Skills for Journalists*. 2d ed. Boston: Houghton Mifflin, 1984.

Bernstein, Theodore M. *The Careful Writer*. New York: Atheneum, 1973.

Bremner, John B. *Words on Words*. New York: Columbia University Press, 1980.

Copperud, Roy H. *Words on Paper*. New York: Hawthorn Books, 1960.

Ebbitt, Wilma R., and David R. Ebbit. *Writer's Guide and Index to English*. 6th ed. Glenview, Ill.: Scott, Foresman, 1978.

Flesch, Rudolf. *The Art of Readable Writing*. New York: Collier Books, 1949.

Fowler, H. W. *Fowler's Modern English Usage*. 2d ed., rev. Sir Ernest Gowers. New York: Oxford University Press, 1965.

House, Homer C., and Susan Emolyn Harman. *Descriptive English Grammar.* 2d ed. Englewood Cliffs, N.J.: Prentice-Hall, 1950.

Shaw, Harry. *Errors in English and Ways to Correct Them.* 2d ed. New York: Barnes and Noble, 1970.

The Compact Edition of the Oxford English Dictionary. New York: Oxford University Press, 1971.

Chapter 7

Consultative Editing

The Editor–Reporter Relationship

It wasn't that long ago that an editor, unhappy with a reporter's story, might roll the story into a wad and toss it into a wastebasket or shape it into an airplane and fly it across the newsroom. As Carl Sessions Stepp put it:

> High-voltage tension pops between many editors and reporters. Nearly everyone who carries a notebook has joined in a besotted, post-deadline session of editor-bashing. And virtually anyone who ever lifted a copy pencil remembers some rattling altercation with an evil-eyed writer.

One journalism educator likened the editor-reporter relationship to the driver-pedestrian relationship: it is bad drivers who treat pedestrians with contempt. And the second edition of Christopher Scanlan's *How I Wrote the Story* includes sections titled "What does an editor do that hinders a writer?" and "What does a writer do that hinders an editor?" There is sometimes bad blood and blood-letting in the newsroom, and people get hurt.

But a new attitude is taking hold. Editors are learning to work with reporters, and vice versa. Copy editors are no longer looked upon simply as the geeks who know grammar and catch misspelled words; they are seen as professionals who understand the process of writing and can help writers produce more effective stories. Consultative editing is part of the editing process.

Consultative editing involves editors from the beginning of the story. Editors and reporters discuss subject matter, reporting approaches, the story's focus, ordering and writing the facts, and revising and editing the result. Editors have learned that analysis beforehand saves time later, especially when the newsroom is on deadline and no one has the time to nurture, only growl. Editors have come to see the reporters in their newsroom as people whose abilities will grow and blossom if carefully nurtured. The nurturing usually falls to the assistant editors, including copy editors, who take care to treat reporters as colleagues rather than as ignoble pedestrians deserving no courtesy.

According to one of the first writing coaches, Donald M. Murray, consultative editing has four main goals:

1. To make use of the knowledge and experience of the writer.
2. To give the writer primary responsibility for the story.
3. To provide an environment in which the writer can do the best possible job.
4. To train the writer, so that editing will be unnecessary.

Roy Peter Clark of the Poynter Institute is another writing coach and consultative editor. He stresses the value of coaching over fixing, the traditional role of editors, as saving rather than wasting time. On deadline, Clark notes, the story gets fixed with short-term benefits. Fixing undercuts the confidence of writers and may turn writers and editors into adversaries. Also, accustomed to having a story fixed, the reporter might not work as hard on good writing and instead become dependent on the copy desk. Finally, the person doing the fixing takes control of a story, usurping the writer's place.

Consultative editing starts when the story is assigned and continues through its printing. Coaching builds confidence and fosters independence and thus has long-term benefits. Writer and editors work with each other rather than against each other. Rather than being a fault-finding tactic, coaching is a strength-building tactic. Writers build on their strengths and have some room to experiment. They maintain control of their story, which is important for their self-esteem and confidence.

The best consultative editing takes place in a one-to-one situation. Such an arrangement minimizes outside distractions and gives both parties time to explore the questions each has. In such a situation, editors can do certain helpful things. These suggestions come from a group of editors and writers at the *Journal-Bulletin* in Providence, R.I.:

1. Confer. Communicate as much as possible with writers. Tell them what you want and don't want. Give them reasons.
2. Listen. Too often an editor gets into a fixed position. Open your mind and be willing to admit you can learn something.
3. Act as the first reader of the writer's material—a buffer between the writer and the reader.
4. Ask the questions and contribute the ideas that may stimulate the writer's thinking and reporting.
5. Be adjustable—willing to change your mind about a story as the writer brings forward new information.
6. Be supportive—not with fraudulent pats on the head, but with useful criticisms and compliments when deserved.
7. Check with the writer—not by nagging, but by giving reassurance that you are available for help. If you have a definite direction for the story, make sure you communicate it to the writer.
8. Don't judge in advance what the writer should produce.
9. Suggest approaches and techniques without demanding that they be used.
10. Offer a different viewpoint on the set of facts the writer has collected.
11. Challenge the writer's assumptions.
12. Find the holes in the story (the writer usually knows they're there, anyway) and demand that they be filled. Better: Ask the writer what he or she thinks are the holes in the story.
13. Help refine the story idea at the point of assignment.
14. Discuss editing changes with the writer during and after the editing process.
15. Provide encouragement for the use of unconventional techniques.

16. Talk over stories before they are written.
17. Make the assignment clear in the beginning. Insist that the writer produce what is asked for, when it's asked for.
18. Ask the questions a reader would ask—after the reporting and before the writing.
19. After thorough discussion, negotiate the length of the story. Give the writer an equal say in this, but when a decision is reached, enforce it.
20. Point out errors that are recurrent.
21. Ask first what the story is about; next what problems the writer is having; and last when the writer can have the story done.
22. Don't be afraid to read the writer's notes—but only at the writer's request. With our computers, that's not as difficult as it sounds.
23. Bring a piece into focus if the writer is struggling or off the mark.
24. Realize that some writers don't talk a good story but can write it.
25. Give story ideas in more detail than "how about a piece on . . . ?"
26. Let the writer come up with story ideas of his or her own. Better: Tell the writer to come up with them.
27. Check with the writer before assuming that the writer is wrong.
28. Give the writer as much time as reasonably possible to write.
29. Point out breakdowns in the logical flow of a story, and suggest alternatives.
30. Suggest information that should be included but is not.
31. Change copy only if the change will make the story more complete, accurate and readable.
32. Remember that psychologically bad editing is far worse than technically bad editing. An editing mistake may be remembered by the writer for a week; a mistake in handling the writer may be remembered for a lifetime.

Still other suggestions abound. Some editors encourage reporters to suggest headlines on stories. This helps the writer understand the focus of the story better. At some newspapers, the writers have formed informal discussion groups. These are not editor-bashing sessions but rather center on writing problems. When a journalist has produced a particularly well-written story, a more formal session might be organized so the journalist can share insight on how she wrote the story.

Practical Guidelines

In order to succeed, writers need encouragement and support from their editors, not harassment. A good editor will recognize when to bend the rules and still get good results. Deadline sounds like a permanent fixture, but a newspaper has several deadlines. A reporter must turn copy in by a certain time, the desk must move copy by a certain time, the pages must be pasted up by a certain time, and the press must run by a certain time. But a reporter writing a breaking story on deadline may produce a better story if given a few minutes alone to organize both notes and thoughts. And so what if the story comes in past the copy deadline, as long as the desk has scheduled time to handle it and the reporter has used the time wisely.

Writers might also be urged to do outlines, especially when writing lengthy, non-deadline stories. Outlines can be of any design the writer is comfortable with. For instance, for this chapter, I had three pages of notes, which guided me to specific pages in my sources and resources. I realized partway through my note-taking that the chapter was taking shape in four parts—statement of the problem, hint at resolution, various tips, and resolution. I set up those headings across the top of a piece of paper and then went back through my notes and jotted abstracts under the appropriate columns. Then I began to write. Sections one, two and three fell under one subhead, and section four became the second division. By the time I neared the end of the third section in my outline, I realized that some points would fit better into section four. I circled them and drew arrows to the fourth column. What I like about my outline approach is that everything is on one page and can be easily moved.

Editors who advise writers also need to go beyond the symptoms and also come up with the cure. One writer was once criticized for writing long sentences. The real problem was the writer's failure to establish a pace throughout the story, to write in a variety of sentence lengths that suited the telling of the story.

Writers sometimes have problems finding a focus for a story. A reporter can gather a lot of information, but that doesn't mean the information has focus. The writer gives it focus. A writer having difficulty finding the focus should begin a story with a sentence like this: "This is a story about trucking companies that ship food to a destination and then load the trucks with garbage for the return trip." Of course, that sentence will not appear in the final draft, but keeping it in front of the writer is a way to help the writer maintain focus.

An editor who has been part of the story from the beginning can help a writer find a focus. One beginning reporter once wrote a series of stories for her newspaper, starting with an advance on a speech by Helen Suzman, then a member of South Africa's Parliament and a liberal who paradoxically opposed some international efforts to end apartheid in her country. Suzman eventually appeared at the local university, and the journalist covered the speech. She noted in a conversation with her editor later that several black South Africans had attended the speech and had disagreed with Suzman, who was otherwise someone considered a friend of black South Africans.

A couple of weeks later the same journalist was working on an in-depth story on apartheid but had a difficult time coming up with a lead. She wanted to show the contradictions in South Africa, even for someone who opposed apartheid. But she was having trouble and went to her editor. "Why don't you open with an anecdote showing how the black South Africans responded to Suzman's speech? That says it all." The reporter did and was able to get a good lead on her story, one with people in it and with a local angle.

Writers also have trouble ordering information. The easiest principle to apply in those cases is to imagine what questions the reader will ask and in what order. For example, when it comes to the refrigerated trucks mentioned earlier, one question that arises immediately is, Isn't that illegal? (At the time, no.) Other questions: Do the drivers clean out the trucks? If so, how? Does that quell possible causes of disease?"

One way of ordering a story is to make sure a thread runs through it from beginning to end. The following example comes from the work of a beginning journalist, Jennifer Tordone, who wrote three drafts of a 2,000-word article in order to get a thread.

This is a story about anorexia nervosa and bulimia. These are the opening paragraphs of the first draft seen by the writer's editor:

Two severe eating disorders, anorexia nervosa and bulimia, are two of the leading causes of death in the United States—yet little is known about these mysterious diseases.

According to the National Association of Anorexia Nervosa and Associated Disorders, there are millions of victims in the United States alone and an estimated six percent of those affected die every year. The association believes that there are about 7 million women and 1 million men or more suffering from anorexia nervosa and/or bulimia in the United States. In the 1987 eating disorders hearing before the House of Representatives, committee members said as many as one teenage girl in eight is affected with anorexia or bulimia.

This is the final paragraph, almost 2,000 words later:

Greene and Schmidt say these organizations have the potential to decrease the prevalence of eating disorders. It is just a matter of time, Greene says, before people become aware of the national sense of the problem and then do something to put an end to it before it is too late.

Among the reporter's sources were various health officials. But she also interviewed members of the local chapter of Overeaters Anonymous, one of whom was bulimic. None of them was quoted in the first draft.

Her editor suggested a different lead and asked the reporter during a consultative session if the bulimic woman she had interviewed might make a good lead. The editor also had some doubts about the ending; he felt it wasn't strong enough, that the story limped to a close.

In her second draft, the reporter began her story talking about the bulimic woman from Overeaters Anonymous:

"Carla" says she never had a problem with her weight.

"I was never told I was fat," she says. "In fact, I may have been a little underweight when I began binging and purging."

A university student who wishes to remain anonymous, Carla says she became bulimic in her junior year of high school.

Carla says she constantly competed with her two older sisters for the better grades, the cute boys and the spot on the cheerleading squad.

"I was never quite as talented as my sisters," she says. "I guess all the luck ran out when I was born."

Although she admits it was frustrating not being as "gifted" as her sisters, she says her father did not care who brought home the "A" or the "C" or who made varsity cheerleading. Her father had no favorites, she says. He treated all of them the same, loving them for the people they were, regardless of their abilities, Carla says.

"My mom is the go-getter," Carla says. "She wanted us to be our very best, but dad just wanted us to be happy."

Her dad supported her in whatever she did, which helped Carla handle the pressure put on her by her mother and sisters, she says. When Carla's father died, however, Carla says her life completely changed.

Carla says she thought she could regain control of her life by watching her weight, something she believed she could successfully do on her own.

"I was wrong," Carla says. "My binge-purge habit began controlling me to the point where it became an obsession."

As a lead, that goes on too long. The reader must go through 10 paragraphs, in effect, a summary of Carla's life, before finding out what the story is about. After much discussion, the writer decided that Carla was the thread for her story. First she shortened her lead, so the reader would know early on what the story was about:

"Carla" says she never had a problem with her weight.

"I was never told I was fat," she says. "In fact, I may have been a little underweight when I began binging and purging."

A university student who wishes to remain anonymous, Carla says she became bulimic in her junior year of high school.

Carla represents one of the millions of people who are bulimic or anorexic. According to the National Association of Anorexia Nervosa and Associated Disorders, about 7 million women and 1 million men suffer from anorexia nervosa and/or bulimia in the United States.

In effect, the writer picked up from the second paragraph of her original story. Three pages later, the journalist wrote about Karen Carpenter, a celebrity who died of anorexia nervosa when she was 32. The journalist wanted to bring us back to Carla, so after a detailed paragraph on Carpenter, she wrote this transition paragraph:

Karen Carpenter's reasons for abstaining from food differ from Carla's.

Carla says she constantly competed with her two older sisters for the better grades, the cute boys and the spot on the cheerleading squad.

At this point, the journalist picks up Carla's story again. But now the reader has more context and understands the many underlying causes of the disease. Having learned about Karen Carpenter, the reader now wants to know about Carla. After all, Carla is a local person. Toward the end of the story, the writer quotes two other members of the local chapter of Overeaters Anonymous. The writer then quotes Greene and Schmidt of the first draft, then closes with Carla:

Carla is still bulimic.

Once anorexic or bulimic, a person will always have the disease but, with help, can learn to control it, she says. Carla says she learned to control her obsession with food through Overeaters Anonymous. A member since her sophomore year at the University, Carla says she started abstaining from food in May 1988. She says

she found out about the group through a counselor at
the Nutrition Peer Education Program.

"It wasn't easy," Carla says. "I started with Overeaters Anonymous in September 1987 but couldn't give
up my habit until almost eight months later."

Carla says she believes she "kicked" her problem,
although she admits her binge-purge cycle is an
addiction that could someday take control of her life
again.

"I'm an addict." she says. "At the very core, I believe
I'm an addict."

Carla became the thread, the ordering mechanism, for this story. Carla
appeared briefly at the beginning. She reappeared after the reader had a
context for the subject, and her reappearance gave the reader more insight
on her problem. Finally, she showed up one more time at the end of the
story. There the reader learns the rest of Carla's story.

By relying on Carla, the writer was following the advice given by
Madelyn Ross, the managing editor of the *Pittsburgh Press*. Speaking to a
public affairs reporting seminar, Ross advised her audience how to avoid
boring stories:

> We need to remember that to tell a story, we have to
> relate it to people. If you don't do that you're telling a
> story of numbers bureaucracy and census figures, and it
> doesn't get to the people you are trying to reach. We
> had a case where a reporter was assigned to write a story
> about a study that listed the kinds of jobs that would be
> available for people in the 1990s. It was boring.
>
> So instead of writing that, he went out to a 6th grade
> class because these would be the workforce of the 1990s.
> He asked them what their hopes and dreams for careers
> were. And they told their stories, very interesting. The
> most interesting part was that it didn't match at all with
> what the experts were saying was going to be available.
> Here we had a whole group of kids expecting to do one
> sort of thing, but those jobs were not going to exist
> when they go to the workforce.

The idea for interviewing 6th graders came out of the consulting process in which an editor and reporter discussed the story before the story was finished. The editor helped the reporter conceptualize the story. They avoided the boring story and also discovered something the numbers didn't reveal.

Relate the story to people. That was also the advice an editor gave a reporter on deadline when the reporter turned in a disorganized fire story. In summary, the story went something like this:

1. Lead: woman and baby killed in fire.
2. Names of victims, time of death; one injured.
3. How they died.
4. How fire began.
5. Detail on how fire spread.
6. Quote on intensity of fire.
7. Scene upon arrival of firefighters; difficulty fighting fire.
8. How the injured person escaped; where woman and baby were found.
9. Injured person tells how he and woman escaped.
10. Injured person tells how woman ran back in for baby.
11. Owner of house and his reaction.
12. Number of firefighters at scene and temperature (freezing).
13. Fire chief thanks everyone.
14. Unidentified firefighter describes house upon arrival.
15. Time bodies found.
16. Problems tin roof caused in fighting fire.
17. Comment of neighbor on how far fire could be seen in night sky.
18. Another neighbor tells how distraught injured man was.
19. Fire chief says thank you (again).
20. Last fatal fire in the county.

What the reporter had done was written a lead and then dumped his notes in succeeding but not always related paragraphs. In a quick consultation, the reporter and editor agreed that the best approach to organizing the story was to keep everying related to people, the dead and injured, together at the top of the story and to put everything related to fighting the fire later on. The logic: The reader would be more interested in the people than the actual fire. Because the story was written on a computer, the reporter could easily rearrange it and insert transition.

Reporters sometimes get so engaged in their stories that they do not see the weaknesses. An editor comes at the story with a fresh viewpoint and can see something the reporter may have missed. For example, one beginning reporter did a brief feature story on parking problems in her town. These are the opening paragraphs followed by the ending:

> In the midst of the noon hour traffic snarl a woman ignores the no parking sign on West Beaver Avenue and parks in one of two travel lanes.
>
> She dashes into the Yarn Shop. Traffic becomes bottle-necked. Emerging several minutes later, she is greeted by blaring horns. After she pulls away, traffic flow resumes.
>
> The same customer does this about every two weeks, according to Rebecca Berg, a Yarn Shop employee.
>
> "Parking is a problem for our customers, many of whom are elderly," Berg says. "But with this customer it's sheer laziness." Berg said the woman shops on her lunch hour and said she doesn't have time to find a parking space.
>
> "I hope she gets a ticket the next time she tries it," Berg said. "She expects us to drop everything when she runs in. I hate that."
>
> Parking is a problem not easily solved. . . .
>
> Scrafford sympathizes with the clerks. "I can't afford the parking garage fee every day on what I make either," she said. "But it's a long walk from my apartment."
>
> Bob Steinbach, manager of Bumblebee's, said, "It's important to see the future needs of the community. We don't want to get caught with our pants down again."

Her editor liked the story, but felt it needed a better ending. In consultation with the writer, he suggested holding back on part of the anecdote in the lead and using it as the close. This is how the story finally ended:

As for the Yarn Shop customer who parks in the travel lane, Berg has a solution:
"I hope she gets a ticket the next she tries it. She expects us to drop everything when she runs in. I hate that."

All the editor suggested was an ending the reader could identify with.

Good editors look out for reporters and work with them, not against them. Good editors nurture good relationships as a way of helping reporters do a better job.

Sources and Resources

Clark, Roy Peter. "Ideas to Improve Writing at Your Newspaper." Handout at Associated Press Managing Editors Convention, October 23, 1981.

———. "Feedback on Feedback." In *Writing & Editing.* Associated Press Managing Editors, Seattle, Wash., September 15–18, 1987, 18.

———. "A Conversation with Don Fry about Coaching." *The Poynter Report* (Spring 1988): 6–7.

———. "Coaching Writers: The Human Side of Editing." *Washington Journalism Review* (November 1988): 34–36.

"Coaching Writers." Unpublished report from a convention of newspaper writing coaches, Poynter Institute, St. Petersburg, Fla., December 3–6, 1985. Copyright 1986, The Poynter Institute.

Fry, Don. "How to Form a Writers' Group." *The Quill* (March 1988): 25–27.

King, Barbara. *A Primer on Writing Coaches and Coaching Writers.* Campbell Hall, N.Y.: Ottaway Newspapers, 1988.

Laakaniemi, Ray. "An Analysis of Writing Coach Programs on American Daily Newspapers." *Journalism Quarterly* 64, nos. 2–3 (Summer-Autumn 1987): 569–575.

LaRocque, Paula. "Suggestions for Coaching Reporters." In *Writing & Editing.* Associated Press Managing Editors, Seattle, Wash., September 15–18, 1987, 19.

Ross, Madelyn. "The Relationship Between Reporter and Editor." Speech to the Roy W. Howard Public Affairs Reporting Seminar, Bloomington, Ind., September 3–4, 1988.

Scanlan, Christopher, ed. *How I Wrote the Story.* 2d ed. Providence, R.I.: Providence Journal Co., 1986.

Stepp, Carl Sessions. "As Writers See Editors." *Washington Journalism Review* (December 1987): 29–32.

Wolf, Rita, and Tommy Thomason. "Writing Coaches: Their Strategies for Improving Writing." *Newspaper Research Journal* 7, no. 3 (Spring 1986): 43–49.

Chapter 8

Headlines

Headlines Are an Aid to Readers

Shortly after Harry S Truman was elected president of the United States, he was invited to speak to a convention of editorial writers. As the Democratic nominee for president, Truman had not enjoyed the support of many editorial writers. Still he had won the election. As he addressed the editorial writers, he paid the usual homage one would to one's hosts and then said, "Still, I'd rather have a good headline writer on my side."

What Truman knew instinctively has since been borne out in research. Readers form their impressions of the news—in fact, believe they are getting all of a story—from the headline. Headlines bear a heavy burden in communicating clearly what's in a newspaper. Whereas a writer might get 10 or 15 paragraphs to tell a story, the headline writer gets space to fit only five or six words and in that space must tell the story.

The headline's most important function, then, is to tell the reader what the story is about. A good headline may also attract the reader to the story. One wonders how many well-written stories go unread because of a poor headline. When a sports editor won a prize for a column he had written, the headline writer took several bows too. After all, he argued, who could resist this headline: "Hot dog vendor peddles inside dope."

The headline serves the reader in a number of ways beyond telling what the story is about and attracting attention. The size of a headline enables the reader to evaluate the importance of a story. When combined with story position on a page, a headline says to the reader, "In the opinion of the editors, this story is more important than that story but not as important as this other story." In this bigger-is-better world, the larger the headline the more important the story. That is why the lead story of the newspaper contains the largest headline on Page One and the most important story on any page has the largest headline. Some newspapers have rules that reserve a certain size headline for the lead story of the day only, and no other page editor may duplicate the size.

A Basic Guide to Writing Headlines

A good headline is a straight line to the reader's mind. A good headline gets right to the point. It tells and sells the story to the reader. As editors have often said, a Pulitzer Prize story is not a prize unless it is read. Getting the reader to start reading is the job of the headline writer. Stories with poor headlines don't get read. In large cities, stories with good headlines can ensure extra street and newsstand sales for newspapers.

In general, headlines are sentences stripped of the frills. That means they usually have subjects and verbs and (if needed) objects. They are written in the present tense, active voice. The best way to write a headline is to put down in as few words as possible what you believe the headline should be. Fitting what you've written will require you to trim some words and collapse prepositional phrases into frontal modifiers. For example, you have a story about a group of U.S. veterans of the Vietnam war who have announced they are going to build a health clinic in Vietnam. You are assigned a two-line head. Your first effort might go like this:

U.S. veterans of Vietnam war
plan to build health clinic in Vietnam

What can you trim and still do justice to the story? Since you're writing a headline for a paper published in the United States, it is unnecessary to identify the veterans with *U.S.* Furthermore, you can reduce *veterans of Vietnam war* to *Vietnam war veterans* or even *Vietnam veterans,* because *Vietnam* when linked with *veterans* says war. Likewise, it isn't necessary to say *in Vietnam* if the word appears elsewhere in the headline. This trimming produces:

**Vietnam veterans plan
to build health clinic**

As you read that over, you have second thoughts. The phrase *Vietnam veterans* could be taken to mean Vietnamese. So you try again.

**U.S. veterans plan to build
health clinic in Vietnam**

That headline does not fit within the width limits assigned by the chief copy editor. How do you trim it? Well, what can go and still be implied? The phrase "to build" seems implicit if not unnecessary. That results in:

**U.S. veterans plan
health clinic in Vietnam**

The bottom line is too long and you must shorten it. Then you realize that you have a prepositional phrase, *in Vietnam,* which can be converted into a frontal modifier. That results in:

**U.S. veterans plan
Vietnam health clinic**

The headline fits and the chief copy editor approves. (See "Headline Styles" and "Figuring the Count" later in this chapter for how to fit headlines.)

You go on to your next story, which is about a woman who adopted a child and then demanded a maternity leave from her employer. She was turned down, so she went to court and a federal arbitrator ruled in her favor. The story reveals that the woman won the right to a one-year leave and that she is glad she fought. If you're not careful, you can miss the point of this story and produce something like this:

**Right to maternity leave
makes Mom glad she fought**

But that isn't really the point of the story. One critical missing element is the mother's adoptive status. Another element worth getting into the lead is the length of the leave. After all, a month-long maternity leave isn't much; a year-long one is. You come up with this as your first effort at rewriting:

**Mother who adopted baby wins the right
to a one-year maternity leave**

The four-word phrase *Mother who adopted baby* can be reduced to *Adoptive mother.*

**Adoptive mother wins the right
to a one-year maternity leave**

Neither *the* nor *a* is necessary.

**Adoptive mother wins right
to one-year maternity leave**

This is still outside the width specifications. In trimming further, consider that the verb *wins* implies *right*. Also, at some newspapers, the rule on numbers in copy is not followed in headlines. The result:

Adoptive mother wins
1-year maternity leave

It passes muster. Next.

Now you're writing another two-line head; this one on the news story about the death of General Maxwell Taylor. He was 85 and a war hero. In your first try, you come up with:

Celebrated war hero
dead at the age of 85

A good part of the second line can go. If you say Taylor was 85, you don't have to say *age,* and, as you know, most headlines don't include articles. But the headline really suffers because no one knows which celebrated war hero died. So, in this case, his name is a critical element and, as it will turn out, his age isn't. This is the final version:

Celebrated war hero
Maxwell Taylor dies

In fact, if this headline were on a page devoted to obituaries, the verb would be dropped, resulting in this:

Celebrated war hero
Maxwell Taylor, 85

Your next effort, on a story about an earthquake in Colombia, produces an indirect headline:

60 dead, 300 injured
as earthquake strikes

That headline does not directly connect the dead and injured with the earthquake; it leaves the reader in doubt about what happened. So you rewrite to make the connection and leave nothing to chance for that reader on the run:

Earthquake kills 60,
hurts 300 in Colombia

That headline leaves no doubt about what the earthquake did and where it occurred. In a present tense, active verb, the headline puts the story out front. If the reader does nothing more than read those seven words, the reader will still know something about the story. That's the mark of a good headline.

The headline about the earthquake demonstrates the wisdom of writing headlines that contain one verb and one thought. On a story about the pope approving a church law that declares women the equal of men, you might create this two-verb, two-thought headline:

Pope signs new law;
women deemed equal

What is the real point of the story? It is not that the pope signed a law, but what the law says. That should be the thought that dominates the headline:

**Pope deems women
equal in new law**

A similar example comes from a story about 10 miners dying after some methane gas exploded. An early effort produced this:

**Mine explosion kills
10; worst in 4 years**

But when written as one thought, a smoother headline results:

**Worst mine explosion
in 4 years kills 10**

A good headline emphasizes the main point of the story and is as specific as it can be. This headline, from a story about a fatal plan crash, emphasizes the crash over the deaths: "Soviet jetliner crashes in Luxembourg, kills 12." To put the emphasis on the deaths, try this headline: "Soviet jetliner crash in Luxembourg kills 12." Speaking of emphasis, this headline suffers from what might be known as a good news mentality: "Two live, 49 die in air crash." Specificity is missing in this headline: "Winds ground shuttle launch." How long? "Winds delay shuttle one day" tells all.

Another mark of a good headline is how well it relates to the lead. Occasionally, a headline writer will base the headline on information deep in the story, which confuses the reader because the headline and the lead don't match. If a headline writer believes the lead of the story is incorrect, the writer should inform the chief copy editor. Also, a headline on a feature story, which often builds to a climax, should not steal the punch line. The writer who spends three pages weaving a story will not appreciate the headline writer who gives the story away in three or four words.

Headline Rules

Headline writing follows a lot of practical rules intended to help the neophyte. Some rules, of course, bend better than others, and some newspapers ignore them altogether, relying instead on intuition. But the newspapers read that way too. Intuition is best applied in unfamiliar situations, which is not what headline writing is.

The best headlines are written in the present tense because the present tense provides the reader with a sense of immediacy. "President signs tax bill" involves the reader; "President signed tax bill" turns the reader away because it sounds like old news.

Frequently, present tense, active voice headlines count better, that is, allow extra room for the writer to say more. This passive voice headline counts 33½: "Vienna's largest store destroyed in fire"; its present tense, active voice counterpart counts 31½. In some situations a difference of 2 would mean a headline that does not fit and is thus unusable.

Do not blindly follow the present tense rule. Headlines containing time elements usually sound better in past tense. For example, "Personal income rises in October" would not make a lot of sense in November. Better to use past tense: "Personal income rose in October."

The headline sets the tone for the story and should be serious for serious stories and light for light stories. When a U.S. diplomat named Richard Queen was freed after eight months as a hostage in Iran, one newspaper headlined the story: "Queen was not treated royally." The headline writer was trying to show off at the expense of someone.

Not every headline needs to have a subject and verb. Headlines on feature stories, in-depth articles, editorials and columns sometimes read better when written as titles. When a former New York gambling czar died in obscurity and *The New York Times* published a retrospective, it was titled "The Lonely Death of a Man Who Made a Scandal." That sounds like a short story.

Regardless of the approach, use only commonly understood abbreviations and then be careful. Is "Reps request inquiry" about Republicans or representatives? More common abbreviations include FBI, CIA, U.S., U.N. and compass points that are part of a name, as in "Rising crime adds to S. Africa's misery." Avoid awkward regionalisms, such as CLUM, which stands for Civil Liberties Union of Massachusetts. And what is the reader to make of "CLEP tests set for 2 dates"? It sounds like a venereal disease.

Headline writers are also very good at making a part stand for the whole. It is not uncommon, when referring to a country's government, to use the name of the capital city in a headline instead of the country's name. Thus, when there isn't room for *Soviet Union,* a headline writer will use *Moscow. Seoul* fills in nicely for *South Korea,* and in states with long names and short capitals, the capital city serves well in a headline.

The need for attribution in a headline parallels the need for attribution in a story. If without attribution, the source of information is unclear or the headline sounds like the newspaper's opinion, then attribution is mandatory. That's one of those rules that doesn't bend. Compare these headlines from the same event but different newspapers: "Reagan knew of contra funding" and "Senator asserts Reagan knew of arming contras." The critical difference is that the second headline contains a source and the first doesn't.

When needed, attribution works best at the end so it does not impede the message:

Authentic letter from
American hostages to
home asks, 'Free us'

'Free us from this
terrible situation,'
hostage letter asks

The headline with the attribution at the end reads better. The first headline buries the news at the end. With attribution, the challenge to the writer is to avoid writing similar-sounding headlines such as these:

Bottled water contains
arsenic, N.Y. officials say

**Upstate valve accused of
leak, NRC official says**

Since the same person wrote those, he could have avoided the repetition by using a different form of attribution:

**N.Y. officials find
arsenic in water**

**NRC aide cites missing
valve as cause of leak**

In headlines with kickers or drops (subordinate headlines), repetition can dull the message because the readers get a feeling of old news when they see words repeated. For example, a page editor ties two storm stories together with a main headline and a drop headline for each story. The main headline says:

Storms kill 10 on Pacific Coast, 6 in Hawaii

The stories contain these respective headlines:

Thousands lose power in icy Pacific storm

Freak winter storm hits Hawaiian Islands

With so many words repeated, it is apparent the writer was not working hard to produce a set of good headlines. This rewrite not only removes the repetition but shows how to link stories with ellipses:

16 die as storms belt Pacific Coast, Hawaii

Thousands lose power in icy onslaught . . .

. . . flooding, high winds, surf plague Islands

Putting an abundance of modifiers in front of a noun can muddle any headline. "Windfall profits tax phaseout pushed back" hides the verb and leaves the reader wondering if *phaseout* might not be it. (The verb is two words, *phase out,* but readers don't always spell when they read.) The writer would not have had a problem if she had used present tense: "President delays windfall phaseout." Given that a tax on windfall profits was a major news item at the time, the reader would understand the rewrite without *tax* and *profits*.

When writing multiline heads, some headline writers attempt to make each line stand on its own. That way the reader is left unsure of how the headline fits together. To write such headlines, the writers avoid bad breaks, the splitting of a phrase whose parts cannot stand alone. One example:

**Pat leaves White
House very sad**

Reading the headline line by line, the reader is jarred:

Pat leaves White

The possibilities at this point are endless, and the reader may stop to figure them out or go to another story, or the reader may read the second line as a unit in itself:

House very sad

The emphasis has now switched from Pat to the House. The House of Representatives? Will the reader re-read? No.

A more typical example involves the splitting of an infinitive between lines.

Senate rejects plan to
end free prescriptions

Some editors frown on such breaks and urge their writers to avoid them. Some editors consider the preceding rule nothing but superstition. Certainly, common sense should remain the primary rule in determining headline clarity. Obviously, this is a bad break:

Tanka aide admits taking $2
million bribe for boss on TV

And an absolute taboo in the category of bad breaks is this:

Psychologist Erich
Fromm dead at 79

Names should never be split between lines of a head.

Headline writers have created their own slang (called headlinese) when they have needed a short word to take the place of a long word that won't fit. Here are some examples of headlinese, all to be avoided: ups, raps, meets, nips, OKs, pens, nabs, fells, hikes, eyes, airs, inks, nixes, taps, tabs, solon, accord, pact, axes, looms, sets, rips. The test of a headline word is, If it is common to everyday conversation, use it. People will understand it.

Because it is uncommon, headlinese is seldom clear, as one 9-year-old showed one day after looking at "A's down Yankees." "Does that mean the Yankees lost?" she asked. When the reader has to ask, the headline is no good. Given the use of horizontal layout in which headlines are easier to write because they go across the page instead of down in narrow vertical columns, writers can more easily avoid headlinese. In horizontal layout no writer can have an excuse for this: "House axes tax slash; vows $ probe." That has an Attila-the-Hun quality to it, which makes it hard to read.

The following headline is hard to believe: "Wrestler nipped in state finals." Does it mean the wrestler was bitten? Some headline writers opt for words such as *cut* for *reduction* and *Mideast* for *Middle East*. But "Troop cut seen in Mideast fray" defies explanation because of the headlinese.

Not all slang, of course, should be avoided. In this headline the use of *up,* as slangy as it is, provides a snappy cadence the headline would otherwise lack:

Federal aid to cities up, but not up with inflation

Headlines that begin with verbs confuse the reader and are best avoided. What is the reader to make of "Charge man with murder"? Who charged the man with murder? And this headline, although it has a national tabloid essence to it, actually comes from a staid small-town daily: "Has her house burned but her cheer's back." Because the headline begins with a verb, it sounds as though the woman intentionally burned down her house, which was not the case.

Just because a headline should not begin with a verb does not mean it should lack a verb altogether. Verbs are the locomotives of thought, and without verbs, thoughts go nowhere. The following doesn't budge: "Growing awareness in U.N. of Third World independence."

A headline must be clear. Fathom this: "Egyptian fat cat class expansion charged." If you figured from that that the rich are getting richer, you have more patience than most readers. Can you understand this one: "Pix Nixed in Cineplex Snit"? This one may be easier: "Prose Pros Nix Phrase Maze." Consider this: "False sex scandal rumored." Why would anyone bother to spread a rumor about a false sex scandal? How far would such a rumor get? "Pst. Wanna hear about a false sex scandal?" False sex scandals aren't any fun.

Colon headlines create problems because of the multiple uses of a colon. Consider these three colon headlines:

Heinz, Green: Similar views on national issues

Vorster: No urban black rule in South Africa

Hearst: 'Rebel in search of a cause'

In the first, the colon functions as an equals sign or replaces a verb. The headline says Heinz and Green have similar views. But in the second, the colon functions as a signal for an attribution tag. In other words, Vorster is making the statement about black rule. And in the third headline, the colon introduces a direct quote about Patty Hearst, not by her. The confusion results from the multiple functions of the colon. Here are some more:

Public: Strong work force needed to keep U.S. great

Suspect: 'I messed things up' in other kidnapping attempts

Studies: Saccharin users face low risks

Social Security: Everyone's involved but few understand system

Austerity threatens Newgate: historian

Some editors wisely ban colon headlines, while others insist that their use be clear and consistent throughout the paper. To achieve consistency means not mixing some of the preceding usages.

Like leads, headlines should be specific. The tip-off to a say-nothing lead is the word *discuss,* as in "City Council last night discussed raising taxes." The same word tips off the reader to a say-nothing headline, as in "Candidates discuss Social Security proposals." A better headline would tell what the candidates said. Similarly, the headline "U.S. Supreme Court upholds FCC stand" says nothing because the reader does not know what the FCC's stand is.

Question headlines are as gimmicky as question leads. Don't try to con the reader into a story with a question headline, such as "Cigarettes harmful to infants?" After all, the headline should be telling the story, not raising questions. "Smoke harms infants, doctor says" would be an acceptable rewrite.

Uncommon words should be avoided:

Androgynous
management
suggested

After that, this headline, with its long word for *dies,* doesn't look so bad:

Councilman
succumbs
at meeting

Obviously, *succumbs* was picked to fill out the line. That's padding, which should be avoided.

Labels usually fail as headlines because they merely sit atop a story and do nothing. Their staticism turns off the reader. Something like "Today's weather" says nothing. What about the weather? That's what the headline should answer.

Single quotation marks take the place of double quotation marks in headlines because the double marks consume space and look unattractive in headline type. Remember this colon head: "Hearst: 'Rebel in search of a cause.'

Forget the style rules when using numbers in headlines. In some newspapers, no number is spelled out in headlines; always use the figure. In other newspapers, the lonely look of 1 has earned it special status—spell out when used alone. Regardless of any other rule, when using the pronoun *one,* spell it out.

And does not appear often in headlines. Instead, the comma substitutes:

Woman shoots husband, drunken friend

If *and* is used, the ampersand is a legitimate substitute at most newspapers. It takes less space.

Headlines, of course, follow the rules of grammar. Logic doesn't take a back seat just because a writer can't make a headline fit. This is a poor headline: "Resident injured in fire, destroys home." It sounds as if the resident had destroyed the home.

Likewise, commas do not disappear, as one did in this headline:

Bullet pierces house
barely misses woman

To avoid *house barely misses woman,* insert a comma after *house:*

Bullet pierces house,
barely misses woman

In Error They Glare

A newspaper's most vulnerable spot is the headline. The qualified privilege that extends to a reporter's story does not protect the headline writer. Good attorneys caution editors that a libel-safe story means nothing if the headline fails. Over the years, letters to the editor of different newspapers have revealed reader unhappiness with misleading headlines. Usually, the writer begins by saying, "The story was accurate, but . . ." and then goes on to complain how the headline distorted the story and gave a wrong impression. If the reader takes in nothing but the headline and the lead, the headline is sure to be remembered. One study of reader satisfaction found that headline accuracy was the single most important predictor of satisfaction with a newspaper. (Second most important was the paper's general appearance, which is discussed in Chapter 10, "Design.")

Reader satisfaction aside, courts have found in favor of plaintiffs in libel suits even when the story was accurate and the headline writer's intention was not to slur anyone. The headline "Bid specs reported 'rigged' " cost a newspaper $10,000 even though the writer was trying to say the specifications favored (were rigged in favor of) some manufacturers over others, not that anyone was fraudulent (which is what *rigged* suggests). Intentions don't count.

A thoughtless headline can deflate any claim of fairness and objectivity when it seems to take sides. For example, "Student protests mar decade's start" was the headline on a story recapping the 1970s. Perhaps it is a matter of perspective, but some would argue that had it not been for student protests, a senseless war would have gone on longer than it did. But, in any case, the headline should have been neutral. Changing *mar* to *mark* would have done that. In another case, when protesters were arrested for trespassing at the Statue of Liberty, a headline writer convicted them before they faced a judge: "Protesters trespass on Statue of Liberty." Another headline writer declared a legal decision at the outset of a lawsuit: "Fallout victims sue government." The second paragraph of the story calls them "alleged victims of nuclear fallout." The court will decide, not the headline writer.

Headline errors also create problems for reporters. Many readers believe that reporters write the headlines on their own stories, so when a headline contains an error, the reporter gets blamed. This creates problems between reporters and sources, with the sources believing that the reporter is not playing fair.

Headlines thoughtlessly placed on a page can combine to give an unintended meaning. For example, stories about prostitutes and a political candidate that appear side by side so that the one headline reads into the other might do this:

Prostitutes identified   Watson runs for office

Even if the reader realizes that Watson is not one of the prostitutes, the damage has still been done.

Headlines containing grammatical or semantic errors are embarrassing. When a woman who had been severely beaten emerged from a coma of two weeks and spoke, one headline writer said, "Comatose jogger speaks to family." The writer didn't realize that *comatose* means "in a coma and unable to speak."

Spelling errors are bad enough in stories, but in headlines they're out there where everyone can see them. When some fraternities decided to hold non-alcoholic parties, a headline writer noted, "Frats set 'dryer' parties into effect." Good news, parents, your sons are doing their own laundry. The right word is *drier*. The headline "Writer dies who wrote war declaration" is awkward because the relative clause (*who wrote war declaration*) does not immediately follow the noun it modifies (*writer*). And this one abuses the language: "Defense Plays Good Despite Flutie's 447 Yards." *Well, well, well!*

Then there's the two-faced headline, such as these from a school board's proposal to restructure the system for students in grades 7 through 12: "School board considers regrouping secondary students into 2s," one headline said, suggesting that all students would be paired off, while another headline said, "Secondary students may undergo change." One editor quipped: "To what? Primary students." And, if you don't like the results of a trial, express your feelings in a headline such as this: "Jury hung in Mesmer murder case." What kind of deal is involved in "Mubarak offers U.S. bases?" Has the president of Egypt been given the right to give away U.S. bases? No; he offered bases in Egypt to the United States. The headline says it both ways.

The more seriously flawed two-faced headline is the one with a ribald meaning. Here are two: "Dick should veto studs, Carson says" and "Dick will fill vacancy, court rules." The reader is expected to know that *Dick* is a governor's first name, but that isn't clear. The headline writer would have done better with "Gov. should veto studs, Carson says" and "Gov. will fill vacancy, court rules." The same headline writer also wrote, "Delinquent water, sewage customers are fingered." The writer meant they were named. The sexual connotations aside, the writer misused *sewage,* which refers to what the system gets rid of. The writer meant *sewerage,* which means the system, for which there are customers.

Consider more two-faced headlines: "Senator undecided on spousal rape." "Officials improve atrocities at Atlanta Zoo," "Mom ponders approach to sexually active son," "Women must realize married men make poor husbands," "Smokers are productive, but death cuts efficiency," "Illegitimate woman doesn't need to hide her past," "Sex education delayed/teachers request training," "Split rears in farmer movement," "Judge to decide if soldier in sex crimes was competent," "Sisters reunited after 18 years in checkout line at supermarket," "People quit burning coal town," "Woman off to jail for sex with boys," "Three are slain in 'crack den' owned by city," "Stalled cars tied to rats," "Illinois high court may rule on cocaine," "Close your eyes and eat abroad," "West Snyder girls have holes to fill," "Supreme Court OKs cable sex," "Coed beats off hooded attacker."

One two-faced headline never saw the light of print: "Leaking is a Washington habit." But this one did: "Doctor discusses disease with lucky victims," in which *lucky* means the victims who didn't die. A copy editor for the late New York *World-Telegram* wrote this headline and readout:

Ford lays off 50,000 men
as strikers cut off parts
Action halts
nearly all
production

The way to keep such headlines from getting into print is to ensure that every headline is read by someone other than its creator. A dirty mind helps too.

Writing Seductive Headlines

A good headline is alluring; it doesn't smack the reader over the head but instead seduces the reader into reading the story. A good headline stimulates readership. A good headline is a pleasure to read even though the reader may not say, "That was a good headline." In fact, the reader never notices good headlines. Good headlines do not call attention to themselves but to the stories they accompany. Copy editors can learn to write good headlines. Headline writing is the same as the finishing polish on a jewel. The attitude of the headline writer helps determine the quality of the headline. A dated headline from *Editor & Publisher* expresses a desirable quality of the headline writer: "Wanted for The Rim: Man Who Writes Like A Poet." The headline is the copy editor's signature on a story.

On a story about a shortage of beef, a writer captured readers with "Don't beef—there isn't much." Who could complain? When a home economist announced that despite rumors the price of hamburger was not going to $2 a pound, a writer caught in the spirit offered, "$2 per pound 'burger report pure baloney." When NBC and the Nebraska Educational Television Network settled a dispute over logos, one headline announced, "All's well that N's well," the dispute having been over the similarity in the stations' N-styled logos.

On a story about the high level of tax revenue that a state had reaped in one month: "In Pa., April is the richest month of all." At another time, the Associated Press reported that residents filing their returns around April 15 wouldn't get their refund until July 4, thus sparking this headline: "IRS: In by the 15th, out by the Fourth." When a U.S. president who had just been shown in photographs slipping on a piece of ice outside the White House later said something he shouldn't have, a headline writer touted the story with "President slips on his tongue." The headline worked because the image of the president slipping on the ice was still fresh. Remember "show and tell" in grade school? One newspaper story suggesting that television programs in which people at home shopped for goods offered on the air wasn't doing too well got this headline: "Shop-at-home program fails to show and sell."

The copy editor bent on writing good headlines does not quit after the first attempt. Second-rate headline writers would accept the following on a story about the R-factor, which tells how well insulation insulates: "Energy department gives insulating tips." For the reader, the headline guarantees instant sleep. A better writer produced, "Insulating means learning the fourth R." Intriguing.

The headline writer goes beyond the obvious to produce a good headline. When a judge ruled that police could not cross municipal boundaries in hot pursuit of speeders, and the newspaper produced a story saying the police were not happy with the ruling, a headline writer wrote,

"Police cool to ban on hot pursuit." The writer of the story praised the headline writer, who replied, "But it was the obvious head." Likewise, a profile on Jim McKay, who, among other things, hosts a television program called "Wide World of Sports," cried out for more than this headline: "Jim McKay: his wide world."

To be understood, a headline should not require reader familiarity with another medium. The headline writer who relies on the reader's knowing some television jingle or watching some television program could write a poor headline if the reader never watches television. This rule, however, carries with it an important exception: The headline a reader can understand on two levels. Such a headline is fine if the reader understands the intended meaning. For the reader who also sees the secondary meaning, it's a bonus. This *Washington Star* headline, about the Milwaukee Brewers, a baseball team, serves as an example: "The Brewers That Made Milwaukee Famous." Seen on a sports page, that headline makes sense. But to those familiar with the pitch for Schlitz beer, the headline reveals more, because Schlitz advertised itself as "The beer that made Milwaukee famous." The reader who doesn't know about Schlitz beer still receives a good headline. Those who know the Schlitz motto appreciate the headline more.

A good headline writer relies on the story, the situation, the opportunity. *The New York Times* one day published a story about how long a person would take to fill out federal forms. The story began on the front page with the headline "An Average Reader Finishes This Article In About 2½ Minutes" and continued to an inside page, where the reader was greeted with this headline on the continuation: "You Have About 2 Minutes Left." These headlines are clever and relevant.

Headline writers always need to be careful that they are not being more clever than clear. The standard headline with a strong verb serves most stories. Few stories in a daily newspaper would benefit from cleverness, so don't attempt to make every headline more than it should be. Mixed metaphors and strained puns detract from headlines. This one, "Curtain rises on Bears' question marks," drew this comment: "Keep curtain risers on the Arts Page, and question marks in the grammar books, and that way you won't mix them." The way to measure a punning headline is to submit it to the groan test—if a second reader groans, scrap the headline; three groans, scrap the writer.

Headline Styles

Headline type comes in many designs (called faces) but only a few are usually used for headlines. Aesthetically, a mix of headline faces on a page detracts from the design by calling attention to the mixture. The mix also detracts from the content of the headlines. An editor striving for a simple, functional look would not mix a lot of headline faces. The editor might use a different face to set off a front-page column or news roundup headline. Or the editor might use a different face on the editorial or lifestyle page. In general, the news department does not use a great many faces because most are set aside for the advertising department, where variety of display type among advertisements helps set the ads off from one another, a preferable result in advertising.

Figure 8.1 shows two type faces and their relative sizes (the figures have been reduced). Compare the Helios with the English. The English type has serifs while Helios does not. (Compare the letter *d* in both, and note the additional lines at the top and bottom of the English *d*. Those lines are serifs.) The serifs make it easier for the eye to pace along a line of type. But because headline type is much larger than story (body) type, the visual aids are unnecessary. Modern headlines are often in a sans serif face.

Modern headlines often appear in what is called down style: only the first letter of the first word of the headline and of proper nouns are capitalized. Newspapers went to down-style headlines because type experts say down style duplicates the way body type is set, which is easier to read. After All, How Easy Is Reading This Sentence, With Every First Letter Of Every Word Capitalized? Down-style headlines avoid the problems of these three up-style headlines:

**Dr. Robert Going
To Speak**

Phils To Name Green Manager

Falling 'Star' Hits Professor Hard

Figure 8.1 Varying sizes of Helios headline type and English headline type. Helios is a sans serif type; English is a serif type. Both are shown in a reduced size. (Courtesy of Daily Collegian Publications, The Pennsylvania State University.)

daily collegian productions
7 Carnegie
University Park, PA 16802
814 865-2533

Helios

72
abcdefghijklmnopqrstuv

60
abcdefghijklmnopqrstuvwxyz

48
abcdefghijklmnopqrstuvwxyzabcdef

36
abcdefghijklmnopqrstuvwxyzabcdefghijklmnopq

30
abcdefghijklmnopqrstuvwxyzabcdefghijklmnopqrstuvwxy

24
abcdefghijklmnopqrstuvwxyzabcdefghijklmnopqrstuvwxyzabcdefghijklr

18
abcdefghijklmnopqrstuvwxyz

14
abcdefghijklmnopqrstuvwxyz

daily collegian productions
7 Carnegie
University Park, PA 16802
814 865-2533

English

72
abcdefghijklmnopqrstuv

60
abcdefghijklmnopqrstuvwxyz

48
abcdefghijklmnopqrstuvwxyzabcdef

36
abcdefghijklmnopqrstuvwxyzabcdefghijklmnop

30
abcdefghijklmnopqrstuvwxyzabcdefghijklmnopqrstuvwxy

24
abcdefghijklmnopqrstuvwxyzabcdefghijklmnopqrstuvwxyzabcdefghijkl

18
abcdefghijklmnopqrstuvwxyz

14
abcdefghijklmnopqrstuvwxyz

Perhaps the reader will figure out who Dr. Going is, but will even the most understanding of fans forgive the Phillies' management for hiring a green manager? Experience should count for something. (Green, by the way, was the manager's last name.) And by now everyone has figured out that Professor Hard does not exist.

A standard headline over the years has been the banner or streamer. It extends across the top of the page from left to right, spanning, for instance, all the six columns into which many newspapers are formatted. The typical banner contains one line. Good headlines, no matter what their size, use as few words as possible. In fact, if a headline sounds wordy, the editor who assigned it might consider increasing its size, provided enough body type exists to balance with the headline.

Headlines come in point sizes ranging, for our purposes, from 14 points to 72 points (see Figure 8.1) and even higher. Before computerized typesetting, headline sizes generally differed by six points at the lower end of the scale and 12 points at the higher end. This has changed with computers, for now a computerized typesetting machine can be commanded to make any size type. If someone produced a brilliant four-column head of 72 points and it was too long, the computer could drop it to 71 or 70 points. This is not the best idea, however. If every headline writer arbitrarily changed head sizes, the page's balance would be off.

Headline assignments are given to copy editors using numbers to represent the number of columns wide the headline must be, the point size, and the number of lines. In addition, the assignment tells whether a headline is to be Roman, *italic,* or **boldface.** The types are mixed to create contrast. Usually one type family will be used, and where contrast is necessary, the headline assigner will achieve it by mixing a boldface and lightface version of the same type. More traditional newspapers achieve contrast by mixing Roman and italic.

Someone assigned to put a boldface banner on a story could get an assignment for a 6-72b-1, meaning six columns, 72-point boldface, one line. Three lines of single-column 24-point italic would come out as 1-24i-3. A four-column 36-point Roman headline would show as a 4-36r-1, and a two-column two-line headline of the same size would be 2-36r-2.

Newspapers stick to a few basic styles. The standard headline, the one that appears on most stories, is a boldface headline of one line when four columns or longer, or of multiple lines when three columns or under.

Usually, a three-column headline would have no more than two lines, whereas a two-column headline would have two lines (usually) or three lines (occasionally). Single-column headlines are two or three lines, depending on the length of the story.

A second style is the lightface version of the boldface headline, which is used for contrast. Newspapers formerly relied on italic type for contrast, but now many use the bold/light approach.

A third style is the combination, or over-under. In this headline, the top line is the larger of two, and the smaller line is usually set in a type half the size of the top line. The larger line can function like a title, and the line beneath tells the story in more typical headline fashion, that is, subject-verb-object. The smaller headline does not have to fill out the line, which results in air that helps set it off. The following is intended to show the thematic approach to writing such a head:

Pageant the road to a dream
Bourne woman hopes for career break

Somewhat related is the reverse kicker, in which the first line uses larger type that does not extend the entire width of the headline. Usually, too, the reverse kicker is a catchy phrase. Here is the setup for a reverse kicker:

Carny Knowledge
Central Florida has a love affair with a fair

A closing note on over-under and reverse kickers: Typically, the second line is half the point size of the first, although some editors ignore that and step up one size from half. Thus, a 48-point reverse kicker might appear on top of a 30-point, instead of a 24-point, headline.

The drop headline is making a comeback—a comeback because it appears to be a variation on the deck style of headline writing. In deck style, a story carries a main headline and several subordinate headlines immediately beneath the main head. They are called decks. The front pages of *The New York Times* and *The Los Angeles Times* exhibit this style, which dates back at least a century. The new form carries only one deck, which editors refer to as a drop. A typical two-deck headline would be a 1-36b-3/1-18-2.

Another version of the reverse kicker is the hammer, which is a reverse kicker but in all capital letters. Such headlines should be used sparingly because all-caps headlines are hard to read. By virtue of their size, hammers impress the reader with their importance, but that can be diluted by having too many hammers on one page. Here is an example of a hammer headline:

STRIKE?
Baseball union leaders call for April 1 contract deadline

The over-under, the reverse kicker and the hammer have spawned other varieties, including a style that Mario Garcia calls tripod heads. A tripod head is essentially a reverse kicker, but rather than having one line above the other, it has the larger type and the smaller type on the same line. For example:

Rules/ *Bumper crop this year*

The word *Rules,* called a banger at some newspapers, is set in 48-point boldface, and the remainder of the head is half the size, 24-point, and either lightface or italic.

The side-saddle headline—placed next to rather than above the story—appears when the story is in such a location that the headline should not clash with a headline below. Typically, that is above an advertisement spanning six columns. In a case such as an advertisement that leaves only two or three inches across the top of the page, using the space-saving side-saddle style is imperative for the editor who wants to publish a lot of story. The alternative is a small (24-point, perhaps) headline, which most editors would not run across six columns because it would be too wordy.

Side-saddle headlines, when used on an open page, appear with boxed stories so that the headline does not conflict with other headlines on the page. The box also keeps the story body type from running into other stories.

The preceding has tried to show that although headline styles may not vary much, their labels do. As with other facets of journalism, individual newspapers have their own names for headlines, and you should not assume that the labels used in this book are universal. What should be understood is the evolution in headline styles and the opportunity of imaginative copy editors to create other styles.

Figuring the Count

Before computerized typesetting, headline writers needed to know how to "count" heads to see if what they had written would fit. Today, a headline writer can put anything on the screen and then ask the computer to measure it. The computer will tell if the headline is too long and by how much. Then the headline writer can decide to squeeze the type or reduce the size (neither is being advocated) or rewrite the headline.

But even with computers helping out, you should still understand the principles behind "counting" headlines. Every headline family counts differently, so the following system represents just one of several in the industry. Learning a new system is not difficult; most copy desks put together a headline chart that gives the size for every headline the system can produce. All the writer has to learn is what individual letters and numerals count. On top of that, the computer tells the writer when a headline does not fit.

Generally, most lowercase letters and figures count 1, even though an accurate measure might show that some letters count three-quarters or nine-tenths. In most headline counting, editors use as a basis ½ , 1, 1½ and 2, and then don't worry about the counts that might fall in between or under. The law of averages helps headline writers.

The letters and figures that do not count 1 include fat letters such as *m* and *w,* which each count 1½, and skinny letters such as *l, i, f, t* and the figure 1, which each count ½. In some systems, the letter *j* counts 1 whether it is capital or lowercase.

Generally, capital letters count 1½, except *M* and *W,* which each count 2. *L, F, T,* which count less in lowercase, also count 1½ per letter. *I* counts 1. Spaces between words can count ½ or 1, depending on how much spacing the typesetting machine has been programmed to allow. Most punctuation counts ½ except *?, —,* and *$,* which count 1.

Given all that, a headline with a lot of skinny letters can squeeze in more than the count seems to allow, and a headline with a lot of fat letters won't allow as many letters as the count says it should. This headline, which was written as a 3-36-1 and counts to fit, probably would not fit because of the many fat letters: "Women march with Mummers."

Those who assign headline sizes know that some counts are virtually impossible to write and that asking a writer to produce a one-line head that counts 18 maximum or three lines of eight counts per line is unfair. Thus, a headline can have too many or too few counts. Each newspaper has its limits, and new copy editors learn them easily and immediately.

Sophisticated electronic editing systems have eliminated the guesswork in writing headlines. A sophisticated system allows for the writing and sizing of the headline.

Depending on the size of the newspaper, a copy editor can write from 10 to 30 headlines a day. The advice of Elwood M. Wardlow, an associate director at the American Press Institute, is for headline writers everywhere: "Remember well: Headlines sell."

Sources and Resources

Bacon, Ed. "Wanted for The Rim: Man Who Writes Like A Poet." *Editor & Publisher* (April 27, 1968): 68–69.

Berner, R. Thomas. "The Narrative and the Headline." *Newspaper Research Journal* 4, no. 3 (Spring 1983): 33–39.

Burgoon, Michael, Judee K. Burgoon, and Steven A. Burch. "Effects of Editorial and Production Practices on Satisfaction with the Use of Local Daily Newspapers." *Newspaper Research Journal* 2, no. 4 (July 1981): 77–88.

Currie, Phil. "How to Make Your Headlines Better: Care Enough to Write the Very Best." *Editorially Speaking* 37, no. 1 (January 1984).

Heinrich, James R. "Reader Comprehension of Verb and Subject Headlines." *Journalism Quarterly* 58, no. 4 (Winter 1981): 639–640.

Johnson, James W. "Footy on the Telly and Other Heady Matters." *The Quill* (December 1986): 14–15.

Marquez, F. T. "How Accurate Are the Headlines?" *Journal of Communication* 30, no. 3 (Summer 1980): 30–36.

Pasternack, Steve. "Headlines and Libel: Is the 'Unit' Approach the Most Effective?" *Newspaper Research Journal* 8, no. 2 (Winter 1987): 33–41.

Tannebaum, Percy H., "The Effect of Headlines on the Interpretation of News Stories." *Journalism Quarterly* 30, no. 2 (Summer 1953): 189–197.

Thornburg, Ron. "Headlines Make the Best Ammunition for Newspapers Hunting Readers." *Editorially Speaking* 42, no. 5 (June 1988).

Wardlow, Elwood M. "Writing Headlines." *Presstime* (September 1986): 16–17.

Chapter 9

News Evaluation

What Makes News

No newspaper can possibly publish every story it receives through local sources and over the wires, so it falls to editors to decide which stories see print. The choice, some days, is easy; other days, it is hard. After all, a newspaper uses perhaps no more than 10 percent of all the wire news it receives; the editor decides which 10 percent along with what local news and how long it all will be.

Editors usually make judgments with the needs of their readers in mind. But, also, editors decide what is newsworthy based on some ideas that have been around newsrooms for a long time. The old saw goes like this: "If a dog bites a man, that's not news; if a man bites a dog, that's news." Following that formula does not make a person an editor, just a cataloger. It has led to the publication of some silly news stories, such as one about a woman who tried to bite a policeman after her dog wouldn't or one about a man who, angered by a howling dog, bit it three times. As the late Adlai Stevenson once said: An editor is a person who separates the wheat from the chaff and prints the chaff.

Similarly, newspapers of old placed a lot of emphasis on crime, which resulted in an unending, unrelated series of stories about, for example, home burglaries, without giving a reporter time to dig deeper to survey the entire scene, to tell the reader about the crime wave and how to avoid it. When you consider how cheap it is to hire someone to merely copy down the police report daily and spit it back at readers, you can understand why the police station became such a great source of news. The analogy today is the newspaper or television station that devotes a great amount of space, time or footage to automobile accidents. Such information is easily and cheaply obtained. Thus, it becomes newsworthy.

Beginning newswriters and editors are often given a list of what constitutes newsworthiness. A list compiled from 14 newswriting textbooks by Professor Wallace B. Eberhard of the University of Georgia produced these terms in describing what makes news: timeliness, proximity–nearness, prominence–eminence, change, action, audience, impact, unusualness, conflict, significance, magnitude, human interest, consequence–probable consequence, sex, children, animals, tragedy, oddities–the bizarre–novelty–rarity, interest, importance, economic impact, familiarity, humor, pathos–pathos/bathos, currency, emotional stimulus–emotion, accuracy, certainty, explanation, clarity, sensationalism, suspense, objectivity, conciseness, irony, drama, surprise, identification, concreteness, personality, progress, disaster, news balance.

As Eberhard pointed out, editors realize that news is more than a list of conditions, elements and qualities. What was the news in the Pentagon Papers case of 1971? After all, the papers revealed history, not current war policy. No reason for secrets there. What the papers really revealed was a government policy of deceit, and by providing that insight into the government, the papers also provided the citizens of the country with a better opportunity to govern, or at least generated a more watchful attitude on the part of the governed toward the government. After all, someone had abused their consent; their news outlets told them that.

But when editors across the country read the Pentagon stories, and many more like them, they probably did not think explicitly of the many points raised here. Such abstractions are not prominent in the publishing of a news report. Instead, an editor examines a story and decides to publish or broadcast it because . . . because it is news.

Several years ago, a member of the Gannett staff reviewed the front pages of all Gannett's (then) 85 daily newspapers. The staff person's job was to see how diverse the editors' news judgments were. The staff person found that the 85 dailies had 42 different lead stories, of which 35 were local. All in all, the 85 dailies covered 300 different stories on their front pages. In effect, what is newsworthy varies from city to city.

News can sometimes defy compartmentalization—the man-bites-dog formula that says news is black and white, either it is news or it isn't.

Just when scholars believe they have figured out what news is, the rules change.

Still, some categories stand out. To be newsworthy, a story must interest many of the readers of the newspaper. That can be tricky. Take *The New York Daily News* and *The New York Times*. The murder of someone in New York City might be a big story in the *News* but get barely a mention in the *Times*. But if some official in a program to eradicate honeybees from Texas died of a bee sting, the *Times* might consider the article worth the lead of its National page and worthy of a reference line on Page One. The *News* wouldn't use the story. The people who read the *Times* know that generally the *Times* is not interested in local news unless it reveals a larger pattern or is national or international in scope. The federal bailing out of New York City was newsworthy to *The New York Times* as much because of its implications for all old cities as because New York City is the home of the *Times*. The same problem in Detroit, Cleveland or Chicago would merit coverage by the *Times* but not by the *News*.

Other news categories include proximity, such as the death of a local person in a local accident or in an accident elsewhere. The dentist who cut down one of only four white ash trees in a small community so he could put in a driveway to his office parking lot was not only news in that community, he was Page One news for three days running. The dentist had offended the community by violating the tree ordinance.

Impact on readers determines a story's newsworthiness, which is why government receives a lot of coverage. The lack of impact is also newsworthy. A bad winter storm that floods Los Angeles and does nothing to San Francisco is newsworthy in both communities, for different reasons. Farmers in Illinois will read with interest about the problems of farmers in Nebraska, because Illinois farmers are trying to learn if the problem is headed their way and if a solution exists.

Weather is always newsworthy. Parents want to know how to dress their children for school tomorrow; farmers want to know if it will be dry enough to harvest or wet enough to get seeds growing. Is an early frost expected? Did the week of rain refresh the diminishing local water supply? Weather coverage, in fact, has improved in recent years. Some newspapers devote an entire page to it, and others at least provide information beyond today, tonight and tomorrow. Any newspaper in a mobile community knows that today's reader may be jetting to Japan and wants to know weather conditions in Tokyo as well as locally.

One need only examine a good newspaper to see how news has been divided into sections. Good newspapers carry the usual news pages and extend their coverage with sections on business, arts, fashion, in-depth sports, science, entertainment and food, to name a few.

News carries with it that implied "Did you hear about this?" News, to paraphrase the legendary editor Charles A. Dana, makes people talk. But, a modern editor hastens to add, "news does not necessarily make people act."

Timeliness often determines news. An event that happened last week may lack newsworthiness, but an event that is 2 years old could be worth Page One. When *The New York Times,* for example, discovered an unpublicized Canadian trial that found that an oil company had once inflated prices, the *Times* ran the story on its front page even though the issue had been resolved two years before. It was news because the issue of price gouging during an energy crisis was a current event that the 2-year-old trial shed some light on. Similarly, confirmation of massive earthquakes in China is newsworthy even when the confirmation occurs years after the event. Any society that operates under a closed-door policy invites the curious to snoop around when that door is opened a crack.

Scientific discoveries, even the hint of some, rate coverage because of the way these discoveries may affect the lives of readers. Any seeming step toward the cure of cancer is sure to generate headlines and magazine cover stories even if the researchers taking the step affirm that it is but a small one. The hint is newsworthy.

Archaeological events, especially those that give clarity to the present, are newsworthy. But even if they do not, secrets of ancient civilizations appeal to the curiosity of many. When Mozart's first symphony was authenticated, it was front page news in *The New York Times.* Likewise, when an American archaeologist discovered chronic lead poisoning after an analysis of skeletons of Romans killed by the eruption of Mount Vesuvius in A.D. 79, that was front page news. A story about a book challenging the work of Margaret Mead, an anthropologist of international repute, also received front page treatment.

State and local news still rank as the major focal points in newspapers. Research shows that no other news outlet provides the state and local news the way newspapers do. The wire services generally provide stories on major state government initiatives, and because whatever the state government does affects everyone, that makes it newsworthy. After state and local news, other newsworthy categories include (in any order depending on the newspaper) crime, education, cultural events, health, social problems, obituaries, labor, environment, sports, disasters, tragedies, politics, business and fashion. On any given day, of course, the editors of different newspapers will rank the events differently, and what might be worth Page One in one newspaper could rate no more than the bottom of the first break (or section) page. By the same token, the editors may have so much news worthy of Page One that they create a second front page to accommodate it.

The use of international news varies, frequently depending on how much the international event affects people in the United States or how much of an investment a newspaper may have made in covering foreign events. The civil war in Vietnam would have meant nothing to U.S. readers until Congress debated whether President Eisenhower should send troops to replace the defeated French. Eisenhower didn't, and Vietnam remained relatively unnewsworthy (unfortunately) for another decade. Nearly two decades after the Vietnam War ended, a page editor on deadline missed a story about the death of a U.S. military adviser in El Salvador and was upbraided for not seeing the parallels between that death and the deaths of American advisers in Vietnam in the early 1960s. If any editing moral can be drawn from this, it is that good editors are steeped in history. They understand that the past is prologue. They reject the notion that today is the only day that counts.

The international scene deserves more attention than it gets, especially in smaller newspapers. As evidence of that, the Hattiesburg, Miss., *American* examined its community to find out how many local connections it had with the Third World. The *American,* at the time a 25,000 circulation daily, ended up publishing a five-day series on how the community relies on Third World markets and how the Third World affects the community. No longer could the editors scorn publishing an international story by saying, "It isn't local." The *American* learned that much international news has local interest.

Any newspaper with television or radio competition finds itself doing well when it plays up state and local news, both areas not well covered by the other two media. With a state capital bureau and backup from their wire services, newspapers can daily present state news packages that include reports on how local legislators vote. The electronic media can present some of that, but not in the convenient, unperishable form of a newspaper. The newspaper that puts its strength into local coverage (broadly defined) increases readership and fulfills an obligation to that readership. That in no way means national and international events should be ignored. Too often, an international crisis springs on newspaper readers because the newspaper has not published background stories about the events leading up to the crisis. The newspaper has failed to keep its readers informed, which is one of the functions of newspapers. International news is more than stories on coups and earthquakes.

Editors who daily evaluate stories for publication or broadcast realize that publishing only the spot, or breaking, news that was once the staple of many news organizations no longer serves the reader well. Editors realize that what makes news is often the story behind the event, the trend, be it a crime wave or a back-to-basics movement in education. Editors now look for stories that tell about people and what makes them act. Editors want stories that tell how people think. Social questions mean a lot to the editors making news judgments. Editors want to know how stories will affect readers, involve readers, attract readers. Does the story say something important and does it say it well? What's in the story for the reader? None of those categories defends gimmicks that attempt to trick readers into the paper; good editors know that news long on tricks but short on substance detracts from the overall news product.

Editors also realize that news can be more than bad or sensationalistic or saber-rattling. They know that behind every story people exist and that the readers want to know about the people in the story as well as the story itself. This attempt to put stories in people terms does not obviate an editor's job to publish the news, nor does it change the substance of news, just the approach. The evolving process of defining news continues today; it is that evolution that makes news evaluation more than just a cataloger's job.

Putting Theory into Practice

Imagine that you are the editor of a 25,000 daily circulation newspaper in a university town of 65,000 people in the center of the state. Your news-paper has television competition from stations in towns 45 and 65 miles away, stations that send crews into your town from time to time. You are 90 miles away from your state capital. The university's football team is always in the top 20, and the university has an otherwise solid sports program. The university has 30,000 students and is the largest public university in the state. You're the wire editor and must make sure nothing of local interest for any department is overlooked. Let's go through some items, compiled from several Associated Press news digests, which should catch your eye.

One story that should be of interest comes from Washington, D.C., with this lead: "In a case that could add to the cost of local bus service, the Supreme Court is considering whether publicly owned mass transit systems should be required to pay federal minimum wages and overtime." You pull it because you know that local government runs the bus service in your town and on campus and that it is federally subsidized. This story, by the way, cries out for a local reaction sidebar.

A federal judge in a nearby state rules that the state's recently adopted plan for inspecting cars violates the Federal Clean Air Act. Because your state is about to adopt the same plan, this story immediately catches your attention. You have an added interest because the judge making the ruling is federal, meaning that the precedent could be applied outside that judge's area. A call to the state transportation people is also in order.

From your state capital comes a story saying that the state's debt to the federal government over the state's unemployment compensation fund will continue to soar this fiscal year, according to federal sources. Certainly of interest.

From Washington, D.C., comes a story about a Supreme Court agreement to decide whether several states, yours among them, will have to repay more than $60 million in education aid the federal government claims was misspent. Who would pay the bill if the court rules against the states? Does this portend a tax increase? And you live in a college town, so education stories are usually of interest. Include this story.

Here's a story from a city 3,000 miles away. The lead: "Researchers say they have developed a low-cost, high-performance solar cell that may convert sunlight into electricity for utilities more cheaply than oil- or gas-fired turbines." Well, you're not in the Sunshine Belt, but you know that among your readers is a small but loyal environmental contingent, and they would certainly want to know more about this.

A story from Battle Creek, Mich., reports that a cereal company is introducing low-sodium versions of two of its cereals in four test markets. This is a consumer story, and that should give it an automatic green flag. Second, many residents are health-conscious, and this is the kind of information that might interest them. And finally, the university has a nutrition department. In fact, a reporter could get a sidebar reaction story from the head of nutrition.

From Jacksonville, Fla., comes a story that the Florida Supreme Court has refused to block the execution of a convicted rapist and murderer. This will be of interest to a university community, which has room for every cause under the sun and even a few on the moon. At least run a couple of paragraphs.

Then there's the story of the woman whose boyfriend sued to halt her from having an abortion. Abortion is a big issue among your readers. Use the story.

You also see this advisory about a feature story that will come later: "At Earlham College in Indiana, a Quaker school where students can major in Peace and Global Studies, officials are coming to the aid of young men who refuse to register for the draft." Given that 48 percent of the student body at your university is male and eligible, you should use this story.

You should also use the story from Cleveland, in fact packaged with the preceding, telling that "a Mennonite college student charged with failing to register with the Selective Service has testified in court that draft registration implies the United States is preparing for war." Be careful, by the way, not to make the mistake of thinking that Quakers and Mennonites are one and the same.

Also consider for the package, from St. Paul, Minn.: "A student group wants a federal judge to block a law forcing college students to register for the draft before they can receive financial aid until he decides its constitutionality."

Then there's the Washington, D.C., story about two congressmen who have introduced a bill to finance repairs of the nation's roads and bridges. One of the congressman comes from your district. Use it.

You also encounter three stories about the National Collegiate Athletic Association, including one that says the NCAA has prepared legislation that would exempt it from federal antitrust laws and protect its monopoly on televising college football. With the university's football team a regular on television on Saturday afternoons, this story is of local interest.

And because it is the primary election season and your state is a swing state, you should run the stories about the three contenders from one party criss-crossing the state just before the election. Also run some wirephotos. After all, it is not for every presidential election that voters in your state might decide who the nominees are.

Then there is a story about Japan restricting imports from South Africa in response to South Africa's apartheid laws. Your readership includes a large number of people interested in this issue.

You also discover that, thanks to a maneuver by your local senator, the state's governing bodies have passed a historic tax reform bill and sent it to the governor at the last minute of the legislative calendar. That's probably the lead, with sidebars, including a telephone interview with the senator.

The good editor recognizes the variety of interests of a newspaper's audience and attempts to provide for all interests.

Hard vs. Soft

One of the important changes in the content of some newspapers in the 1970s was a new emphasis on so-called soft news. Soft news sometimes showed up as a feature story on what to wear when sledding or as a gossipy tract on show business people. But hard news became soft news in the hands of skilled writers who put feature rather than hard leads on stories, who deferred time elements and put the emphasis on people. Typically, sportswriters excelled in this field because they had been doing it longer.

Some newspapers went overboard in soft news and turned their front page content over to magazine-style stories. The readers, though, did not want to be puffed to death; they still wanted to know what happened in the world, and they didn't want to have to hunt through a collection of stories on rock stars and recipes to find that. The newspapers had put too much soft news on their front page, or throughout the paper, at the expense of hard news. Editors forgot that *The National Observer,* which distinguished itself with what many would consider a soft approach to news, died in the late 1970s just as many newspapers were joining the soft news parade. Some editors missed the message.

Just because a news story is not breaking news does not mean it is not important. In-depth stories, for example, provide an extra dimension for readers. They are not soft news. They can show up as an in-depth look at credit policies at local banks, an analysis of cancer research, a look at the housing market. Consider some of the stories cited in Chapter 2, "The Copy Editor and Technology," stories that were possible because of computer analysis: in Rhode Island, a scandal in the state's mortgage agency; in Atlanta, evidence of discrimination by banks in granting home loans to whites and blacks; in Rhode Island, the revelation that several school bus drivers had bad driving records; in San Jose, Calif., an account of the secretly owned properties of a Philippine dictator.

The lack of a breaking news focus should not detract from the value of any story. The reader has to know what the city council did last night, of course, but reporters, under assignment from editors, should be examining the action for its long-term implications, and when those implications are found, editors should be willing to display the story on Page One, if appropriate.

Brief vs. Long

An editor cannot know in advance how long a story will be, and the reporter who covers a news event sometimes can only estimate how long the resulting story will run. But both, through careful overall scheme, can package news to make reading it easier. Some of what they can do is discussed in Chapter 10, "Design." But for this discussion, editors should set limits on story length and then encourage reporters to break up long stories into sidebars or related stories. *USA Today* does this, although some critics say to a fault.

Although that solution means packaging differently, it also suggests that readers do not need all of a story, only parts of it, and that individual readers will need different parts. Thus, editors and reporters must present the entire story but in a form that allows the readers to choose among a variety of information. One example out of a pool of many good examples comes from the Stockton, Calif., *Record.* It published a series called the "Roots of Violence," in which it examined a crime in a story on one page with expert analysis neatly packaged on the facing page. The editors, by the way, used literary techniques and created engaging stories that compelled readership. The overall approach allowed the reader to digest the story in easy doses.

Reporters can still be allowed to write long stories, after which editors can cut them apart and repackage them, but that consumes valuable time, both in the writing and in the editing. Better to establish a clear policy that encourages reporters to discuss story length in advance of writing so that editors can make decisions early in the cycle (see Chapter 7, "Consultative Editing"). Editors and reporters should remember that newspapers are quickly read and that unnecessarily long stories impede readers.

The Want to Know vs. The Need to Know

Readers can be a notoriously fickle bunch and can throw curve balls to editors attempting to learn what readers want in their newspaper. The 1970s preoccupation with soft news at some newspapers went over the brink and brought out readers complaining that their newspapers lacked news.

By the same token, those same readers seemed to complain about an overemphasis on some government reporting. Those who complained should not be faulted, but their editors need guidance on how to better present the news. The reader who asks, "Why am I reading this? I don't need to know it," reflects poor presentation on the part of the newspaper. Often the reader does need to know the information but has not been told that. Government stories, especially, can appear as mundane outlays of words or as a gaggle of officials trading barbs, and the reader will be none the wiser as to the story's value (if any). A college newspaper published a story about the questionable use of funds by a branch of the student government, and readers complained that the paper was "crucifying" the student leaders. The newspaper's stories failed to say, "The money in question came from student fees. The cost of this venture came from your pocket."

Too frequently, decisions are made that affect people, but they never realize it until it is too late because the newspaper failed to make the issue clear. Any time an editor reads a story and asks, "Why does the reader want to know this?" the editor has placed the burden of proof on the newspaper. Such stories need more polish so that the readers can understand the relevance for them.

Overreliance on Wire Service Budgets

The wire services daily provide clients with a list of what they consider the top stories of the day. The lists are called budgets, digests or directories. The stories listed have usually received more reporter attention and are longer than the average wire story. What the wire services are providing is an advisory service, not a newspaper content service, and they are making decisions far removed from the editor's community.

Wire service budgets and directories reflect a big city, East Coast mentality that does not apply in Austin, Texas, or Butte, Mont., or Bend, Ore. The wire services who say a major snowstorm on the East Coast is a top story are not aware of what is happening in small communities across the country and are not trying to supersede local judgment. Editors should take the wire services' lists as suggestions and build their paper around local needs and local interests.

A Member of the Community

The best newspapers cover their communities with a critical eye. Boosterism has no place in the news pages. In some cases, newspapers dig deeply to see how the community works. The best newspapers not only document the problems but also dig for solutions or potential solutions. The implications of such reporting are not lost on readers, who then see the newspaper as working for them. Community concern in a newspaper makes the reader say, "The paper's on my side."

Newspapers have shown this involvement in many ways and will continue to show it as new ideas bear fruit across the nation. *The Los Angeles Times* started an obituary page to report the deaths of local people who may not have been famous but who led interesting lives. In Lansdale, Pa., the *Reporter* publishes an elementary-level newspaper with specific lessons enclosed for grades kindergarten through fourth. For adults, the *Jacksonville* (Fla.) *Journal* publishes an advertising-free tabloid newspaper providing parents with suggestions on helping their children learn. School teachers prepare the stories. In Harrisonburg, Va., the *Daily News Record* scientifically polled its readers to learn how they felt about the newspaper's coverage of a controversial brewery that had been proposed for the area. The newspaper also asked how readers felt about the brewery, a question no government agency had thought to ask the community.

Some newspapers around the country present zoned editions to provide better neighborhood coverage in their county. Each section contains detailed local news of interest only to a particular part of the county. Some sections feature personal news many newspapers overlook, such as Scout news and school honors.

One section of town that newspapers have been accused of overlooking is the section where the poor live. In Monroe, La., the *Morning World* published an in-depth look at the community's housing in a 12-page special section. The newspaper learned that almost 40 percent of the community's housing was substandard and that the community's building code was not enforced. The research took three months. Nine months later the *World* followed up its study to see if anything had been done. After stirring the pot, the cook also has to taste the soup.

One ambitious in-depth look at a community occurred in Fort Myers, Fla., where the *News-Press* published a report on that city's black community. The report included not only criticism of government leaders but of the newspaper itself for failing to cover the community. Generally, the newspaper covered minorities but the coverage lacked a commitment to their needs as people and had, instead, treated them as just another reader to sell a newspaper to. The *News-Press'* nine-part series, which included editorials, ran for a week, but it involved eight months of work. It was conceived to go beyond the myths and stereotypes of the community to find out what influenced the lives of the people. The *Asbury Park* (N.J.) *Press* published an ad-free tabloid called "West Side Story: Profile of a Black Community." It was an attempt to see whether conditions that had triggered riots a decade ago had changed.

Still another ambitious report came from the *Columbia* (Mo.) *Daily Tribune,* which examined in a 24-page tabloid the effects of a tank-car spill of 20,000 gallons of chlorinated phenolic chemicals. Titled "The Sturgeon Spill, More Questions Than Answers," the report admitted it could not answer all the questions raised, but like a good member of the community the *Tribune* was willing to lay out those questions. The town of Sturgeon at the time of the crisis numbered 800 people, yet the *Tribune* dispatched two reporters and a photographer on the assignment. A year later the paper conducted a follow-up and learned that the problem had not been solved.

In other towns, newspapers serve their communities with critical analysis. In Huntington, W. Va., in the early 1980s, the *Herald-Dispatch,* concerned about the declining business volume in downtown stores and the feeling of stagnation in the community, published a Sunday section titled "Huntington, How Are You?" a frank look at the town. The Stockton *Record*'s five-part series on violence (cited earlier) is another example of a newspaper serving its community.

Less spectacular but still as community-minded are the consumer pages that provide critical information for consumer use. The consumer page that serves up puffballs when it could be throwing hardballs doesn't rate a place in the community. But the page that names names, even at the risk of losing advertising, puts its honor on the reader's side.

These varied examples show one of the strengths of great newspapers: their ability to cover their areas with concern and sensitivity, to praise as well as criticize, to expose as well as propose, to admit doubt as well as show the way. Such newspapers lead with their strength, the local story, and show readers that the newspapers are working in the readers' best interests, not the publisher's or the advertisers' or the local politicians'. The newspaper does not do this because it will make a lot of money (most people in Monroe and Fort Myers and Asbury Park are not wealthy, and the people in Sturgeon too few to have an impact on the papers' treasuries) but because a good newspaper values its community consciousness.

A First Amendment Obligation

Editors who complain about closed-door meetings but never send a reporter to attempt to get through the closed door do not discharge their First Amendment obligation; instead, they duck it. Such editors no doubt write editorials bemoaning the public's lack of access to government and suggest that someone should do something about it. Sadly, the editors never suggest that they themselves should do anything.

All news media, of course, should never presume to serve as the public's surrogate, although that has happened. In such a self-anointed role, when journalists sit in on private meetings and do not report the outcome, who then is served? Obviously, not the public.

The news media must realize, though, that because of their resources they serve as the public's representative at public events. Their presence assumes an interest on the part of the public, the missing audience. Having taken on this representative role, the news media must carry through; that is their First Amendment obligation.

The news media must also provide the information each member of a democracy needs to properly discharge his or her role in society. That means the news media must search out and bring clarity to obscured events. Some editors would complain that such proposals are expensive, but they would be those who have for too long filled the news media, in print and on the air, with easy-to-get stories that require little legwork and that can be mechanically put together without much thought. The people who do such work receive low pay, and it is no wonder. The commitment to quality goes beyond one day's news to a feeling that the flow of democracy turns on a continuing obligation to observe and report for everyone. The editors who decided to publish the Pentagon Papers were exercising their First Amendment obligation to the fullest. Similar situations may arise daily throughout the world of journalism, and good editors rise to the challenge.

Sources and Resources

Broder, David S. *Behind the Front Page*. New York: Simon and Schuster, 1987.

Eberhard, Wallace B. " 'News Value' Treatments Are Far from Consistent among Newswriting Texts." *Journalism Educator* 37, no. 1 (Spring 1982): 9–11, 50.

Epstein, Edward J. *News from Nowhere: Television and the News*. New York: Random House, 1973.

Fry, Don, ed. *Believing the News*. St. Petersburg, Fla.: Poynter Institute for Media Studies.

Gans, Herbert J. *Deciding What's News*. New York: Pantheon Books, 1979.

Goleman, Daniel. "Down with Reptilian News!" *Columbia Journalism Review* (September/October 1989): 60.

Goltz, Gene. "Weather Pages." *Presstime* (March 1987): 16–19.

Hamilton, John Maxwell, and Frank Sutherland. "The News of the World Is Right Here on Main Street." *The Quill* (March 1985): 14–17. (The five-day series ran in the *American* on Nov. 11–15, 1985.)

Kovach, Bill. "International News is More Important Than Ever, but a Tight Economy Makes It Tough to Cover the Stories." *ASNE Bulletin* (April 1989): 24–25.

Manoff, Robert Karl, and Michael Schudson, eds. *Reading the News*. New York: Pantheon Books, 1987.

Miller, M. Mark, Michael W. Singletary, and Shu-Ling Chen. "The Roper Question and Television vs. Newspaper as Sources of News." *Journalism Quarterly* 65, no. 1 (Spring 1988): 12–19.

Newsom, Clark. "Special Sections Return Their Popularity." *Presstime* (October 1982): 56–58.

O'Mara, Richard. "The Tyranny of the Proximate." *The Quill* (June 1985): 30–33.

Rosenblum, Mort. *Reporting the World for America.* New York: Harper and Row, 1979.

Ruth, Marcia. "Covering Foreign News." *Presstime* (April 1986): 28–35.

Schierhorn, Carl. "A Day in the Life of Gannett's Front Pages: Study Shows Diversity in Story Selection, Play." *Editorially Speaking* 39, no. 2 (March 1985).

Thornburg, Ron. "Interest in Business News Hasn't Peaked, No Matter What Direction the Market Takes." *Editorially Speaking* 41, no. 10 (December 1987).

Ungar, Sanford J. *The Papers and the Papers: An Account of the Legal and Political Battle over the Pentagon Papers.* New York: Dutton, 1972.

Chapter 10

Design

The Way It Is

The operative difference between yesterday's newspapers and today's is more than the difference between the meaning of two words, *layout* and *design*. The modern newspaper is better planned than its predecessor; editors pay great attention to the package, from length of story to style of caption. That is design. The concept behind modern newspaper design envisions a visually pleasing product that will attract readers and draw them into reading the newspaper. The modern product must appear pleasing enough to compete with television, radio, magazines, children, home chores, social functions and whatever else people can do with their available leisure time. Newspaper design continues the concept of good editing, which is done with the reader uppermost in mind. Today's editors polish words and then create attractive formats for those words to appear in.

Design gives order to a newspaper and sets priorities. A poorly designed newspaper tells the reader that the editors don't care; a well-designed newspaper, on the other hand, tells the reader how much attention the editors pay to the product, how careful they are with their work. The design tells the reader what the newspaper is worth. The design also gives the paper its personality. Simplicity, clarity and focus guide the editor in designing the daily news package.

The modern format derives its attractiveness from a modular design in which all columns of type in a story are the same length. The stories, for the most part, run across the page rather than down. Those stories that go down the page without subheads are short—eight inches or less. White space has replaced column rules. The columns of type are wider and the type is larger, all of which make the paper easier to read.

Deep vertical modules have not disappeared altogether. When used at a great depth (more than eight inches), they often appear in the form of photographs, which the eye can easily scan, or in the form of news roundups with subheads. In fact, pages without vertical modules appear listless because they lack the tension necessary to attract the reader. One critic calls pages lacking vertical modules "layer cakes" because that is what they look like. The necessary tension comes from the contrast between the horizontal and the vertical. A page of all horizontal modules bores the reader, so vertical and horizontal modules are set against each other.

The Mechanics of Design

Laying out a dummy and keeping a copy schedule are necessary bookkeeping chores that keep the daily production schedule moving and provide a view of how the day's issue is shaping up. The copy schedule is a list of the stories, photographs and other graphics elements scheduled for a particular page or section. The dummy is an editor's sketch of how the elements on the copy schedule will come together on the printed page.

Design editors may rough out a page before actually fitting it together, but they send a precise, polished dummy to production. Editors with pagination systems don't worry about polished dummies on paper; theirs appear on the screen (see Figure 10.1).

The less sophisticated pagination systems present the user with a dummy sheet on a VDT screen. Stories are set in place with a cursor but the user does not see the actual stories. All that appears on the screen is the slug of each story. The user trims all stories as needed and, once completed, signals the computer to print out the page with everything (except graphics and photographs) in place.

More advanced models actually display the type on a screen, thus allowing an editor to edit the story at the same terminal used for design.

Figure 10.1 Page One of the Pottsville, Pennsylvania, Republican *as it is being designed on a computer terminal. This particular screen displays the page dummy to the right and the story being put on the page to the left. (Pottsville,* Republican *Pennsylvania photo.)*

To get around the graphics deficiency, such equipment allows a user to define the shape of the graphic so type can flow around it. Later, the graphics and photographs are added to the page.

The system that will eventually appear in newsrooms will allow editing, photographic manipulation, and story and graphics placement all on the same terminal or unit. Then the editor will retain control over all aspects and phases of designing a page.

In the meantime, let's do a page and see what choices the design editor at *The Seattle Times* makes. It is the weekend of the NCAA basketball tournament in Seattle and the week of a disastrous oil spill in Alaska. In effect, both are local stories. Also, it is the day before the return of daylight saving time. Editors at the story conference have agreed on the following front page stories: a locally reported story that the FBI is investigating the oil spill in Alaska (25 inches) and a second story, combined from various wire services, announcing that the Alaska governor has tentatively accepted clean-up assistance from the Soviet Union (20 inches). The spill stories come with a local photograph (size to be determined) and the need to announce a third story inside. The editor also has a local story revealing that a local man was arrested on murder charges 12 years after the fact (15 inches), and a combination local and wire story announcing that the president has agreed to transfer some federal money from one pot to another to keep an experimental anti-AIDS drug available (15 inches). Oh, by the way, it is April 1, and the editor has a 10-inch story about someone in Britain flying a hot air balloon disguised as a flying saucer. The dominant photograph shows the winning cheerleaders of a national collegiate competition and passers-by going through the motions in downtown Seattle. The photo editor has decided it will run at slightly over four columns by six inches. The photo and a feature story on the basketball tournament will be packaged, with the type set in bastard measure and the photo and story contained in a box. The page must also carry a nameplate, skybox on the basketball tournament, a weather box and an index.

Some decisions have already been made for the design editor. The nameplate will occupy the upper left corner of the page and will run three and a half inches deep. The skybox runs next to the nameplate. Likewise, the weather box and the index run at the same size daily, and the editors have decided that the way to remind everyone of daylight saving time is to run a one-column box that is three inches deep. When the weather box and the index are stacked, they take up a little less than two columns by three inches. Placing the daylight saving time box next to them fills out almost three columns wide by three inches deep.

With the oil spill the lead news of the day, the design editor needs to come up with a way of packaging the two stories and the photo. The editor decides to run a banner headline with two-column drop heads on the separate stories and the related photo between the two stories. This photograph will be small—two columns by three inches—so it does not compete with the dominant photograph of the cheerleaders.

The design editor now needs to balance the space between the lead stories and the photo-news feature package. Since the feature package will include a headline, the design editor must also account for an inch of space above the photograph. As far as the feature story is concerned, the design editor wants to get about two inches per column underneath the headline. The design editor knows that to run less than two inches will make the story appeared jammed.

Let's review the feature package. There's one inch at the top for a headline, six inches in depth for the photograph, a half inch for a headline and two inches for the story. Figuring in a half inch for white space, the total depth of the feature package is 10 inches.

The design editor has already placed the weather, index and time boxes at three inches high. The editor now draws a line across to represent the bottom of the feature package, then goes up 10 inches on the dummy and draws a parallel line representing the top. With this decision made, others fall into place.

For example, the design editor now knows how much space remains for the lead stories. Along with a reference box to the third story, they are squared off across the top and run almost six inches deep. This leaves some space down the side and underneath the feature package, next to the daylight saving time box.

The April Fools' story is hardly worth a major display, and so the editor places it underneath the feature package at the bottom of the page. The local murder gets placed to the right of the feature package and in effect becomes the second lead. The design editor also assigns the murder story a larger headline than the AIDS story and makes sure that more of the murder story appears on the front page than the AIDS story. Space allotted to a story on the front page is a sign of its relative news value on a particular day.

All stories are continued ("jumped") to other pages in the front section. The design editor's dummy can be seen in Figure 10.2, and the finished product in Figure 10.3.

The copy schedule maintains continuity on the desk, especially if several editors are involved and if several editions or sections are planned. The editors who put out the state edition may not be the ones who edit the late-night final, and they'll need a copy schedule to keep track of the earlier work. Even on a small newspaper, a single editor should keep at least a rough schedule, just to have an idea where the stories for that day's issue are.

The desk editor fills in the copy schedule as each story goes to a copy editor. A story not logged in at the time an editor decides to use it could get lost. Special instructions remind everyone if a story has an accompanying photograph or if it is set wide measure or if it has a side-saddle head or subheads. The page editor has assigned subheads for the news roundup, and the copy editor who does the roundup will produce a 20-inch piece with subheads intact. They won't have to be inserted later.

Doing copy schedule work on a VDT system has its advantages. An editor can tell the computer how many inches are available and the computer can tell the editor how many inches have been used every time a story or photograph is logged into the copy schedule. It is the same principle as keeping a running checkbook: You always know what kind of shape you are in.

The Package Concept

In another time newspapers were figuratively thrown together without much thought as to what went where after Page One. Local and foreign news might appear on the same page with a feature story. Smaller newspapers published local obituaries on the front page.

Today, though, the product is well planned. The newspaper not only has a purpose, it projects that purpose. It has become a package of information. Many newspapers package all types of related information, such as obituaries and other milestone-type information, on one page. Special pages extend beyond obituaries and include pages or whole sections dedicated to certain kinds of news, such as foreign or sports. In essence, the

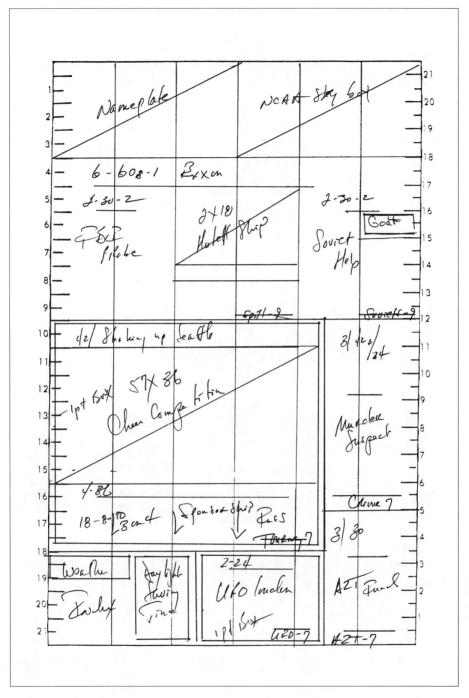

Figure 10.2 Dummy of Page One of The Seattle Times. *(Copyright 1989, The Seattle Times Co.)*

Figure 10.3 Page One of The Seattle Times. *It exhibits many of the attributes of modern design. Note the use of a dominant photograph, or center of visual impact (CVI), the modular shape of stories and packages, the use of skyboxes, refers, and drop headlines. Also note the use of boxes and graphics. (Copyright 1989, The Seattle Times Co.)*

concept behind the typical metropolitan Sunday newspaper now shapes dailies everywhere. Newspapers have become compartmentalized. The reader can find various calendars of events in one spot; all general news together; features in still another but unified spot. Larger newspapers contain sections or parts of sections on the arts and entertainment, on business and lifestyle.

Within a section, and even on a single page, editors practice packaging. An editor might have three related stories about an issue and run them together in a box, perhaps using one large headline for all three stories and then separate headlines on each story. Such a package can include a photograph or photographs. Realizing that not every worthy story can fit on Page One, some editors package a second front page.

Good packaging also means making sure that stories with inappropriate relationships are not placed together. One example: A newspaper publishes a photograph of two deer hunters from the Florida Everglades. One of the hunters has a dead deer next to him. Below the photograph is an unrelated story with this headline: "82-year-old woman hurt during shootout with cops."

Related to the package approach are section flags, refers and summaries of contents, which help the reader sort out the information. They are discussed later.

Editors also provide their readers with a large number of news stories by packaging them in roundups on a special page. In addition, editors break stories into sidebars not only to rid themselves of bulk but so readers can focus on all or parts of an event, as their interests dictate. Magazines have long used sidebars as an effective way of telling a long story through a variety of short stories.

Present-day newspaper packaging is evolving. Who knows, one day editors might decide to publish only current information on their early pages and put background later in the paper, where the reader who needs it can find it and the reader who doesn't can skip it. For that matter, maybe all background information will be stored in a computer, subject to accessing on home computer terminals only by those who want it.

Elements of Design

The standard newspaper format is six columns, although on any given day a design editor is sure to mix it up with some odd measure (also called bastard measure). Some newspapers, however, use a five-column or a four-column format. The five- and four-column formats, though, allow for few stories and, as will be noted again, publishers and editors are seeking formats that remain attractive while carrying enough stories to attract the reader not only to the front page but to the newspaper.

Some editors do not agree on whether to continue stories from Page One to later pages. The reader should not be made to turn any page to finish a story. Television and radio news programs do not require the reader to work so hard, the argument goes, so newspapers shouldn't either. But other editors say that necessity dictates continuing stories, especially if the editors are to get a reasonable number of stories and useful graphic elements on the front page. To ease the burden on the reader, some editors who jump stories put them on the back page of the first section, which makes turning back and forth easier. Research conducted at Indiana University suggests that jumped stories lose a higher number of readers than non-jumped stories, that stories perceived as boring lose readers regardless of whether they're jumped, and that subject matter can override the question of whether a story is continued. If the reader is interested in the subject, the reader will follow the story to the end, jump or no.

To achieve unity, designers concern themselves with three elements—art (any visual elements), type (including headlines) and air (white space). Other elements include color, boxes and rules, and section flags. Also important is production quality. No matter how well-designed the page, it will not work if the photographs are spotty or the type is crooked. Quality of the finished product, of course, directly relates to the quality of the design editor's work.

One element not always considered with the others is advertising, yet poorly planned advertising display detracts from the effort of the news design. Horizontal placement of advertisements presents a sensible news hole for the news designer to use without detracting from the sales pitches. After all, the reader buys the newspaper for the advertisements too and will want to read those. No doubt a well-designed page works to the advantage of the advertiser a lot better than a page laid out blindly. If a page looks ugly and the reader skips it, the reader skips the news *and* the advertisements. When advertisers become aware of that, they will pressure newspaper advertising managers to pay attention to good design.

Good design is a collaborative effort. Editors, photographers, artists, reporters and page designers work together to package the best newspaper they can make. The page from *The Seattle Times* shown in Figure 10.3 is a modern front page, to which you should refer from time to time as you continue through this chapter.

Type

Using the wrong type face for a newspaper story can put off readers as much a dull headline or a dull lead. Story type faces (more commonly called body type) need serifs, distinctive markings at the tops and bottoms of letters. Those markings provide fixation points for the eye to set upon when reading horizontal lines of printed matter. They represent what in the handwriting of another period would be the beginning and finishing strokes of a pen. Sans serif type, on the other hand, is optically evenly weighted (the strokes of the letters are the same thickness), which creates a lack of the contrast so necessary for the eye to distinguish between letters.

Likewise, the space between lines should provide the eye with enough room to return from the end of one line to the start of another without encountering and being distracted by the second line. Lines too close together don't allow the eye to move uninterrupted to the next line. The typical leading in a newspaper is one point, meaning a story will be set 9 points on 10 points (or 9 on 10), which ensures a half point of space top and bottom and a point of space when two lines appear one above the other. The wider the line of type and the larger the type size, the more leading is necessary. The most common body type sizes range from 8-point to 11-point, although as the population grows older and natural eyesight problems occur, editors would be wise to opt for larger type.

The maximum length of a line of type is from 16 to 18 picas. Newspapers occasionally violate that dictum to create, say, a two-column box that might run 25 picas wide. At that width, the type size should be no smaller than 10-point. Too many stories set beyond the maximum length tire readers.

The smallest body type used is 5- or 6-point, which frequently appears on sports pages for box scores or other statistical matter. Some sports editors place all their statistical matter in 5- or 6-point boldface type (for legibility) and keep it confined to one page or a section of the page called "the scoreboard" or "for the record." Some news editors, unfortunately, set lists such as court proceedings and meeting or state house schedules in small type and then wonder why nobody reads them. The small type (so-called agate) is hard to read and is best avoided. Given the high median age of newspaper readers and the rising median age of the country as a whole (33 in 1990), editors will no doubt have to discontinue using small body type altogether because the older reader will have trouble reading quantities of it. Some editors believe that only the most rabid fan spends any time reading small type on the sports page.

Newspapers also use as another typographical device the setting of columns in ragged right. Most newspapers justify their columns of type so that each line aligns with the preceding line on both the left and right sides. That requires frequent end-of-line hyphenation, too much of which diminishes readability. Ragged right, on the other hand, requires little or no hyphenation and injects more air (white space) onto a page. Ragged left typesetting of body type should be avoided because it deprives the eye of a common return point for line after line of reading. To avoid fatigue, the eye needs the common return point.

In selecting type, be it for a story or the headline on a special page, beginning editors often make the mistake of selecting an inappropriate face. For any story, the type should be easy to read.

In order to set off a story, to make it stand out from other stories, editors use wide measure. Wide measure, also called bastard measure or odd measure, is any non-standard width in the newspaper. Preferably it should be wider than standard. Wide measure is an attractive and easy way to set off a story, but a page filled with a variety of wide measures appears disharmonious.

Air

Air in a newspaper provides a subtle background for the other design elements on the page. To be legible, type needs the right amount of air between letters and lines. Some editors try to crowd out air because they feel they must squeeze in every last letter. But lack of air will make the page illegible.

When the spaces between columns are wide enough, air functions as a divider. Skinny column rules, which once separated columns of type, were dropped in favor of wider strips of air between the columns. But the one pica of air that keeps lines of 9-point type from running into each other is not enough to separate two headlines. Headline type needs a larger divider.

Like any other design element, air must be used consistently. A page with a lot of air at the top and crowded graphics and type at the bottom does not show a consistent use of air.

Modular Format

A modular page is not only easy to read but also imparts unity. Unity is the result of making good use of the elements of design. The page becomes a unified collection of modules (stories, photographs and graphics).

Behind the modular approach is knowledge of the Golden Rectangle, a proportion said by the Greeks to be the most pleasing. The proportion approximates 3 to 5. Any page full of modules strictly patterned on that proportion, though, would lack the tension necessary to stimulate the reader to dig into the page.

In part, that tension comes from violating the Golden Rectangle principle by creating modules that defy the 3 to 5 proportion. Vertical more than horizontal elements best violate the principle, and photographs more than stories appeal to the eye in such cases. A deep photograph or other graphic is easier to read than a deep column of type. When a deep column of type is used, subheads help break up the gray and make the module less formidable.

If possible, no module on a page should be the same size as any other. Each deserves its own distinctive size. A page of many-sized modules generates the tension mentioned earlier. If a design editor is not careful, the editor can create a boring page by having only two, or mostly two, types of modules. Typically, such a page would have a lot of four-column modules and two-column modules. Such a page lacks tension. Also to be avoided are square modules; square modules are static.

Photographs

Photographs attract the eye more readily than type. A story with a photograph has higher readership than the same story without a photograph. Photographs represent an important element not only in conveying news but in contributing to the overall appearance of the page. The dominant photograph on a page serves as a center of visual impact, a CVI. Every well-designed page has such a center.

Photographs deserve the same kind of play a comparable story would get. If it is a major news photograph, play it big. The reverse is not quite as true, though. Tiny photographs in a large format such as a newspaper format lack communicative quality. Even a bad photograph looks better played large.

Photographs are discussed more thoroughly in Chapter 11, so just a few comments appear in this section. Photographs should not be used to prop up a large headline unrelated to the photograph. Sloppy layout editors will stick unrelated headlines and photographs together and confuse the reader, who will try to figure out what the headline and the photograph have to do with each other.

Conventional wisdom says photographs should be anchored to the top or bottom of a page or to a nameplate or headline but should not be allowed to float unconnected. Photographs surrounded by stories but unconnected to anything confuse the reader; thus, the anchor advice is sound, although like any other advice it should not be followed blindly. When violating the rule, some editors box the photograph and its caption, and place a headline (sometimes called a catchline) above the photograph. Whatever approach is taken seems to be more a matter of training the reader than following an absolute.

Finally, never publish on the same page two photographs of the same size. They will offset and diminish each other's impact. One must dominate. "Mug shots" (photographs of a person's head and shoulders only) do not come under this rule. Also, mug shots should not be used merely as a design device. They are useful to help the reader identify people in the news. And make sure when using a mug shot that its tone is consistent with the story. If the story is about a tragedy, don't use a mug shot showing someone smiling.

Caption Styles

A photo caption's first function, of course, is to complement the photo-graph, not to look pretty. But a caption whose design gets as much earnest attention as its message will add immeasurably to the appearance of a newspaper. Generally, a caption must contrast with the body type. If they are the same column width or same type size, the caption will be lost. What is desired is a caption that stands out so the reader can easily find it. It is not difficult to avoid the same column width as the body type's, especially when the caption is set in wide measure. Also, to help contrast, the type should be larger than the body type, meaning, for instance, that a 9-point body type mixes best with a 10- or 11-point caption.

Captions sometimes appear in (horizontal) stacks, the visual equiva-lent of columns, although every effort is made to minimize the number of stacks so that the reader finds the captions easier to read. Several of those efforts will be discussed presently. Editors attempt to balance the stacks of a caption by having each stack match line for line. With a com-puter system, that job is easily accomplished.

Air plays an important role in displaying captions. To help float the caption in a background of air, a design editor can indent all captions a minimum of one pica on each side. Captions so indented stand out better than those that run from one edge of the photograph to the other.

The standard caption style begins with a legend (or lead-in) in all capital letters. For better effect, the legend should also be in boldface type. For example:

CHEERS FOR GORBY: Cheering crowds hold pho-tographs of Soviet President Mikhail S. Gorbachev as he leaves Stuttgart, West Germany, following talks with representatives of Baden Württemberg. The talks were held on Wednesday.

Most non-traditional caption styles are merely a variation of the traditional. Two other traditional captions are the nameline and the one-liner. Newspapers use either a larger or a bolder type to make namelines contrast with body type. The one-liner usually appears in a type larger than normal caption type. Editors use one-line captions when they must span a great distance with few words. The editors know that using the regular caption style would result in a caption a half stack short of covering the distance.

Then there are the variations on the all-caps legend. In these, the legend is set in headline type and appears above the caption.

Cheers for Gorby

Cheering crowds hold photographs of Soviet President Mikhail S. Gorbachev as he leaves Stuttgart, West Germany, following talks with representatives of Baden Württemberg. The talks were held on Wednesday.

Besides being more eye-appealing, this style also puts more air into a page design. It is a good style when consistently used throughout the paper.

Given a five-column photograph but not many words for a caption (although more than enough for a good-looking one-liner), the editor opts for the caption that appears at the side of the photograph in the sixth column. The rules that affix the caption to the photograph are optional unless confusion would result.

Boxes and Rules

In newspapers, boxes function as containers of information. Boxes are useful in packaging. They're found around any type of story and are frequently used to yoke a story and a related photograph or photographs (see Figure 10.3, page 206). An editor may box a short late-breaking story to give it more attention. Boxes are also useful to set off features, series roundups and briefs.

Some boxes have squared-off corners while others have rounded corners. Rounded corners break up the straight lines of a page, but they are harder to paste on and are unpopular with production people.

Boxes are sometimes used with photographs. Some newspapers wrap a box around a photograph and its caption. Still other newspapers place a hairline rule around the edges of a photograph when the edge is hard to see, or box a photograph when it is not related to a story.

Because boxes are visual elements, some editors try to keep them from bumping into each other and from being next to photographs. The editors feel that boxes side by side or next to photographs compete with each other. But boxes have made an interesting contribution to page design. Boxes now get used when they are needed to help package the news, and little concern arises if two boxes appear side by side. The more important element is presenting the news intact, and boxes help do that.

The semibox, or half-box, results when rules are used top and bottom but not at the sides of a story. One popular rule in such cases is the Oxford rule, a two-point line parallel to a one-point line.

Graphics

In their drive to deliver their message better, newspapers have added a new position to the news desk, that of the graphics editor, graphics journalist or graphic artist. In another era, an editor assigned a story to a reporter, who wrote it. The story was then shown to a photographer, who took photographs, and to an illustrator, who was expected to produce illustrations. Today the editor assigns the project to a reporter, photographer and graphics journalist, who work together to produce a unified result. Also, the graphics journalist is no longer concerned with just illustrating the story. The important thing is telling the story. Graphics are words turned into pictures and, as one editor said at an American Press Institute seminar, graphics are visual sidebars to stories.

When the use of graphics wasn't as common as it is today, the standard graphic was probably the pie, which newspapers broke out whenever they had a budget to display. One pie would show the sources of revenue as slices and what percentage each one represented, and the other would show expenditures as slices and how they were apportioned.

Thanks to personal computers, pie charts, bar charts and fever charts are easily produced. Graphics now routinely show up in almost any story that needs visual help yet lacks photographs. Even with photographs, some stories still need additional visual cues, and entry points and graphics serve that need. Furthermore, the people making the graphics are not necessarily artists from the nation's fine arts schools but copy editors from the nation's journalism schools.

Assigned one day to show how House Republicans intended to reduce the deficit by $30 billion, a team of student journalists created a $30 billion dollar bill and then sliced it proportionately into pieces to show a breakdown in the budget-trimming proposal. Another team, given a *San Jose Mercury News* story on curveballs, created a graphic that provided an aerial view of a pitcher throwing a curveball. The graphic showed visually that a curveball doesn't break at the last minute but is on an arc from the time it leaves the pitcher's hand and, if gravity did not interfere, would come full circle and hit the pitcher in the back. The graphic included some type to explain the main point and a shadow box called "curveball facts."

Maps make excellent graphic elements and are available from a surprising number of sources, especially the wire services but also state and local government offices. In addition, personal computers can store maps for use at any time. When publishing a story about an unfamiliar location, for example, a newspaper can use a map to provide a perspective.

Another type of graphic that is easy to create is the information graphic. It can appear in different styles but commonly appears as a box containing brief biographic information about the main subject(s) of a story. Some information graphics include a mug shot of the subject. The graphic can be shaded or presented in a shadow box, and if the paper is using spot color, outlined in spot color.

Graphics come with pitfalls. Just as stories need to be simple, so do graphics. A writer shouldn't use mixed metaphors; a graphic artist shouldn't mix type faces. Communication suffers.

A good graphic shows the information, the data, in a way that enables the reader to absorb the information, not ponder the design. If a graphic puzzles the reader, it is a bad graphic. A good graphic uses enough data points so that information is not distorted. If you want to plot two years of gradual circulation growth to look like two years of rapid circulation growth, put in four data points instead of 24 and see what happens. No nuance remains.

Ensure that the representation of numbers is proportional. Graphic artists use a variety of symbols in place of numbers. For example, an artist might want to show the federal deficit as a brick wall being built up brick by brick by brick. All bricks, though, should be the same size and have the same value so the overall effect is not distorted. Also, don't vary the design; vary the data.

Just as the copy desk must concern itself with the accuracy of words in a story, so it must concern itself with the accuracy of graphics.

Extracted Quotes

When an editor believes a story contains a compelling direct quotation that helps tell the story, she will extract it from the story and set it in larger type. The quotation also remains in the story, of course. Extracted quotes should contrast with the body type. Some editors achieve that with boldface type; others use italic. Still others use a different type or a small version of the newspaper's headline type.

Extracted quotes are miserable failures if they appear after the quotation in the story. Such failures occur when extracted quotes are used throughout a story in the same manner as subheads, to break up the gray. There's nothing wrong with breaking up the gray, as long as the breakers appear logically. The reader who reads a quote in the body of the story and then encounters it set off in larger type finds the placement illogical.

Refers

The word is pronounced REE-fer and it has nothing to do with cigarettes. Refers point the reader to related stories elsewhere in the newspaper. They are part of the package concept. One typical refer style says "See related story on Page 7." Such a refer does not direct the reader well because the reader has to figure out which story on Page 7.

The editor who wants to serve the readers repeats the headline of the story referred to and then gives the page number. When the readers turn to Page 7 and see five stories, they will know which one they were directed to. Typographically, refers are much like extracted quotes and can be handled in a variety of ways.

Nameplates and Section Flags

Some newspapers have gone quasimodern, that is, adopted a six-column, no-column-rules format but retained their nameplate, which was set in Old English type around the turn of the century. The editors who argue against changing their nameplate contend that the readers need the old style to maintain identity with the newspaper. The editors say this with a straight face even though, for example, professional sports teams, which have enjoyed increasing fan loyalty, are not bashful about changing uniforms and team logos every five years.

Modern editors not only have redesigned their nameplates to fit the times but also have installed section flags or logos to help the reader through the paper. Using section flags represents a segment of the package concept, of thinking through the entire product and telling the reader where each section is.

The newspaper's section flags create an image consistent with the front page nameplate. The section flags don't have to be the same as the nameplate but they should project a relation with the nameplate.

Modern section flags also appear in the same place as the nameplate, at the top of the page. In the late 1960s and for most of the 1970s, the floating nameplate and section flag were popular. They could be moved around the top half of the paper. Then some newspapers stopped doing that. Redesigned nameplates were kept at the top of Page One, and the section flags were made in the image of the nameplate and kept at the top of the section. Occasionally a newspaper will lower its nameplate and run a single story above it. That doesn't happen on inside pages, although there's no reason why it couldn't.

The Summary of Contents

The package concept that lies behind the better newspapers manifests itself early in the paper in the form of a summary or what can also be a detailed table of contents. The summary tells the reader what is in the package and provides a brief summary of the entire day's news. The summary has to be complete enough to tell the reader what is inside and that what's inside is worth turning to. The summary promotes the contents of the newspaper. It sells the inside.

Summaries are put together in various ways. The most common is by the location of the news, such as local, state, and so on. Other summaries merely tell what's inside without any categorization. Still other summaries are broken up by subject matter—politics, religion, entertainment, lifestyles. Other summaries combine elements of location and subject.

Another type of summary is one that appears above the nameplate and highlights three or four major stories in that day's paper. Called skyboxes, they are not intended to represent the entire contents but merely a few stories, perhaps the most notable of each section. Skyboxes are graphically more involved than summaries and can include photos. The person responsible for filling the skybox should make sure the stories highlighted are substantive. Nothing is quite so silly for readers as to see a story promoted in the skybox and then turn to the section cited and find the story in the lower half of the page with a small headline on it.

A good summary is well written. Treated as an afterthought, a summary reveals an uncaring newspaper and suggests that the contents are no better. The summary should be intriguingly written; it should give more than the one-sentence lead of every story in the paper. In fact, one difficult summary to write would take the form of a story; items would be related and transition provided between items. But making the summary an attraction as just described also means giving someone the time to write it, and it means putting the paper together soon enough so that the writer has a sense of the total package. The idea is good but executing it is time consuming.

Color

Two types of color appear in newspapers. The full color photograph is called process color, and the color border on a box, for example, is called spot color. Process color is much more expensive than spot color and needs more planning. Often the fault with color photographs is that they are used just because of their color. The color photograph that engenders the reaction "good color" instead of "good photo" suggests where the editor's priorities are. They certainly aren't with the news. A good color photograph should appear in a newspaper because it has something to do with the news, not because it's colorful. Now that more and more newspapers are able to process color photographs in-plant, newspapers should be trying for more spot news color photographs.

Spot color has also been misused. In some cases, it appears in headlines, giving the newspaper page the appearance of a circus poster. In other cases, the same color shows up every four or five pages, as though the editor required that color be used even if no one had a reason. Overused color shows up in every other graphics element on a page. All that color spoils the impact. Finally, the spot color on the front page matches the spot color in a later advertisement, meaning the advertiser paid the paper's color costs that day or that the only reason the paper uses color is because an advertiser also uses color. Not very original.

The best spot color is functional; it is not used for its own sake but because it can help make a story clear. Different colors can be used in a map to distinguish areas from one another. A zoning map in color would certainly aid its user. Whether color is flamboyant or useful depends on how an editor uses it. The difference in application shows a difference between bad and good editors.

The Future

In redesigning a newspaper, editors have been faced with a problem: how to do it so the new design causes the least shock to the reader. Editors assume that readers are conservative and don't like surprises. A conservative approach calls for redesigning from the inside out or a section at a time, leaving the hard news section for last. It results in a gradual change that will not affront the reader. Also, mistakes don't glare as brightly with the gradual approach. A radical approach is to redesign in one giant step—overnight. Editors who inform readers about design changes and their reasons ahead of time usually win reader acceptance quickly.

It is hard to say which way newspaper design will go. Today's styles, while innovative, have their roots in old newspaper or magazine design. The box approach is a modern application of column and cutoff rules. Content is changing in the face of static circulation, rising competition from other media and different modes of news delivery. A lot of what happens to newspaper design will be determined by which medium newspapers feel the most pressed by. Newspapers will adapt their design to compete.

A concentration on design could be a problem if editors concern themselves only with appearance. Design should never come at the expense of content or dictate news play. No editor should feel bad about ripping apart a good design in order to provide worthwhile fast-breaking news.

Another concern that future design editors must face is the rising cost of newsprint, the paper on which newspapers are printed. Gone are the days of cheap paper and lots of air and few stories on Page One. Publishers are demanding good looks tightly packaged. Seven to nine modules seems a fair compromise if jumps are allowed. Prohibiting jumps reduces the number of modules and decreases the variety of news.

It has long been suggested that the newspaper of the future will carry a front page that is nothing more than a table of contents of the major stories of the day, which appear throughout the paper. Whether the reader would accept such a newspaper day after day remains to be seen.

Sources and Resources

Anthony, Jay. "How Editors and Artists Handled the Challenger Tragedy." *APME News* (June 1986): 4–7.

Anthony, Jay, and Kate Newton Anthony. "Typefaces, White Spaces, Splashes of Color." *Washington Journalism Review* (May 1985): 30–37.

Bain, Chic. *Newspaper Design and Newspaper Readership: A Series of Four Experiments*. Research Report No. 10. Bloomington: Indiana University, 1980.

Berner, R. Thomas. "The Golden Rectangle in Newspaper Page Design." *Editor & Publisher* (August 21, 1976): 30–31.

Click, J. W., and Guido H. Stempel III. "Reader Response to Front Pages with Modular Format and Color." *ANPA News Research Report,* no. 35 (July 29, 1982): 2–4.

Garcia, Mario. *Contemporary Newspaper Design: A Structural Approach*. 2d ed. Englewood Cliffs, N.J.: Prentice-Hall, 1987.

Garcia, Mario R., J. W. Click, and Guido H. Stempel III. "Subscribers' Reaction to Redesign of the St. Cloud Daily Times." *ANPA News Research Report,* no. 32 (September 3, 1981): 2–7.

Goltz, Gene. "Contending with 'Jumps.' " *Presstime* (August 1987): 28–29.

Govier, Wendy. "Knight-Ridder Graphics Network Takes Off." *Knight Ridder News* 2, no. 2 (Summer 1987): 14–17.

Hanson, Barry. "A Reader's Visual Aids." *AP World,* no. 1 (Spring 1989): 3–8.

Holmes, Nigel. *Designer's Guide to Creating Charts and Diagrams*. New York: Watson-Gutpill Publications, 1984.

"If Page One Sings and Dances, the Whole Show Should Be a Hit." *Editorially Speaking* 43, no. 3 (March/April 1989): 1–8.

Jacobson, Alan. "The Importance of Stylebooks." *The Journal of the Society of Newspaper Design* (March 1988): 12–15.

Lombardo, Barbara. "Personal Computers, Graphics: A Marriage of Convenience." *APME News* (August-September 1986): 6–8.

Morison, Stanley. *Selected Essays on the History of Letter-Forms in Manuscript and Print,* ed. David McKitterick. New York: Cambridge University Press, 1982.

Tankard, James W., Jr. "Quantitative Graphics in Newspapers." *Journalism Quarterly* 64, nos. 2–3 (Summer-Autumn 1987): 406–415.

Thornburg, Ron. "Adding Graphics to Your Newspaper Makes for Powerful Show-and-Tell Journalism." *Editorially Speaking* 41, no. 9 (November 1987): 1–8.

Tufte, Edward R. *The Visual Display of Quantitative Information.* Chesire, Conn.: Chesire Press, 1983.

Utt, Sandra H., and Steve Pasternack. "Front Pages of U.S. Daily Newspapers." *Journalism Quarterly* 61, no. 4 (Winter 1984): 879–884.

Wanta, Wayne. "The Effects of Dominant Photographs: An Agenda-Setting Experiment." *Journalism Quarterly* 65, no. 1 (Spring 1988): 107–111.

Webb, Craig L. "Syndicated and Computer Graphics." *Presstime* (August 1985): 26–28.

Zunn, Clyde Z. *Eyesight Problems and Newspaper Readership.* Research Note No. 8. Newspaper Readership Project, Newspaper Advertising Bureau, New York, 1982.

Chapter 11

Photographs

Photographs Have a Purpose

Photographs are not just something to fill in space or to make pages attractive. Photographs function the same way stories do: they tell the news. If the overall news package is to succeed, editors must give the same attention to photographs as they give to words.

A photograph with a story ensures a higher readership than the story run alone. The reader sees the photograph first and is attracted by it to the story. Often a good photograph can lift a story from the routine or save a writer weak in description. Photographs freeze the action and allow the reader to study the event. The reader can take a few seconds or many minutes, and the longer the reader spends with the photograph, the more the reader will get out of it.

One example of the value of photographs appeared on the front page of *The New York Times* on October 13, 1981. It was a week after the assassination of the Egyptian president Anwar as-Sadat. The *Times* acquired photographs taken before and during the assassination and then asked three security experts to examine them. The experts agreed that there had been a breakdown in security. In all, the *Times* published 10 photographs. The story about the photographs was the lead of the day. It carried a four-column headline: "Photos Show Cairo Security Breakdown, Experts Say." The *Times'* package was another validation of the value of photographs.

Too often photographers are unfairly accused of trying to be artistic rather than journalistic. That happens. But the good photographers are photojournalists; they know they are helping to tell the news, and they photograph accordingly. That their work rises above the mundane should not detract from its news value. When their photographs fail as a news conveyor, editors should reject the work in the same way as they would reject a story that fails. It is, of course, easy to require a reporter to rewrite a poor story, but it is impossible for a photographer to reshoot a news event already a part of history. For that reason, a photographer who produces high-quality work is worth more than a reporter who has to rewrite. Getting it right the first time is an essential ingredient of good photojournalism.

Good editors respect good photographers the way they respect good reporters. Good editors would no more butcher a photograph than a story. Mutual respect inspires editor, reporter and photographer to strive for all-round understanding and quality. To engender better use of photographs, editors have added a new position to the news staff, that of photo editor. At larger papers, the person is a photographer; at smaller papers, a copy editor may double as photo editor. No matter, the mission is the same: to enhance the visual personality of the paper and then protect it against those who would reduce a photograph one or two columns just to get in more words.

A photograph worth using is worth using at a size that will engage the reader. And if a story needs five or six photographs to be told well, an editor should use them. It is similar to using sidebars to help tell a news story.

In selecting photographs, editors should not be swayed by what kind of photographs win awards. According to Lil Junas, one-time Arkansas News Photographer of the Year and author of *Cardon Creek, A Photographic Narrative,* photographs showing tragedy and violence win awards more readily than any other type of photograph. Junas studied the Pulitzer Prizes and the Pictures of the Year (awarded by the National Press Photographers Association and the University of Missouri School of Journalism) and found that 54 percent of the winners showed tragedy or violence. With the Pulitzers only, tragedy or violence among the winners rises to 63 percent. A look through back issues of *Editor & Publisher,* a trade magazine for the newspaper industry, supports Junas' research. Prizewinning or major news photographs depict assassination, violence, death, mass suicide, protests. *E & P* headlined one presentation of photographs this way: "Mostly grim."

But the attitude of judges and editors may be changing, for another issue, while still showing photographs of grim scenes, also heralds a photographer who produced an unobtrusive yet touching essay on a child dying of brain cancer. For that, George Wedding, then of the *Palm Beach Post,* received the World Understanding Award from the National Press Photographers Association, the University of Missouri and Nikon Inc., a camera manufacturer. Another photograph, this one from the portfolio of Chris Johns of the *Topeka Capital-Journal,* shows a father kissing his child through the plastic wall of a bubble that protects the child from infection. A tender moment hard to put in words.

Words cannot substitute for the good photograph. For example, in 1976, *The New York Times* used these words in a story about Vice President Nelson Rockefeller: "After protesters showed they were able to drown out his speech, Mr. Rockefeller then gestured three times with his finger." Did he point? Beckon? Raise his pinky? Flash the V for victory? The words don't tell. A photograph of Rockefeller gesturing was taken by Don Black, then of the Binghamton, N.Y., *Sun,* and the photograph moved on the Associated Press and United Press International wirephoto nets. One of the papers receiving it was the *Times.* Rockefeller was also a former governor of New York, and since he had gestured in New York, a student of journalism might assume that the *Times,* prideful of itself as a paper of record, would publish the photograph. Not so. The *Times* turned down the photograph because it was not tasteful and because the gesture could be explained in words. But the words alone do not make clear the gesture or the fact that it was obscene.

Photographs that do not communicate include those of a line of people receiving a check or being sworn into office or being congratulated for something. These are derisively referred to as "stand 'em up and shoot 'em" or "execution at dawn" or "grip 'n' grin" photographs. Given a choice between a photograph of the president of the United States addressing a group as part of an event to show off newly installed solar panels at the White House, or a photograph of the president showing off the solar panels, a good editor would choose the second picture. The second picture shows more than a head, a microphone and the presidential seal; it shows the president doing something. As in writing, avoid clichés.

An editor must also decide what effect the shape of a photograph will have. Horizontal photographs generally produce a calming effect on the design, while vertical photographs, because of the contrast they offer, stand out. Such an effect will not happen every time, but an editor should remain aware that horizontal and vertical photographs often give off different sensations.

Photographs in series or semiseries help the reader understand an event by giving a sense of a continuity. Series photographs are especially popular in sports, where the sequence details a particularly spectacular play. When the action is moving from left to right, run the series horizontally on a page. When the action is moving right to left, run the series vertically, which is easier on the reader.

Taste and Ethics

A distasteful or unethical story must be read before anyone will react to it. A newspaper can publish such a story, but few may notice because the story hides among the advertisements and carries a bland headline that attracts no attention. A photograph, though, requires no effort of reading; it can be taken in with a glance and its impact imparted immediately. A photograph needs no headline, and a reader does not have to read five or six paragraphs to learn the details. The photographic story yields news in an instant; one sweep of the eye usually makes the story clear.

What does the reader make of a series of photographs that shows firefighters searching a creek for the body of a boy who fell through thin ice, one of them carrying the boy's body to the shore, the dead boy's mother tearfully watching the unsuccessful rescue attempt?

The first question that might arise is how intrusive was the photographer? If the photographer was heavy-handed and pushy in getting the photographs, the family's privacy has been shattered and later apologies will not change that fact.

But what if the photographer shot the scene from a distance, did not poke a camera in anyone's face and did not behave obnoxiously while trying to get the photographs? The next issue, then, is whether by publishing the photographs the newspaper invades the family's privacy. Is the photograph worth it?

What of a photograph of the body of a woman who has been hit by a train? Her body lies across the tracks, and the camera angle makes it appear she was decapitated. In that case, the family and friends expressed their dismay to the newspaper. They were right. The dead woman was elderly and was suffering from mental illness. The photograph added nothing to the printed account of her death; it merely heightened the family's anguish.

The *Poughkeepsie* (N.Y.) *Journal* also was criticized for publishing a photograph of a man who had been shot and was near death as paramedics attempted to save him. The photograph, taken by chief photographer Robert V. Niles, shows a man who was shotgunned in the stomach and who died about four hours later. But what if the man had not died? Would that have softened the impact of the photograph? Would it mean something to readers to know that the victim was under indictment on a drug charge? In other words, does the victim's possible criminal background make a picture of his dying fair game for publication? What if he had been the mayor of Poughkeepsie? What if he had been a nobody? Also, what of the man's family? Must they be subjected to such a photograph? Editors must consider many things before deciding to publish such a photograph.

In Fort Myers, Fla., the *News-Press* published a photograph of an injured child and her distraught family watching paramedics work on her while a helicopter prepares to land and take the child to a hospital. The child, who had gone into a street to retrieve some books she had dropped and had been struck by a car, was alive when the *News-Press* published the photograph. She died a few days later. Only one complaint reached the managing editor, photographer Acey Harper says, and that was to say that the photograph was in poor taste. On the other hand, Harper says, a police sergeant and a paramedic both praised the paper for publishing the photograph because they felt it worked to promote safety.

One photograph that received a lot of complaints showed the body of a boy who died during one of the eruptions of the volcano in Mount St. Helens, Washington, in 1980. The photograph was labeled unimaginable, repulsive, callous, gross, cruel, tacky, in very poor taste. One of those who complained was the boy's grandmother, who knew only that the boy, his brother and his father were in the eruption area. Nobody knew their fate until *The Seattle Times* published the photograph on Page 2 of its fourth section almost two days after it had been received on the wirephoto net.

The *Times'* executive editor, James B. King, said he approved the publication of the photograph because it showed a human victim of the volcano. Said *Times* day picture editor James C. Heckman: "Thousands of words about gas velocities, air temperatures and ash falls don't begin to tell the story of the violence and instant death as that one picture." All in all, those who defended publication saw the photograph as news, as a graphic and poignant element in a larger tragedy.

The photograph, by the way, was taken by a photographer from the *San Jose Mercury News,* which devoted approximately one-third of its front page to the picture. The photographer was the same George Wedding mentioned earlier for receiving a World Understanding Award.

Consider Figure 11.1, which shows a man screaming as firefighters pull him from his smashed van. He sustained two broken legs. The photographer, Thelma Robinson of the *Centre Daily Times,* State College, Pa., had to argue with her city editor to get him to persuade his editor to publish the photograph. No one doubted it was a good photograph, but some of the editors were reluctant to publish such a photograph of a local person. What if he died after press time? The editors solved the problem by calling the hospital; upon learning that the victim's condition was good, they talked to him and got his oral permission to publish the photograph. The newspaper did not need the victim's permission because the accident occurred on a public highway, which the courts recognize as fair game for newspaper coverage. But by getting permission the editors stilled one potential source of criticism. (No complaints were received.)

A couple of weeks later, the same editors had to decide whether to publish a mediocre photograph of a woman trapped in her wrecked automobile. They easily rejected the photograph. Unlike the man in the first accident, who was not at fault, the driver in this case had been the subject of a police chase, had been in three minor accidents before her big crash and was legally drunk. The police planned to press charges. The editors felt that by publishing the photograph they would be adding to the person's problems, so they chose to publish just a story. Publishing the photograph would not have served the public interest. It is not, however, an invasion of privacy to publish a photograph of a current accident that occurs in public. Publishing it months or years later, however, could be an invasion of privacy because the photograph is no longer (current) news.

Newspapers have been successfully sued for using a photograph to illustrate an article when the photograph was unrelated to the article. One newspaper, the *Harvard Crimson,* was sued after running a file photo of two former undergraduates with a story on prison reform. One of the *Crimson's* editors had bars drawn on the faces of the two men in the belief

Figure 11.1 The local accident photograph raises ticklish problems for editors of small-town newspapers who live in the same community as the injured people. Although the major questions an editor should worry about are quality and accuracy of the photograph, the close-to-home issue must also be addressed. (Thelma Robinson photograph, Centre Daily Times, *State College, Pennsylvania.)*

that the men would be unrecognizable. They weren't—and the *Crimson* settled out of court.

More clear-cut examples of privacy invasion arise with non-newsworthy photographs shot at a distance with a telephoto lens, which enables the photographer to see something not visible to the eye of a passer-by. Clearly, such photographs are not ethically obtained. Publishing them compounds the sin. Long-distance photographs worth using are those that might show illegal activities and thus have news value.

Editors supporting the publication of photographs later considered by some to be an invasion of privacy or tasteless defend publication on the ground that the photograph serves a greater good. When Stan Forman of the Boston *Herald-American* photographed a fire escape breaking away from a building and casting two people to the ground, one to her death, the resulting flurry included an inspection of all the city's fire escapes. Some editors used that to defend publication of the sequence (which won a Pulitzer Prize). Some editors use the same defense in publishing gory accident photographs. People will drive more carefully after seeing such photographs, the editors argue. That hasn't happened, perhaps because readers have become jaded from seeing so many accident photographs.

Other editors would argue that they are not in the "social good" business, just the news business. They would say they publish photographs because the photographs are news and not because the photos might solve some social problem. They are right. If an editor publishes a photograph with a greater good in mind, might not the same editor withhold a photograph because it might represent a greater evil? Editors must avoid a child-care mentality when editing newspapers. The major criterion for any photograph should be its inherent news value. A photograph of a body crumpled up after falling 10 stories lacks the news value of a photograph showing the body falling, unless the victim is newsworthy (a public official), in which case any photograph might be used.

Such a situation occurred on January 22, 1987, when the treasurer of Pennsylvania, R. Budd Dwyer, called a news conference the day before he was to be sentenced for his role in a kickback scandal. Instead of announcing his resignation, Dwyer pulled a .357 Magnum from a manila envelope and shot himself. The photographs available to newspapers across the country ranged from Dwyer pulling the gun, to Dwyer just as the bullet came out of the top of his head, to Dwyer bleeding from the nose and mouth with his body slumped on the floor. The photo most favored by editors surveyed by the Associated Press Managing Editors was one of Dwyer with the gun in his right hand and his left hand extended toward the photographer in a gesture saying "keep away." The choice of most editors was not to show the actual suicide or the aftermath.

One newspaper that used a photograph of Dwyer with the gun in his mouth and his body on the floor seconds later was the *Philadelphia Inquirer*. The editor of the editorial page, Edwin Guthman, explained in his Sunday column that using only the photograph of Dwyer waving reporters away "would not really convey what had happened." Guthman, who was responding to readers' complaints, said that the senior editors who made the decision to publish the photographs noted the public circumstances of Dwyer's suicide. "In agony," Guthman wrote, "Dwyer was trying to make an appalling statement, and however deranged he may have been, we did not want to tamper with the force of what he was attempting to convey."

Case-by-case judgments arise in many decisions on the selection of news photographs. In the early 1960s the Associated Press transmitted a photograph of a Vietnamese monk who had doused himself with gasoline and then lit a match. The photograph showed the monk in flames. Some editors rejected the photograph because they published morning newspapers and they did not feel it appropriate for a breakfast audience. The same editors undoubtedly would not have used it in an afternoon paper because it would offend the dinner crowd. Other editors used it because the act of self-immolation showed the emotion of protest in Vietnam at that time. That was its news value. It showed something people in the United States would never have understood from words alone.

A later Vietnam photograph, this one of a police chief executing a suspected Viet Cong officer with a pistol shot to the head, appeared on the front page of *The New York Times* and the *Washington Post,* among others. (The *Times* had rejected the monk photograph.) NBC showed footage of the execution but cut away when the footage showed the corpse and blood rushing from the head of the corpse. The NBC producer made a decision between news and gore; he edited out the gore and kept the news.

Some editors would argue that distance between the reader and the event makes the photograph easier to use. A newspaper would reject the photograph of a local woman's body lying on railroad tracks but might show the photograph of firefighters removing the body of a youngster, his face clearly showing, from the waters of a river where his school bus had plunged—in Spain.

Overall, editors must ask themselves if any photograph, no matter what the content, contains newsworthy elements, adds insight to a problem or puts a story into context enough to make it publishable. If a photograph has voyeuristic rather than news value, the editor has good reason to reject it. (See Figures 11.3, 11.4, and 11.5, and the accompanying column from the Easton, Pa., *Express* (Figure 11.2) in which managing editor Bruce Frassinelli explains how the editors of his newspaper decided which photographs of a tragedy to publish.

The ability to change photographs through computer enhancement also raises ethical questions. Newspapers, magazines and the wire services can improve the quality of a photograph through computer enhancement, a process that speeds cropping and enlarging, makes those procedures more precise and removes them from the confines of a darkroom to a television screen. Computer-enhanced photographs are nothing new; they are a product of a space age that propelled camera-bearing craft into space. Those spacecraft transmitted to earth photographs of the distant planets; the weak images were fed through a computer, which turned them into photographs.

The negative aspect of the electronic manipulation of a photograph occurs when the photograph's content is altered. Thanks to digital retouching equipment, an editor can remove something objectionable in a photograph and introduce an image from another photograph. Newspapers need to be alert to the potential for abuse and unethical manipulation.

Soon to be available is the camera that sends photographic images to a computer via telephone or satellite, thus allowing the editor in the main office to select the photographs. Missing from the process are film and the chemicals needed for processing. Another new technology allows printing of photographs from a videotape. Electronic transmission of photographs eliminates time-consuming mechanical processes from the photographic procedure and offers more time for a human brain to evaluate and creatively select photographs.

Figure 11.2 Column by Bruce Frassinelli. (Copyright 1989, Easton, Pennsylvania.)

Photo of Minsi Lake tragedy struck a nerve

Decision to publish is praised, condemned

When I decided to publish the photograph of a rescue worker carrying a lifeless child across the ice of Minsi Lake on the front page of The Express on Monday, Jan. 16, I knew that some readers would strongly disagree with my decision. I expected a few would support the decision, too.

I spent most of Tuesday on the phone discussing the decision with readers. What I found extraordinary was the need by many adults to talk about the incident in which a mother and two of her children and another child fell through the ice of Minsi Lake in Upper Mount Bethel Township, Pa., on Sunday, Jan. 15, and drowned.

While the photograph may have sparked the phone calls, at least a dozen of those who called were just as interested in coming to grips with the tragedy by talking about it.

I learned that not only were children — particularly the dead children's schoolmates — profoundly affected by the loss but so were many adult readers, regardless of whether they knew the victims or their families.

"I have a child that age," said a shaken Palmer Township, Pa., woman. "I kept thinking, 'My God, suppose that would have been her? What would I have done?'"

Express photographer Sue Beyer returned from Minsi Lake with a number of photographs showing different aspects of the attempted rescue, retrieval of the victims and efforts to revive them.

Choosing best package

Express editors meet on the morning of publication to decide which stories, photographs and graphics will appear on the front page. It was obvious that the dramatic story from Minsi Lake would be a front-page story. We also decided it was the most important story we had that day and its placement as the "lead" was underscored with a six-column headline.

Next came the question of how to illustrate the story. We had several photographs of rescue workers with the retrieved children. One showed a close-up of a child's face. We immediately rejected that one. One showed rescue workers huddled around one of the victims on shore, performing lifesaving techniques. Another showed two rescue workers carrying a ladder across the ice to save a fisherman who attempted to go to the aid of the four victims but who also broke through the ice. We decided to use these two, along with the controversial photograph. Each, I felt, told an important part of the dramatic story.

We also published a map showing where Minsi Lake is in relationship to some Slate Belt towns (Bangor, East Bangor, Roseto) to help readers unfamiliar with the area.

The words, photographs and map were important components in

JAN 2 9 1989

Bruce Frassinelli

LETTER FROM EDITOR

bringing readers the full story and impact of this tragedy.

Capturing the drama

The photographs have much to tell, for they are instants of people's lives captured on film. These frozen frames move readers — fellow human beings — who vicariously share those moments.

But why use the photo of the rescue worker rushing the child across the ice to waiting rescue personnel?

This was an indispensable part of the visual image of the story. It captured graphically the drama of those tense moments, how several volunteer rescue squads pooled their resources in a game but vain effort to save the four.

At the time our photographer froze that image, the child was still presumed to be alive. Frantic efforts to revive the child continued all the way to the hospital.

Most but not all of those who criticized the decision were either relatives or friends of the family. I can understand that reaction. At the time of my decision, I knew that its publication would weigh most heavily on those closest to these victims. And they would be viewing my actions in that capacity. I, on the other hand, had to make a decision based on what I thought would be appropriate coverage for all of our 100,000-plus readers.

Carolyn Gara of Hampton, N.J., aunt of one of the children who died, commended The Express on the use of the photograph. "That picture said everything," she said. "Even though it was a difficult experience for the family to go through, the look on that rescue worker's face as he carried that little body told a story that no words could ever tell."

Sending a 'message'

Most of those who called to commend the decision to publish said that they hoped it would send a "message," that it would help point out how dangerously thin the ice on lakes and ponds could be during such a relatively mild winter.

"If that photograph can save one child's life, then it was the right thing to do," said a reader from Bangor.

"My 6-year-old son looked at the picture and asked me why the man was carrying the child," explained a mother from Nazareth. "It gave

me a chance to discuss the situation and talk about the dangers and how it's important to read and obey signs," she said.

Another mother from Nazareth said her first reaction was to throw the paper into the garbage so her 5-year-old child wouldn't see it. And she did. It was now the next day when she was talking to me.

"I didn't sleep good last night, thinking about those children who died," she said. "But, you know, now I'm kind of sorry I threw the paper away. I think I should talk to my daughter about this in a couple of days. I think that would be helpful and valuable."

I offered to send her a tear sheet of the front page. She accepted.

Branded a 'scavenger'

But these were the exceptions. One caller accused me of being "a scavenger trying to pick clean a kid's bones to sell a couple of lousy papers." Another said Express editors "have no heart."

It's not easy to hear these deprecating remarks and remain unmoved, but I know that much of it comes from emotionalism and anger.

A Hunterdon County reader wondered how many of the editors who voted The Express as one of the three best newspapers in its circulation classification in Pennsylvania would have run the photo with such prominence on their front pages.

Aren't reporters "sufficiently adequate in their profession to warn people of the dangers by the mere use of words?" he asked.

Deciding on using a photo such as this is not easy. Don't think it didn't occur to me to take the easy way out and discard the photo. But my job is to make the best decision I can based on sound journalistic judgments — even in cases such as these where an answer can be right or wrong, depending on one's point of view.

Photos showing the consequence of tragedy may have a sobering effect on the public and could make people more safety-conscious, yet the flip side of publishing such photos is to add to the shock and grief of the family and friends of victims.

One thing I've noticed is a relationship between readers' reactions to a picture and its proximity to them. A local photo can raise cries of protest while a similar picture from the other side of the country or world draws no outrage.

Local photographs are debated passionately as we editors try to explain the function of news pictures to puzzled and angry readers. We are chastised as unfeeling and accused of sensationalism.

"You're just trying to sell newspapers," angry readers tell us.

Bum raps to be sure, but that goes with the territory, too.

■ Bruce Frassinelli is managing editor of The Express. You can write to him at Box 391, Easton, PA 18044-0391, or call him at 215-258-7171 or 800-397-9777.

Figure 11.3 Faced with a variety of photographs taken at a tragic drowning, editors of The Express *chose the photo shown above and the two on pages 235 and 236, as explained by managing editor Bruce Frassinelli. (Photographs by Sue Beyer. Copyright 1989* The Express, *Easton, Pennsylvania.)*

Picture Pages

Picture pages represent the essence of photojournalism, the melding of pictures and words to depict a spot news event or a feature. Although the length of the word story can vary, the best picture pages contain short word essays and rely mostly on the visual to give the message. Putting a limit on anything can backfire, but the best picture page usually contains no more than five or six photographs.

Figure 11.4

Some newspapers routinely fill up a page of unrelated photographs of news events and call that a picture page. But the picture pages that a photojournalist would want to produce to tell a story would stick to a single subject. Multitopic picture pages lack the thematic unity so necessary to retaining a reader's attention. A picture page should be a visual essay, not a set of visuals.

The concept behind designing a picture page is the same as that used in designing a front page—the page must have a lead. That does not mean, however, that the photograph in the upper left-hand corner is the lead or that the largest photograph on the page is the lead. Often, the lead (or dominant) photograph is the most striking in content, size or position but is not necessarily the largest. For example, the lead photograph could be

Figure 11.5

one column by 21 inches deep or six columns by three inches deep and not be the largest photograph on the page. The atypical size would make it stand out.

Those who design picture pages should forget column sizes and use a blank piece of paper on which to make a dummy. That way they are apt to present the photographs in a visually better size than the standard column size might allow. Furthermore, a five-column photograph centered over six columns visually breaks from the traditional columns and frames the picture in a background of air. In other words, pictures are floated on the page rather than held to standard columns. In a well-designed picture page, each module, including type, lines up with at least one other module. That helps give the page unity.

Most photographs on a picture page need a caption, not because the photographs need the words but because captions guide the reader through the page. Captionless picture pages, or pages with one caption referring to all pictures on the page, function like ships without rudders—they are aimless and readers avoid them because they lack time to figure out what is going on. Occasionally a self-explanatory photograph, especially one that is not central to telling the story, can appear without a caption.

For the most part, photographs look best in rectangular rather than square shapes. The pictures on a picture page about bowling need not appear in the shape of bowling pins or bowling balls. Also to be avoided are mortises, cutouts and insets, all of which detract from the photographs. Type on top of photographs can be overdone, as can reverse type. Keep air to the outside; don't trap globs of empty space between pictures or in the middle of the page. In all, those who design picture pages should strive for clean presentations that do not mutilate the pictures and words on the page or the newspaper's reputation.

The Mechanics

Sizing

The tools of photo sizing are the pica stick, the proportional scale and two Ls, which are optional. The Ls are cut from very heavy paper or cardboard (so they can endure many handlings) and enable an editor to move them about the surface of a picture to see how it will appear if cropped a certain way. Other editors use pieces of paper, which are not as convenient or durable.

The measuring area of the standard pica stick is 12 inches long and is broken into inches down one side and picas down the other. A pica is a printer's measure equal to approximately on-sixth of an inch. An inch contains six picas. A pica breaks down into points, of which there are 12 in one pica. The point, of course, is the same point used to measure type. Thus, a 36-point headline is three picas deep. Six picas, or 72 points, equal an inch. In 12 inches, there are 72 picas.

The proportional scale, more commonly known as the wheel, has on its face two scales, both of which are marked off in inches. Ignore that fact, and simply interpret the numbers on the wheel as referring to picas. After all, the wheel is a proportional scale, and the sizing of photographs is an exercise in changing proportions. It doesn't matter how the measurements are labeled.

To change the size of a photograph, an editor must first know its width and depth in picas. To change a photograph 30 picas wide and 42 picas deep to three columns (41 picas wide, for this exercise) the editor would find 30 on the inside scale of the wheel (called Size of Original) and line it up with 41 on the outside scale (called Reproduction Size). In the window appears the percentage the reproduction camera must be set at to blow up the photograph to the size wanted by the editor. This percentage must be marked on the photograph. To learn the new depth of the photograph, the editor looks at 42 on the inside scale (without further moving the wheel) and sees what it lines up with. That number (57, in this example) is the photograph's new depth. The photograph would be marked 3×57. (When not dealing with standard column widths, an editor marks a picture size picas by picas.) A photograph can be reduced using this same method.

Cropping

The art photographer has time to pose pictures and produces work that seldom needs cropping. But the photojournalist takes pictures on the fly and often has to settle for a poor vantage point. Just because the action doesn't take place where the photographer is doesn't mean the editor won't expect a good photograph of the action. Don Black was quite a distance away when he took the photograph of Rockefeller, and he used only 20 percent of the negative to produce the final print.

Black, like most photographers, did his cropping in the darkroom. But often cropping is done on the desk, especially when an editor sees something croppable in a photograph that the photographer did not crop out. A photograph should not be cropped just to make it fit into a page. Cropping should be done to make a picture better, in much the same way as an editor removes words here and there to make a story better.

Figure 11.6 A photograph frequently needs cropping to improve it. In the photo above a distracting reflection on the left and some grayish-white areas at the top and bottom can profitably be cut from this photograph. A tightly cropped and more interesting photograph results. See Figure 11.7 on the next page. (The Bettman Archive photo.)

Examine Figure 11.6. It shows a British soldier standing guard outside a clothing store in Belfast, Northern Ireland, while next to him two shoppers look into a window. To the left is a distracting reflection of nearby people. At the top of the photograph is something white that will no doubt wash out in reproduction and thus should be cropped out of the picture. The sidewalk, although it will reproduce adequately, is distracting foreground and should be cropped as close as possible to the people in the picture. That will bring the people closer to the reader. Likewise,

Figure 11.7 (The Bettman Archive photo.)

the area to the right of the soldier adds nothing and should be trimmed away.

That leaves a photograph with three adults, Figure 11.7. Contrary to what you may be thinking, that is not dishonest cropping even though what remains is not the original photograph. What if the photographer had turned in a photograph of just the two men? Nobody would have been aware of what had been trimmed away, either in the taking of the photograph or in the darkroom. The photograph represents a slice of Belfast, not all of it. Any photograph is only part of a larger whole.

Cropping should remove that which distracts the reader from seeing the main point of a photograph. Beyond normal cropping (removing extraneous background and foreground) is radical cropping, which offers the reader atypical perspectives.

Inexperienced editors make many mistakes in cropping photos, especially if they lack a photographic background or an appreciation of the visual. Beginners tend to want to reduce photographs rather than crop them to the desired size. Too often a beginner will reduce an entire photograph rather than crop out of the photograph the uninteresting and distracting. A reduced photograph means a reduced image and a loss of detail.

To tell the production department which part of a picture to crop out, an editor marks the margins of the photograph. An editor never marks on the surface of a picture because the editor may have a change of mind about the size and will need to remark the photograph. Pencil and ballpoint pen marks will not come off the surface of a photograph. Other than crop marks, all instructions to the production department are usually placed on the back of a photograph or are written on an order tag attached to the photograph.

Caption Writing

Captions rank right behind headlines as the most highly read item in a newspaper. They convey information in a few sentences and cannot suffer from ambiguity. They serve the reader much as headlines do, and for that reason copy editors should give them as much attention.

A good caption with a photograph completes the thought the photograph starts or provides something the photograph doesn't, such as a name. The caption gives the photograph context and explains anything not immediately clear to the reader. Just like a story, a caption requires strong, active verbs. A caption is usually written in the present tense because it describes the photograph the reader is looking at and conveys immediacy. Frequently, a time element does not appear in a caption, especially if a story accompanies the photograph. If a time element is needed, it does not appear with the present tense verb in the opening sentence. It appears in another sentence or in a subordinate clause.

Editors who write captions always have the photographs before them as they write. Wise editors avoid mistakes by seeing what they are writing about. A chief editor, for example, may crop a photograph and not tell the copy editor, who then writes the caption from memory. The newspaper will look silly if the caption mentions someone or something that has been cropped from the photograph.

Here is the caption that accompanied the wirephoto from Belfast shown in Figure 11.6:

> TIGHT SECURITY IN EFFECT
> BELFAST, N. IRELAND: Security forces throughout Northern Ireland were put on alert April 17 for possible reprisal attacks for the death of an IRA official and the 60th anniversary of the bloody Easter uprising. The current alert is in addition to the tight security measures put into effect in and around the city's shopping center last week. Here, an armed British soldier stands guard in front of a clothing store as two pedestrians check out the window. Protestant militants marched throughout Northern Ireland April 19 under the watch of the strong security forces seeking to prevent any violence.

The caption does not refer to the photograph until the third sentence. After the first sentence, though, the reader may assume that the wrong caption appears with the photograph and go on to reading something else. What that caption needs is an introductory sentence about the picture:

> A British soldier stands guard outside a store in Belfast, Northern Ireland, unnoticed by two shoppers and

their child. The guard is one of the British security forces put on alert throughout Northern Ireland yesterday.

Now the first sentence tells about the photograph, and the rest of the caption provides the context. In essence, the wire service's sentences were reordered. Also, whoever rewrites the original would reduce its length. A good caption does not make the reader linger but provides quick information and lets the reader continue. Three short sentences make a good caption length.

The success of a caption begins with its legend or lead-in. In the case of the preceding caption, the wire service provided the legend "Tight Security in Effect." Because that legend does not fit the picture, though, the copy editor who rewrote the caption would also create a more germane legend. One of these legends might do: "On Guard," "At the Ready," "On Alert," "Guarded Shoppers," "Guarded Irish Shoppers."

The legend (or its equivalent) should be as seductive as a headline. That's one reason names do not make good legends. The good legend sums up the photograph and entices the reader to read the caption. On a photograph of a woman being arrested for throwing an egg at a politician, a novice wrote, "Egg Thrower Arrest." Well, that sums it up but it's hardly enticing. A possible replacement: "Egg on Her Face." Among other things, the legend turns around a cliché and uses it as an appropriate metaphor.

Also make sure that the legend and the caption fit. A beginning caption writer turned this in:

FLYING FINISH: Pilsdon High's Austin Williams stumbles to second place . . .

The legend and the main verb (*stumbles*) contradict each other. This is a caption on the photograph of the finish of a race, and one assumes that a flying finish is good. But *stumbles* tells the real story, and the caption writer needed a legend that conveyed what the picture showed.

Good headline writers make good legend writers, for they know their mission and they approach it with zeal. A dull headline writer usually produces dull legends.

Caption writing, like headline writing, has its own set of rules, some of which duplicate other aspects of newspaper production. Some editors would distinguish between captions written for photographs that accompany stories and photographs that stand alone. Captions on photographs with stories should avoid duplicating the headline but rather should further explain the story. Remember, as the Belfast caption demonstrates, a photograph is part of a story, and the caption needs to explain both the part and the context. Don't include some mundane fact from late in the story.

Here are some other caption guidelines that can apply either to photographs with stories or to photographs standing alone. As noted, use the opening sentence to describe the photograph and write it in the present tense. Unless you can find a clever way to subordinate the time element, don't use it, because the sentence will not make sense with a present tense verb and a time element, which will function as past tense.

In describing the action, don't state the obvious. Rather, explain what is happening. In the Belfast caption, for example, stating the obvious could include something like this: "A soldier with a rifle in his hands and a beret on his head stands with his feet apart." What the caption should tell the reader is who the soldier is, what he is doing and why.

Identify every recognizable face in a photograph. The standard form is to say (*from left to right*) but a more interesting way cites some form of action a person is taking: (smiling), (frowning), (walking away).

A caption writer should not editorialize. Present the facts as neutrally as possible and let the reader make the judgments. The caption writer should not attempt to enter the mind of a person in a photograph and tell what the person is thinking.

Make sure the caption is consistent with the story. Don't have a caption saying 20 people died in an accident and a story saying 10. And don't spell the same word differently. In the caption of a photograph of a wrecked plane, the writer said the plane belonged to Japan Airlines. The photo showed the company's name painted on the fuselage: Japan Air Lines. Which is correct? the reader asks.

Be honest about the source of a photograph. If the dictator of a country provides a photograph of his torture-free prison after having been accused of conducting torture in the prison, note that the dictator provided the photograph. It would probably be necessary in such a situation to state that the dictator would not allow news photographers inside the prison. Another time to reveal the source comes when the newspaper is using a file photograph. When the mug shot of an 85-year-old person who just died makes the person look 55, the newspaper should indicate the age of the photograph. That's usually done by noting the year the photograph was taken.

A camera can lie, and the perspective it provides might not be honest, especially if a telephoto lens (which makes subjects appear closer to each other than they are) or a wide-angle lens (which distorts) is used. Explain such distortions in the caption. At the same time, when the staff photographer produces a work of art, do not tell the readers what f-stop and shutter speed the photographer used. The work of art arose in the eye of the photographer, not in the mechanics of the camera, and by providing mechanical information, the newspaper contributes to the delinquency of amateur photographers who would rather imitate than create.

Finally, rewrite wirephoto captions. They are turned out rapidly and sometimes carelessly. Check captions against stories, which are sent later in the cycle than the photograph. The story may have updated information; in fact, check for the latest story. A thoughtful copy editor who takes an extra minute to do the job well can always improve such a caption.

Experts say that people have become more visually aware. A good editor recognizes that the best stories are told not one-dimensionally but with as many dimensions as the editor can muster. Photographs represent one of those dimensions and deserve equal treatment with words.

Sources and Resources

"A Public Suicide." In *1987 APME Report: Photo and Graphics,* 3–9.

Baker, Robert L. "Portraits of a Public Suicide: Photo Treatment by Selected Pennsylvania Dailies." *Newspaper Research Journal* 9, no. 4 (Summer 1988): 13–23.

Currie, Phil. "The Ethics of Photographs: To Shoot or Not Shoot Tragic Pictures?" *Editorially Speaking* 35, no. 4 (April 1982).

Elliott, Deni, ed. *Responsible Journalism.* Beverly Hills, Calif.: Sage Publications, 1986.

Faber, John. *Great News Photos and the Stories Behind Them.* 2d rev. ed. New York: Dover Publications, 1978.

Fedler, Fred, Tim Counts, and Paul Hightower. "Changes in Wording of Cutlines Fail To Reduce Photographs' Offensiveness." *Journalism Quarterly* 59, no. 4 (Winter 1982): 633–637.

Fink, Conrad C. *Media Ethics in the Newsroom and Beyond.* New York: McGraw-Hill, 1988.

Geraci, Philip C. *Photojournalism: New Images in Visual Communication.* Dubuque, Iowa: Kendall/Hunt Publishing Co., 1984.

Goodwin, H. Eugene. *Groping for Ethics in Journalism.* 2d ed. Ames: Iowa State University Press, 1987.

Gordon, Jim. "Judgment Days for Words and Pictures." *News Photographer* (July 1980): 25–29.

Guthman, Edwin. "Why the Inquirer Ran Those Budd Dwyer Photos." *Philadelphia Inquirer* (February 1, 1987): 7–F.

Hartley, Craig H. "Ethical Newsgathering Values of the Public and Press Photographers." *Journalism Quarterly* 60, no. 2 (Summer 1983): 301–304.

Hoy, Frank P. *Photojournalism: The Visual Approach.* Englewood Cliffs, N.J.: Prentice-Hall, 1986.

Klaidman, Stephen, and Tom L. Beauchamp. *The Virtuous Journalist.* New York: Oxford University Press, 1987.

Kobre, Kenneth. *Photojournalism: The Professionals' Approach.* Somerville, Mass.: Curtin & London, 1980.

Kochersberger, Robert C., Jr. "Survey of Suicide Photos Use by Newspapers in Three States." *Newspaper Research Journal* 9, no. 4 (Summer 1988): 1–12.

Lambeth, Edmund B. *Committed Journalism: An Ethic for the Profession.* Bloomington: Indiana University Press, 1986.

Lasico, J. D. "Photographs That Lie." *Washington Journalism Review* (June 1989): 22–25.

Leckley, Sheryle, and John Leckley, eds. *Moments: The Pulitzer Prize Photographs.* New York: Crown Publishers, 1978.

Meyer, Philip. *Editors, Publishers and Newspaper Ethics: A Report to the American Society of Newspaper Editors.* Washington, D.C.: American Society of Newspaper Editors, 1983.

Rivers, William L., and Cleve Mathews. *Ethics for the Media.* Englewood Cliffs, N.J.: Prentice-Hall, 1988.

Sandeen, Rod. "Hey, Hold Still Just a Minute, Please; I Want to Take Your Environmental Portrait." *Editorially Speaking* 42, no. 8 (October 1988).

Singletary, Michael W., and Chris Lamb. "News Values in Award-Winning Photos." *Journalism Quarterly* 61, no. 1 (Spring 1984): 104–108, 233.

Swain, Bruce M. *Reporters' Ethics*. Ames: Iowa State University Press, 1978.

Wolf, Rita, and Gerald L. Grotta. "Images: A Question of Readership." *Newspaper Research Journal* 6, no. 2 (Winter 1985): 30–36.

Chapter 12

Wire Services

The Two Major Wires in the U.S.A.

The state, national and international news that appears in most of the newspapers in the United States comes from two major wire services: United Press International and the Associated Press. These two wire services provide about 70 percent of all the news heard or read in the United States. Larger newspapers, and television and radio stations, subscribe to both, which permits editors to choose the better story or combine elements from both. Smaller news media, though, often rely on one service only, primarily because of cost but also because two would transmit more copy than any newspaper or station could print or broadcast.

The two services differ in structure and reputation. The United Press International (formed in 1958 with the merger of United Press and the International News Service) is intended to be a profit-making venture. It is privately owned and has endured several ownership changes and questions about its financial solvency, which have lowered its credibility with many users. The Associated Press, on the other hand, is a non-profit cooperative of member newspapers and broadcasters. Any budget surplus is used for development. Nobody receives stock dividends.

The wire services, while covering much the same news, still exhibit differences. Substantive differences are difficult to describe, because each service's reputation can vary from state to state and decade to decade. At one time UPI was known as "a writer's wire" because that service's stories were frequently more interestingly written, whereas the AP's stories tended to follow the bland inverted-pyramid formula. AP has since cast off its reputation for dullness. The quality of state government coverage varies from state to state, and editors subscribing to both services develop a feel for which service is better for their paper and then seldom check the other service for stories in the state government category. It is human nature to do that, but it is not good editing.

Both wires initiated the electronic changes discussed in Chapter 2. In the early 1970s both realized they could meet deadlines faster and produce more efficient reports if they converted to electronic editing systems. They also introduced high-speed service, higher-quality wire-photos and satellite delivery of the news. Newspapers started changing over when they saw the benefits.

Newspapers that had never before purchased wirephotos acquired the service because its quality virtually matched photographs produced by the newspaper's photographer. With VDTs installed, newspapers could receive news at 1,200 words per minute rather than 66 words per minute, as on a Teletype. This allowed the wires to expand their coverage and upgrade their services. (Eventually, transmission speeds on standard news circuits will reach 10,000 words a minute.) The high-speed service not only delivers faster, it also delivers better. Rather than wasting time with new leads that member newspapers had to affix to earlier stories, the wires can now send a completely rewritten story (slugged "writethru") in seconds, thereby saving newspaper editors time in updating the day's edition. The high speed also enables newspaper groups and chains to set up their own delivery system by using an open channel in the wire services' trunk lines. Similarly, syndicates that provide feature and column material to newspapers use other channels to send their fare, thereby cutting down on mailing costs and reducing their reliance on the sometimes unreliable mail service.

In addition to providing radio stations with printed news copy, both AP and UPI furnish full audio services. These include hourly national and international newscasts, special reports, sports, stock material information and live broadcasts. High speed capability has also allowed the AP to split its service to radio and television stations, which ended the problem of serving different media on one wire.

Organizational differences between the wires mean more to wire service employees than to users, so a detailed description is omitted here. Both wires have bureaus throughout the United States and the rest of the world. The bureaus within the United States are capable of taking over and distributing most of a day's reporting when equipment or electrical problems plague headquarters.

The news of the world, filtered through bureaus, reaches the main distribution center of each wire service by entering a vast computer storage center for later retrieval and redistribution by the slot editor. That editor, who must stay on top of incoming stories and new leads, works with the news editor, who decides which wire a story goes on (A, sports, financial, etc.) and what priority it receives. The news editor also assigns work to rewrite (copy) editors, who fix poor writing and remove local references from stories so that they are fit for understanding by a large, diverse audience. The news editor also checks the finished work of these rewrite editors. The file editor actually assigns the story to the designated wire after checking it. The supervisor, in the meantime, reads all stories and puts together that day's digest, or budget, for members.

In deciding which stories rate budget treatment, the supervisor hears from the many bureaus around the world. Bureau editors who feel they have submitted excellent stories will lobby the supervisors to get those stories listed on the budget. The newspaper analogy is the story conference, where section editors jockey to get their stories on Page One. Daily the many editors of a wire service meet to decide how to process the news flow. For these meetings, the bureaus are linked through telephones so bureau editors can participate.

The editors of one wire service, of course, are always scheming to beat the other wire service. No wire service editor likes to hear that the other service placed a certain story on the wires first. Even though the receiving newspaper may not go to press for four hours, and the difference between the delivery of the two stories is three minutes, the wire editor who comes in second feels chagrined. The wire editors believe that a newspaper subscribing to both services will use the story it receives first. At the same time, being first is a good selling point for a wire service bureau chief dealing with a potential client: "Look how many times we beat them." Every day wire service editors check metropolitan newspapers to see how the papers played wire service stories. The editors keep a tally to see which service gets used the most.

In addition to having bureaus abroad in order to get foreign news for U.S. newspapers, the wire services also provide news to foreign countries. The Latin American desk at the AP, for example, translates stories into

Spanish and Portuguese. UPI offers a Spanish code converter that provides stories in Spanish (right down to the punctuation peculiar to that language). The stories can be processed in electronic systems.

Domestically, AP and UPI provide a variety of wires to fit the needs of large and small newspapers. The A wire, the main wire that gives the top news first, is offered in high and slow speed. It provides news faster and in more detail than smaller wires. Usually, only large newspapers need it or can afford it. Smaller newspapers subscribe to a state or regional wire. Depending on the area, the regional wire might serve three small states or just one. In larger states, the regional wire might be split into eastern and western or northern and southern divisions (called legs) so that the wire services can provide more localized news. In Pennsylvania, which has a split AP wire, "more localized news" means Philadelphia stories for subscribers on the eastern leg and Pittsburgh stories for the western leg.

In a widely used related service, participating newspapers feed electronic carbons of some stories with statewide interest from local computers over telephone lines to a central AP computer, from which they are redistributed to AP members. Because of the direct and quick link through computers, participating newspapers have increased their contribution to the daily wire report, and editors believe that all-around AP coverage has improved.

A wire considered especially important to larger newspapers is the financial or stock wire, which distributes the stock tables at high speed. The AP provides a wire that moves the stock tables at 9,600 words per minute, a boon to afternoon newspapers with special deadlines to get the day's stock report published on the same day. Another wire, this one especially useful to morning newspapers, is the sports wire, which provides individual game stories and statistics not found on a regional wire. Morning newspapers, known for having a heavy sports orientation, receive an abundance of sports stories not provided on smaller wires. The sports wire selection allows sports editors to present a package of stories tailored to local interest rather than relying on the roundup stories a small wire provides. The roundup stories traditionally lead off with the big winners or the division leaders, meaning that a small-town fan whose big-city sports team is not doing well won't get in-depth coverage from a regional wire. After all, who wants to read about losers?

The availability of wire service news is not without its drawbacks. As told so well by Timothy Crouse in *The Boys on the Bus,* reporters for major newspapers tend to write their stories to agree with the wire services' emphasis. Such a unity of emphasis contravenes the Founders' intentions in shaping the First Amendment, which they hoped would protect a multitude of conflicting ideas. This pack mentality, of course, is not the fault of the wires. It is the fault of newspaper editors who are afraid to be different.

Some critics of the wire services suggest that they are nationally oriented, homogenized, often shallow and bland. Given the changing newspaper scene, the wire services will no doubt continue to upgrade their writing and try new writing styles and reporting approaches. In fact, the wires may have to lead in this area because newspapers outside the major cities tend to be conservative and slow to respond to new trends. Even though journalists from both wire services have won their share of Pulitzer Prizes, the "shallow" label will always be with the wires. Though they have attempted to provide more than spot news coverage, their strength lies in quickly turning out current information.

The two wire services have also been criticized for stereotyped coverage of international events, of covering in detail spot news such as terrorism, flood, famine and pestilence but seldom bothering to cover in depth the many stories that would provide U.S. audiences with an informed view of the world. In addition, developed nations get better coverage than developing nations. Poor international coverage also reflects a cultural problem. Wire service editors know their audiences and do not go against the tide of cultural ignorance they represent. Larger newspapers supplement their international coverage by subscribing to foreign news services such as Agence France-Press, Reuters, Hsinhua, and Telegrafnoie Agentstvo Sovetskovo Soiuza (better known by its acronym, TASS).

Supplementary Wires

Newspapers that want to round out their wire coverage subscribe to supplementary wires. Newspapers that belong to chains or groups receive additional wires such as the KRTN News Wire, the Gannett News

Service, the Christian Science Monitor News & Photo Service or the
Newhouse News Service. Some of the supplementary wires operate as partnerships. The KRTN News Wire comprises Knight-Ridder,
the *Chicago Tribune* and *The New York Daily News* and other newspapers owned by the Tribune Company as well as several independent
newspapers. Another partnership that also provides a wire service for
anyone who wants to buy it is the Los Angeles Times–Washington Post
News Service. An individual wire service that rates highly with some
editors is the New York Times News Service. The Register and Tribune
Syndicate Inc. provides the Christian Science Monitor News & Photo
Service. The Newhouse wire is available through the Field News
Service, which also provides stories from the Chicago *Sun-Times* and
the *Baltimore Sun*. The Reuters News Agency, which has an international
clientele, has an exchange agreement with Canadian Press, a national news
agency similar to AP and UPI.

   The content of the news provided by these many wire services varies,
but with the exception of the British-based Reuters service, the idea behind them is the same: supplement wire service coverage with columns,
features and stories the two larger wires don't provide. The supplementary
wires do not try to compete with AP and UPI; they try to complete them.
New York Times News Service subscribers like not only the in-depth
articles and analyses the service provides but also the editorial package,
the *Times'* columnists who appear regularly on that newspaper's op-ed
page.

   By combining the services of two or more newspapers, the supplementary wires increase their reach across the nation and the world. The
Los Angeles Times–Washington Post service combines 50 bureaus and
then adds contributions from *Newsday* and the *Dallas Times-Herald,* Agence
France-Press and the *Guardian* of London. *Newsday's* contribution includes
a bureau in China.

   Knight-Ridder established foreign bureaus both as a way of improving its international news coverage for the KRTN wire and as a way of
offering reporters of Knight-Ridder newspapers an opportunity for overseas assignments. Member newspapers provide correspondents to staff the
bureaus. Also, Knight-Ridder, like other groups and chains, provides
subscribers with stories from member newspapers. Such service increases
the mix of any user's content. In addition to the supplementary wires,
there are many syndicates that provide a variety of copy ranging from

astrology to youth issues. The crossword puzzle, horoscope, comics and some of the columnists on newspaper editorial and feature pages are provided by syndicates.

Using the Wires

People just learning the skill of fielding a baseball are always told to charge a ground ball when it is hit toward them rather than waiting for the ball to get to them. "Play the ball; don't let the ball play you," learners are told. The analogy applies to the wires: Editors should use the wires to their best advantage rather than just stuffing wire stories throughout the paper wherever a convenient hole pops up.

No editor should thoughtlessly publish any wire story. Suppose the story has a local angle deep within it? The story should be rewritten so that the local angle appears either near the beginning or as a sidebar. And what if the two wires offer non-duplicate stories on the same topic (i.e., written from different angles)? A good editor would combine the best of both instead of rejecting one story outright. What if a wire story is written so poorly that it needs rewriting? Either complain to the wire's editor or have a copy editor rewrite it, but don't publish as is, because the critical reader will consider the story an error made by the newspaper, not by the wire service. And it is the newspaper's error.

Beginning desk editors should also guard against the bulletin mentality of both wire services, which in the heat of competition may offer something "sensational" that turns out to be a dud—after the presses are running. In the early 1970s, a wire service bulletin from Athens telling that air raid sirens could be heard over the telephone from Cairo conjured up the image of Israeli jets about to devastate the Egyptian city. The newspapers printing that bulletin looked stupid when the wire service reported, after deadline, that the air raid sirens had sounded in error.

During the 1980 Republican convention, both wire services announced that Ronald Reagan had selected former president Gerald R. Ford as his running mate. Approximately an hour and a half later Reagan chose George Bush. Both services quoted by name people they considered reliable sources, but the sources were wrong, and it speaks poorly of good journalists that they didn't query their sources deeper and harder. It was, said Louis D. Boccardi, then vice president and executive editor of the AP, "a chaotic moment." For that reason, more caution should have been exercised.

In a more tense event, freedom for 52 Americans held hostage for 444 days in Iran, both wire services announced the freedom of the hostages almost an hour before their planes took off from Iran. Because neither wire service was allowed to have correspondents in Iran, they had to rely on foreign journalists, who themselves were not permitted near the airport to witness the release of the hostages. Perhaps the release time would not have been so critical were it not for the fact that the United States was about to inaugurate a new president, and it was significant if Iran freed the hostages during the outgoing president's term or at the start of the new president's term. Those newspapers that published premature wire service reports on the hostages' release provided inaccurate information.

Spot news no longer sells newspapers the way it once did. Radio long ago replaced newspapers in the spot news category. In fact, radio, because it provides only a headline service, requires newspapers to publish more than bulletins. Modern newspaper editors realize that their job is providing the well-researched, detailed stories that lie behind the hasty headlines of another medium.

Wire service editors do not expect local editors to unquestioningly publish everything. When asked, wire service editors shrink from providing advice they sense would replace local judgment. The wire services expect local editors to make creative use of their reports. In fact, local editors may freely rewrite, without credit, any wire story they want. Some newspapers do that to an unethical fault, going so far as to put a local byline on a minimal rewrite and presenting it as staff work. The remainder of this chapter provides future editors with advice on how to use the wires properly.

What the Symbols Mean

The wire services use many symbols as a shorthand method of telling editors a lot of information about stories. Most of the symbols used by AP, UPI and many of the supplementary wires are the same because of the American Newspaper Publishers Association, which urged standardization for the sake of multiple-wire users and users with automatic story-sorting systems.

Two standardized symbols are the priority code and the category code. On hard copy (paper copy from a Teletype machine), they can be found on the line that follows a story's transmission number. On a VDT, the transmission number and the priority and category codes appear together on a single line. Editors using VDTs must know the codes so that they can spot high-priority or special section stories merely by examining a directory, that is, without having to open every story and read the lead. Of course, systems that sort stories by computer route the story to the correct page editor automatically.

The priority codes are:

f   flash
b   bulletin
u   urgent
r   regular
d   deferred
a   advance for weekday use
s   advance for weekend use

The wires seldom use the flash code, which would interrupt any story as it is running. Flashes have appeared on stories about the safe landing of astronauts, the assassination of a president, the nomination of a candidate, the death of a pope, the release of 52 Americans held hostage in a foreign country. The bulletin code appears on stories of bulletin importance or on advisories that need quick attention. The urgent code appears on prime news and corrections. The regular priority code appears on scheduled stories—most of the stories on the wire. The deferred code, when used, appears on stories of secondary importance. Stories marked with the *a* or *s* code are sent "hold for release (date)."

In addition to the priority code, each type of story has a code by which a computer can sort and route to a particular queue:

a   any domestic news not from Washington
b   special events
c   regular features

e   entertainment or cultural
f   financial
i   international (including the United Nations)
k   commentary
l   lifestyle
n   regional (such as a state wire)
p   national politics
q   result or period score of a single sports event
s   sports
t   travel
v   advisories
w   Washington
y   for internal routing among wire bureaus or
     for reruns

Thus, a copy editor looking at an AP directory of stories on a VDT and seeing this computer-generated transmission number from the A wire— a056-uw—would know it belongs to an urgent Washington story. The story might already be in a Washington file created by the newspaper and fed by an automatic sorter that would direct any *w*-designated story to it. A sports editor seeing a 114-uq would know it is probably a single-line final score (Ithaca 61, Georgetown 60); the computer (if programmed for this) routes all *q*-designated information together to compile a list of scores.

The next line of importance is the keyboard slug line, which starts with one of three cycle designators—AM, PM, or BC—codes that indicate, respectively, stories for morning newspapers, afternoon newspapers or both cycles. Next comes the keyword, the story's slug in 21 or fewer characters. During the Olympic games of 1980, however, the AP inserted between the cycle designator and the keyword a special identifying slug (OLY) to enable automatic sorting systems to route all Olympic stories to one directory. On a daily basis, entertainment features from AP carry an ENT code. The keyword slug is important because it remains the same on all new leads, adds, inserts and substitutes. Following the slug is a word count, no more than 450 a take.

Besides that, the wires tell if the story is budgeted—Bjt (AP) or sked (UPI)—and how many takes the story is, for example, 2 takes. The word count follows in a cumulative setup—450, 675—to tell the editor the total number of words in the first take and the total number of words in the story. A first add to such a story includes Bjt.1stAdd,225. Starting with a number, here is a regular sports story for an afternoon newspaper, from the budget, two takes long:

        a041–rs
        PM.Cowboys,Bjt,450,600

The second take (also called the first add):

        a042–rs
        PM.Cowboys,Bjt.1stAdd,150

During the morning, the wire service sends a new lead. To make the lead easy for identification, the wire editor uses not only the exact slug of the original story but also the number of the story, called now the reference number:

        a102–us
        PM.Cowboys,1stLd,a041,200

Instead of Bjt, that section of a wire story could contain any of these: Advisory, KILL, WITHHOLD, ELIMINATION, Insert, Sub (for substitute), Correction, Writethru (meaning an earlier story has been completely rewritten) and Box (for boxscore).

Stories that are two or more takes long contain special instructions at the end of the first take and the beginning of the second. Here is part of a two-take story:

        CLEARWATER, Fla. (AP) — Bake McBride spent
        the kind of winter during which reading a good book
        was his only peace of mind.
            . . .

"I even played when I messed my knee up, some 40
games. That's just the way it is. There isn't anything I
can do about it."
MORE

1st Add,250
CLEARWATER, Fla.: ABOUT IT."
McBride claims that he has yet to reach his potential
as a . . .

Notice how the second take includes the dateline and repeats the last two
words of the first take. When the words do not match up, it usually means
the first take was not fully transmitted.

Wirephotos typically begin with the initials of the originating station
followed by a figure. Next comes the dateline (which, unlike a story,
contains the date) and then the caption. AP introduces captions with an
all-caps legend it calls an overline. ("Use verbs in overlines, avoid labels
and lifeless phrases," the stylebook correctly advises.) The end of the
caption includes a credit, the initials of the caption writer, and for AP, the
day of the week the caption was written (1 means Sunday, and so on) and
the time the caption was written. Following that is the source of the
photograph (such as stf for staff or mbr for member and the name) and
finally the year of transmission.

Budgets, Directories and Advisories

The wire services announce their wares early in the morning and afternoon cycles by sending a list of top stories and photographs. The AP
updates its story lists three times during each cycle. These lists are commonly referred to as budgets, digests, directories or schedules. They are
broken down by topics, give a story's slug, and tell briefly what the stories
are about and how long each one is. Wirephoto directories are not always
as detailed, although some include information on whether a photograph
will be horizontal or vertical.

Some of the words common to these directories include *developing,
will stand, should stand, with separate. Developing* means a continuing story,
one the wires expect will provide new information and new leads (if not
writethrus) during the cycle. A local editor handling an early version of a
developing story would not bother to edit the story because a new version

might replace it and make the editing unnecessary. Similarly, an editor does not dummy a developing story on an early page (a page that is made up early and cannot be changed later).

Good for early page use, though, are those stories marked *will stand.* That means the wire service editors are not planning to update the story, have not even assigned a reporter to keep up with the story. A *should stand* story means the wires don't expect an updating, but anything can happen. In fact, the people who assign such pieces of advice to directories cannot predict the future, and any story can become the opposite of a wire editor's expectation. For example, a reporter sent to cover a natural disaster (marked *developing*) might not be able to get new information to a bureau because of a lack of communications facilities. The best editors expect the unexpected and do not fret when it happens.

With separate means the story includes a sidebar. A *roundup* usually covers all aspects of a major topic, although most of the aspects get brief coverage, as in a roundup of all professional football games played on a Sunday. One game is highlighted; all others get a subhead and a paragraph. The wires also provide *analysis* and *commentary;* stories so marked should receive the same designation in print so that readers don't think they're getting straight news.

The wires send advisories for various reasons, from alerting editors to additional potential stories to giving directions on how to obtain press passes for special events. Some advisories announce the travel plans of presidents and would-be presidents. Advisories tell editors of news conferences that may produce stories for their editions or of court decisions that may come down in time for today's paper.

Finally, the wire services send corrections, and the alert wire editor checks periodically to make sure nothing is missed.

New Leads

A new lead updates a story already on file and presumably places the most current important information at the beginning, or top, of the story. This is the way the AP moved early information on the launch of the shuttle Challenger on Jan. 28, 1986:

> CAPE CANAVERAL, Fla. (AP) — Shuttle Challenger rocketed away from an icicle-laden launch pad

today, overcoming finicky weather and faulty equip-
ment to carry aloft a New Hampshire schoolteacher as
NASA's first citizen in space.
 MORE =

AP-NY-01-28-86 1138EST

But before the AP could move more, the Challenger exploded. This was the next lead:

CAPE CANAVERAL, Fla. (AP) — Space shuttle
Challenger exploded today as it carried schoolteacher
Christa McAuliffe and six crew members into space
today.
 MORE =

AP-NY-01-28-86 1141EST

PM-Space Shuttle, 1st Add
URGENT
CAPE CANAVERAL
There was no indication of the fate of the crew but it
appeared there was no way they could survive.
 It was the first such failure in 56 such U.S. man-in-
space missions.

AP-NY-01-28-86 1143EST

New leads appear in sequence, beginning with 1stLd and continuing until the end of a cycle, when new stories are written. New leads are necessary for stories written in advance of an event (the announcing of economic statistics, for example) because they provide background or context that fleshes out the newer information. When wire editors antici-pate a new lead, they will say so in their budgets or advise at the top of the stories on which they expect to put new leads. Such stories are marked *may be topped.*

New leads, as noted before, carry the same slug and provide the number of the story they go with. A new lead gives pick-up instructions at the end, telling the local editor where the old and new should be joined. As a double check, the wire story also provides the first two or three words of the pick-up paragraph.

Sometimes the new lead for, say, a Washington dateline story comes from somewhere else. A story about the president embarking on a seven-nation tour would begin with a Washington dateline. When the president reaches the first country (Cuba, perhaps), the wires would send a new lead telling of the president's arrival. The new lead would have a different dateline (Havana, in this case). To avoid confusion, the wires would include the following phrase on the new lead, *precede Washington.* That tells local editors that the original story carried a Washington dateline, not a Havana dateline.

Editors using electronic systems find that processing new leads is simple. Rather than fumbling around with two parts of a story—one of them already in type in the production department—an editor can summon a copy of the original story and affix the new lead, then send the new version to the shop with instructions to kill the original. The speed of electronic printing equipment makes that process simpler and faster than it was when stories were sent on 66-word-per-minute Teletypes and type was set on a Linotype machine.

New leads can create problems for sleepy editors who do not reread stories after a new lead has been affixed. Editors should reread to ensure that in writing a new lead the wire reporter did not repeat information from the earlier story, information that may appear late in the story. Typically, a person's full name and identification are repeated. In such cases, the alert editor deletes the information from the original story because it is needed early in the story.

Developing Stories

Stories in which developments change throughout a news cycle become developing stories, marked by new leads, inserts, subs, writethrus and hold-for-release leads. Inserts are used to add secondary or clarifying information to a story. Substitutes clarify information or update stories, such as the disaster story cited in Chapter 3, in which authorities identified six dead people and speculated on the identity of the seventh body. Once the seventh person's identity was known, the wire service sent a substitute paragraph to replace the one containing the speculation. Inserts and substitutes carry information telling local editors which paragraph precedes and follows and which paragraphs an editor should delete. Corrections carry the same directions.

As more newspapers acquired electronic systems and high-speed wire input, writethrus became more common and new leads appeared less frequently. That happened because wire service reporters and editors could more easily redo a story and send it without delay on a 1,200-word-per-minute circuit than they had been able to do on a 66-word-per-minute circuit. Thus, the wires will eventually remove the inconvenience noted under "New Leads" of dealing with pieces of a story. Instead, a complete story will replace the original.

Hold-for-release leads appear on developing stories when the wire editor is fairly certain of what development will occur next in the ongoing saga. A typical example of the 1960s and 1970s was the U.S. space program, about which the wires would write leads based on what was scheduled to happen. (NASA had every moon trip timed to the second, it seemed.) Such leads would be marked "Hold for release, expected release time 1:30 p.m." For the editor with a 1 p.m. lock-up (meaning all pages are finished and headed for the press; no changes can be made), the temptation to use a 1:30 lead and thus publish as fresh a story as possible was overwhelming. But the editors who, for example, used the hold-for-release lead that said the United States and Russia had linked in space were confounded when the hook-up did not go smoothly—the wires killed the advance leads and substituted different leads. At the Republican National Convention in 1980, UPI sent a lead declaring Reagan had picked Ford but told subscribers not to release it until after midnight. One daily went to press 15 minutes before midnight, with erroneous news. The rule of thumb: Don't use leads designated for release after the newspaper's deadline.

The typical advance story is a column or feature article sent on, say, Tuesday for use on Sunday. The wires send advances so newspapers have stories for earlier pages, including those pages made up a day in advance. More important, sending stories in advance helps the wires cut down on jams on slower circuits. Another type of advance story comes on a special Sunday feature filing, and its day and cycle of release are marked. A story for use in a Wednesday afternoon newspaper would say "For release PMs Wed., March 10." A newspaper publishing the next morning (March 11) could also use the story, but the PM paper gets first crack. Wirephotos accompanying advances are clearly marked, giving not only the date of release but the byline and the slug on the story.

Another type of advance is a story sent early in a cycle for release later in the same cycle. The story gets advance status because some or all of the story is based on something that is scheduled to occur later in the cycle. For example, someone who will appear before a congressional hearing might provide reporters with an advance copy of a statement prepared for the hearing. The wire service reporters write a story based on the statement and then, once the statement is given, a wire editor will send a bulletin clearing the story for use.

A related type of advance includes the caution "For release at 1:30 p.m. EST—time set by source." The source could be investigators for the Nuclear Regulatory Commission who have not yet reported to their superiors. Because early promulgation of the information might result in a more accurate and understandable story, the source provides copies, but on the condition that the public not get the news until a certain time. When the information seems absolutely newsworthy, some newspapers might violate the advance status by rewriting the story in the conditional mood.

> Investigators hired by the Nuclear Regulatory Commission were prepared today to warn that nuclear accidents like the one at Three Mile Island "could have happened in a lot of places."

That approach is fraught with ethical and practical problems, especially if the scheduled story doesn't come off. Same-day advances, like hold-for-release leads, deserve cautious treatment, and smart editors use no advance whose release time has not yet come.

Combining Stories

Equipped with a VDT that can display separate stories simultaneously in their own windows on the screen, an editor has the opportunity to compare competitive wire service stories and combine their best aspects into one story. In some cases, combining stories leads to a complete rewriting, a job handled by a copy editor, not a reporter. In other cases, combining stories means inserting paragraphs of one wire service into the other wire service's story. The copy editor must create transition so that the story does not come off as a collection of unrelated paragraphs.

Another form of combining is really the insertion of a parenthetical paragraph that might point out a discrepancy between two stories. For example, UPI says 15 people were injured in an airplane crash, and the editor has decided to use UPI's story. But if AP's account says 13 people were injured, the editor might insert in the appropriate place in the UPI story, "(The Associated Press reported 13 people injured.)" If the two stories contain many discrepancies, it is best to query both services for an explanation.

When an editor combines two stories, he or she must decide how to handle the byline and dateline. Combined stories should no longer carry the names of the individual wire service reporters because they did not produce the final story. Usually, a newspaper will change the byline to "From our wire services" or "By the Associated Press and United Press International" or "Combined from wire reports." The parenthetical credit in the dateline is removed.

Combined stories require extra checking for repeated facts and names, names without identification, and inconsistent spelling and style. Neither wire service presents style-perfect copy, and the copy editor must watch for inconsistencies between the two. Caution is also necessary with copyrighted stories from supplementary wires. The copyright covers the form the news takes, not the news itself, so a copy editor combining such stories may freely rewrite but may not reproduce verbatim without credit.

Creating Summaries

Although newspapers are usually thought of as publishing long stories about the news, many newspapers distill less important news into summaries. Readers don't need all the news in great detail every day, and not every newspaper always has enough space to print the news in detail.

Creating summaries may mean rewriting two wire stories into one or condensing just one wire service's account. A summary is not created merely by using the first two paragraphs of a collection of stories and throwing the rest away. A good summary captures the essence of the story, giving the reader 10 inches of information in two inches of type.

A model of good summary writing is contained in the *Wall Street Journal,* whose inside-page editors daily write a Page One column called

"What's News——." Half of the column is an index to stories inside, and the rest is a summary of important news that gets no further detail inside.

Here is the beginning of an inside-page story from the *Wall Street Journal:*

> CHICAGO — International Harvester Co. is approaching a critical point this week as it seeks to pull off one of the biggest financial juggling acts in corporate history.
>
> The maker of trucks, farm machinery and construction equipment is scheduled to meet here Thursday with more than 200 bankers, and many people think the company's survival is at stake. The bankers, all of whom have lent the company money, will hear details of Harvester's recently announced plan of debt restructuring and will have their first chance to haggle about the proposal.
>
> The restructuring promises to be arduous and explosive. Harvester wants a $4.7 billion financing package in place by May 15, replacing hundreds of short-term bank credit arrangements with three "umbrella" agreements—one for Harvester, one for its credit corporation and a pact to sell $1.5 billion in receivables to some of the larger banks.

This is how an editor condensed that for Page One:

> International Harvester will present a $4.7 billion debt restructuring plan to its lenders Thursday. Harvester wants to replace myriad short-term agreements with three major ones for the parent, its credit unit and the sale of $1.5 billion in receivables.
> (Story on Page 2)

Note how tightly written and to the point the summary is. The editor who wrote it did not zip through the chore. According to the authors of *What's News—Dow, Jones Story of the Wall Street Journal,* the *Journal*'s front-page column takes six or seven minutes to read but is written over a

16-hour period each day. "It's written to be easy to read, not a word wasted," the book's authors say.

No beginning editor should assume writing such a summary is easy. The beginner should expect to spend a lot of time learning the art of summary writing.

Localizing Stories

If the federal government announces a series of grants for 15 states, the wire services are not going to put the state of local interest in the lead. That's up to local editors. The process is known as localizing, that is, giving the national story a local angle. A local angle could also be something more specific, such as a grant for a local organization or person.

Disaster stories provide opportunities for localizing. Suppose a plane crashes and 200 people die, including five from, say, Nebraska. Nebraska newspapers using the story would rewrite the lead to emphasize the local angle:

> Five Nebraskans were among 200 persons killed when the first Chinese excursion plane to fly the route of the Long March crashed today, Hsinhua, the New China News Agency, reported.

In addition to changing the lead, the local editor would also ensure that the names of the five Nebraskans appeared early in the story, probably in the second paragraph.

Localizing state stories might mean rewriting to get the name of a local person or organization on top. It would also mean calling that person or organization for more details, an assignment that could go to a reporter or to a copy editor. For example, a lobbying group has just released a rating of your state's representatives in Congress. How did your local representative rank? Rewrite the story to get that either in the lead or near the top.

Any story can be overlocalized, such as reporting the injury of a local person in an accident in which 50 people died and not mentioning the deaths until the third or fourth paragraph. One newspaper supposedly localized a story about President Kennedy flying from Washington to the

U.S. Air Force Academy in Colorado with a headline that ran like this: "Kennedy to speak at Academy; will fly over Iowa en route." When a Russian space station was falling to earth, one newspaper headlined the story, "Space station won't fall on valley."

Another type of localizing occurs when newspapers use wire service stories as pegs for local stories, sometimes generating a complete local story and at other times just rewriting the top. Alert copy editors watch for wire stories with potential local angles. For example, a story that says people who paid in advance to go to the Olympic games in Moscow might not get their money back raises the question: Any from my town? Call local travel agencies and then follow up with calls to the affected people. What does an increase in the prime lending rate mean to local banks? How are local farmers affected by changes in grain futures? Will a cut in the defense budget affect the nearby Army base?

Every good editor should remember that the wires provide not only state, national and international news but also an opportunity for local journalists to show their reportorial skills. Good editors know that the wires are their servants, not their masters, and they use the wire reports accordingly.

Chapter 13

Newspapers under Fire

The Decline in Readership

Those who thought television had devastated magazines and had taken large bites out of newspapers in the 1960s learned in the 1970s that newspapers were in worse condition than first believed. Reborn as specialty publications, magazines made a comeback, but daily newspapers, as reflected by their circulation figures, stood pat. The population of the country grew, but daily newspaper circulation failed to keep pace, a shortfall with roots in the late 1950s. It was not until 1980 that circulation reached the level of the 1960s, approximately 62 million a day. A decade later, circulation was at 63 million, up 1 percent at a time when the number of adults had increased by 34 percent.

For some newspapers, especially those in metropolitan areas, the decline was cataclysmic. Some went out of business, especially in two- and three-newspaper markets, and sister publications were consolidated while others suffered from a weakened financial base infected by 10 to 25 percent circulation declines. Advertisers, among others, were not happy. But advertisers were not the only ones who complained; editors began to realize that the slipping base of readership detracted as much from the editorial product as it did from the advertising product and that the two had to survive together. Publishers initiated countless studies to find out what had happened to the readers. Editors soon found they had to stop blaming television for the decline in readership.

Various researchers learned that young people saw newspaper editors as cigar-smoking, middle-aged, isolated people who were more interested in protecting the status quo than in challenging their readers. This image flourished at the end of the Vietnam War and the Watergate scandal, both of which triggered distrust of public institutions. Television, of course, deserved some of the blame for the readership decline, but not as much as editors attributed to it. Some studies suggested that people who rely on television for news rely as much on newspapers. If anything, television should have helped readership. Of course, television implanted in society a visual awareness that was not satisfied by dull-looking newspapers of gray columns of type and small photographs. In that regard, television affected readership.

Editors soon realized that many things competed with newspaper reading for people's free time. Yes, television competes, and so does radio, and so do the many specialty magazines. But so do gardening or working at a hobby. Who wants to read a newspaper delivered in the late afternoon as the last few rays of sun remain for weeding or raking or just relaxing? The product no longer seemed relevant.

Readers also sensed alienation; they felt the newspaper was not a member of the same community. Words like *uncaring, unresponsive, inhuman, out of touch* appeared regularly when researchers asked people why they didn't like their daily newspaper. The readers sensed that newspaper editors didn't care much for the reader beyond making the reader a statistic in the circulation manager's book. Such a feeling came naturally as the consumer movement grew and editors ignored or played down the issues the movement raised. "Why shouldn't they?" a cynic asked; "they want to protect their advertisers." Editors were seen as taking care of their advertisers at the expense of the consumer, the person who bought the newspaper. The same feeling prevailed among readers whose newspapers faintly covered local government by relying on handouts from politicians or by failing to examine deeply the empty words of some leaders. Also working against newspaper credibility was chain ownership. As chains bought more and more newspapers, readers began to feel that all decisions, even the editorial stands, were made at corporate headquarters and with only the balance sheet in mind. Against this groundswell of alienation and declining circulation, newspaper editors acquired a new attitude and a new desire to create something that readers would buy and read.

The Medium Reacts

One startling thing editors learned from reader attitude studies was that the reader spent a certain amount of time each day with the news media, and that was it. The image of someone reading a newspaper for an hour or so no longer held up. Twenty minutes became the accepted maximum time, and some researchers suggested half that time. Thus, if the newspaper did not arrive at the time the reader usually set aside to read it, the newspaper might go unread while a television or radio station or magazine might get more attention. What editors had to do was design a product that would make the readers want to read. One successful method of getting back readers has been the mini-newspaper, which takes the concept of a zoned newspaper one step further by creating within the main newspaper a second newspaper designed only for a segment of the readership. Metropolitan newspapers especially, faced with competition from suburban dailies, have used this approach. Suburban dailies, meanwhile, have made sure they are filled with local stories that the metros do not cover. Every newspaper is aiming, to quote Phil Currie of Gannett, to create "a sense of place."

Other responses have included new feature items or a greater emphasis on good writing. Stories about the self sprang up during the so-called Me Generation of the 1970s, not only because readers were self-centered but also because they wanted information to help them cope with life. Newspaper attempts to become a bigger part of readers' lives included expanded letter-to-the-editor columns and other forums that invited reader comment. Taking a hint from the specialty magazines, some newspapers enlarged their coverage of leisure activities so that readers would need the newspaper to learn where they could spend leisure time. More consumer-oriented stories filled newspapers, and suddenly readers found they needed their local daily. Many newspapers started business sections, doing more than just running business stories from the wires but also focusing on local business matters. Some newspapers started science/ environment and entertainment sections. Some geared up to do more specialty reporting, to go beyond city hall coverage. Many also started Sunday papers, even in markets once thought too small to support such a venture. And, believe it or not, many newspapers started to admit mistakes and regularly publish corrections, something not as common before the 1980s.

Other changes came about. Newspapers started looking better as graphic artists became as important as editors. Some newspapers added special sections and others redesigned their packages. Color became more prominent. Newspapers started thinking about the untapped younger market. They learned, for example, that only about one-third of people between 18 and 29 read newspapers and that teenagers in general were not inclined to become newspaper readers. More newspapers became involved in the NIE program. Newspapers In Education, which promotes newspaper use in schools. Other newspapers became sponsors of high school newspapers, even providing newsroom space and computers for high school journalists.

None of these changes came without their critics, who saw the newspaper turning away from its First Amendment obligation to inform the public and toward a soft-news approach of pabulum, an orientation of personalities, personalities, personalities, and no news. Some critics called the new content "mush" and said it was edited for people whose brains were equally soft. Mediocrity, not excellence, became the byword of journalism, the critics charged, and some complained that newspapers, attuned through market research to what their audiences wanted, had softened their editorial bites so as not to offend anyone. Whatever happened, a new approach to newspaper publishing had occurred. Little was left to chance.

Readership Surveys

Not so very long ago, editors prided themselves on the fact that they had their fingers on the pulse of the community. "I know what my readers want," they would say, backing up their claims with nothing but hot air. The decline in readership proved that many editors had no idea what their readers wanted.

Interestingly, the readership surveys that evolved out of the readership decline showed that the results of the intuitive approach to editing newspapers was often far from what readers wanted. The only thing on which editors and readers agreed was the need for local news, although no researcher to date has determined just what local news is. (Is it a report on local government or a blurb on some 6-year-old's birthday party?) Depending on which survey you read, one area that does not interest a lot of readers but does interest a lot of editors is sports. The surveys that learned such information did not take into account that many editors once worked the sports beat, which was the route to the top in the newspaper for some years. The editor had covered sports; therefore, sports were important. Those sports pages that took a turn for the better also covered participatory sports, the kind readers could appreciate because they could be part of it.

Newspapers were latecomers in making use of scientific surveys and other kinds of research. Magazines, for example, not only rely on surveys but some have their own research departments, which work with all other departments in the magazine, not just editorial. Magazine surveys take various forms, including the insertion of questionnaires that ask readers if certain articles were helpful. Some magazines send issues to selected readers for evaluation, and others rely on personal interviews. Television and radio have long relied on surveys to determine content. Market-savvy radio station owners learned in the 1960s that intuition was a poor way to sell a product and turned to surveys to see what kind of format (i.e., rock, country and western, all news) appealed.

Now newspapers have joined the list of media relying on surveys, although newspapers often use what they learn not so much to change the product but to retune or fine-tune it or perhaps even to justify what is already being done. Readership surveys pinpoint problems; they do not provide answers. When a particular type of coverage receives much criticism, an editor evaluates it not with an eye to getting rid of it but with an eye to improving it. Research tells editors not where to go but how to get where they want to go. City council meetings will always be part of a newspaper's local fare, but how the newspaper reports the meetings (more graphs and sidebars, perhaps) may change because of reader unhappiness revealed in a survey.

Readership surveys have already uncovered some interesting problems. Readers believe that local news leans too much on governmental and political events, which are easy to cover but which can lack the importance that more grass roots or in-depth coverage might turn up. Readers believe that newspapers lack positive news about the community, and others say newspapers are written for journalists and government officials, not for readers.

Depending on the market and the newspaper, a readership survey reveals different things. One local newspaper conducted a survey and learned that its readers had a high interest in world affairs, national news, local/community news, state news, opinions and editorials, home and cooking, death notices, crime and police reports, notes about local people and local government. The same audience had a low interest in religion and church, business and economy, weddings, high school sports and coverage of organized recreation sports.

Emphasizing the high-interest areas, the newspaper improved its editorial page, added a weekly food section and now does a more thorough job of covering local government. In the low-interest areas, the newspaper has retained its religion page, added a business page and included a business section in its Sunday paper, cut down on the length of wedding coverage and maintained coverage of high school sports.

Non-readers of the newspaper had a healthy interest in sports, including the local university's sports teams; in television and entertainment news, and in personal health, medicine and weather. Non-readers were not that interested in arts and culture, farm and agriculture, local university news, outdoor and recreation news, science, real estate, professional sports, other colleges' sports and women's sports.

Among the high-interest areas, the newspaper beefed up its sports section, added a weekly television guide and published a daily listing, created a weekly entertainment section, and followed every other newspaper with a better daily weather package. In the low-interest areas, it added a monthly real estate guide, made its arts and culture coverage part of its entertainment coverage, modified its coverage of local university news unless it had an impact on the area, and stayed the same in covering women's sports.

The newspaper did not blindly follow the results of its readership survey but instead worked with the information in the survey to fine-tune the newspaper seven days a week. Thus, just because an area had low interest did not mean it got dropped. Its status depended on how it played against everything else in the paper.

Good editors no longer rely on intuition. Today they routinely seek reader response. Some sent questionnaires to people named in news stories as a way of checking the accuracy of stories. Some solicit reader opinion on a broader scale, and others have hired in-house critics (called ombudsmen) to evaluate the newspaper's work and, in some cases, report to the readers in columns published in the newspaper. Some editors have kept their fingers on the pulse of the community by regularly walking the streets of their town and soliciting face-to-face reader opinion. Other editors have formed readership and focus groups to regularly critique the newspaper's work.

Marketing

Readership surveys have shown editors they don't know that much about their readers. The readers, the surveys show, come from all walks of life and often change during the day. The businessperson going to work in the morning wants stock tables but going home that night might want information on gardening or lawn care. Making the news product appeal to such a person requires marketing a product whose content has first been shaped by editors who know what their readers want.

Marketing takes several forms, including the weekly meeting of editors and circulation department personnel to delve into reasons readers give for discontinuing the papers. Another approach personalizes reporters and photographers, but that runs the risk of creating a "star" system in which the reporter or photographer rather than the news is important. Such hype smacks of an image orientation rather than an information orientation.

Some newspapers promote heavily, touting in Monday's paper what special features will appear the next day and throughout the week. Some newspapers use radio and television to promote themselves, something they would have never done when those two media were in their infancy and considered beneath newspapers.

The good marketing newspaper keeps readers attuned to what changes the newspaper might be making. When a newspaper builds a new plant, installs a new press or switches from afternoon to morning publication, the newspaper heavily promotes the changes so the reader knows what is going on and feels a part of it.

That type of promotion aside, editors have segmented their markets in various ways to find new readers and regain lost ones. The segmentation breaks the market along geographic, demographic and psychographic lines.

GEOGRAPHICS. Dividing the audience according to where its members live is nothing new. Magazines have been delivering audiences to advertisers like this for years, and newspapers have taken up the form through zoned editions, that is, editions in which part of the product is devoted only to one zone among many. Newspapers in cities with large Hispanic populations publish editions in Spanish. Newspapers that circulate in more than one county produce special news tabloids for each county.

The aforementioned mini-newspapers represent another geographic approach, and the future holds promise for more such newspapers because electronic equipment makes storing and reusing stories so easy. Editors can easily package and repackage great quantities of news merely by pushing buttons on VDTs.

DEMOGRAPHICS. The magazine industry, with its many specialty publications, has shown newspapers that there's more than one way to sell a product. Newspapers, especially in competitive markets, no longer think of themselves as aimed for a mass audience but instead tailor themselves to a coalition of certain groups within the mass. Special editions appear only when those groups are active: The newspaper carrying stock tables in the morning for business people may market itself for leisure time activity to those same people as they're homeward bound at night. The working woman wants a much different newspaper than her housewife predecessor did. Senior citizens represent still another possible news market segment.

PSYCHOGRAPHICS. Still another marketing technique is to peg a newspaper's appeal to distinctions in lifestyles and personalities. Such an approach accounts for the success of specialty magazines and points the way some newspapers might go. One experiment in this area was Consumer Extra, an adless, separately sold tabloid published by the Louisville *Courier-Journal and Times* in 1979. The consumer-oriented newspaper fell short of its 15,000 break-even circulation goal, so its creators folded it. But the possibility of creating similar magazines and selling the main newspaper to those individuals who would also subscribe to preferred special supplements for an additional fee is not that far off.

Format Changes

The newspaper industry, generally conservative, responded to the decline in readership in several ways once considered radical. Format changes spelled the difference for some.

In one-owner, two-newspaper towns, the morning and afternoon editions were consolidated into a morning paper. In many instances, this meant a larger news hole for other papers to fill. Thriving suburban dailies started Sunday editions to keep out city newspapers, and some papers switched from afternoon to morning publication.

Other format changes include special sections or columns on recreational sports, celebrities, medicine, food and fashion, consumerism, teenagers, leisure and love, gardening and grooming, television and travel, pet care and home repair, investments and hobbies, and the inclusion of comprehensive calendars of cultural and leisure activities. News about religion has been increased; reviews of books have (unfortunately) been cut back. Additional sports columns and news features have found their way into print, and most newspapers that weren't six columns took on the eye-appealing format. Section logos were created to help the reader find the news faster, and photographs and graphics received better display, sometimes through the use of color.

From Afternoon to Morning

A wire service story written at 8 a.m. for use in a newspaper that would publish at 2 p.m. and be read at 6 p.m. might begin this way: "Theodore Rand's second murder trial today was in the hands of the jury." Unsure what would develop between 8 a.m. and 6 p.m., the writer had to use past tense to describe an event that was continuing all day. The same writer writing for a morning newspaper would be writing the story at the end of the day, when the news cycle is usually spent, and would not have faced the problem of how to cover an event that could be superseded.

The one major problem afternoon newspapers face is timeliness. News often breaks in the afternoon, in time for the 6 o'clock news on television but not in time for the 2 p.m. press run, which has been preceded by an even earlier copy deadline. Thus, many afternoon newspapers, no matter how well put together, read like rewritten morning newspapers and taste like day-old bread. The readers learn from their afternoon newspapers what they could have read in the morning or seen on television the night before. Why buy a rehash?

Many reasons for converting from an afternoon to a morning publication exists. Those who have studied morning and afternoon markets say that morning papers have been more successful. Traffic jams that delay the delivery of evening newspapers don't occur in the middle of the night, when morning papers are delivered. Energy is saved when presses are run at other than peak hours (such as 2 a.m.). Most people are sleeping while a morning newspaper is being produced, making its content fresh to them when they awaken. Morning readership doesn't face the competition for time that evening readership does. Advertisers in a morning paper can anticipate same-day response because readers can see an advertisement in the morning and buy that day rather than waiting, and maybe forgetting, overnight. An advertisement published in the morning is assured a longer shelf life, which enhances its sales ability. The freshness of news in a morning paper makes it more attractive to readers.

Papers that have switched to morning publication find they can package better and that the quality of writing must be better. The reader has no time for long stories, which means reporters must break their once long reports into brightly written sidebars to allow the morning reader to pick and choose among the issues.

What Lies Ahead

Trying to predict the future provides more than its share of work for some people, including those in marketing, especially any form of marketing that relates to newspapers. Some of what they foresee is obvious—more working women and more senior citizens were evident in the 1970s. More working women means, among other things, a rising interest in business news, because working women will probably also invest in the marketplace. Working women, too, are expected to read more newspapers, to watch less television and to be more interested in a variety of topics, from consumer safety to the environment. Newspaper advertising that does not stereotype women as housewives will appeal to working women.

With the teenage population declining relatively in the United States, all news media will have to serve a more mature audience. But newspapers first will have to find a way to get adults to read the newspaper. Service industries will have to expand to care for an older population, and the increase in the work force suggests more leisure time—trends that newspapers must keep abreast of if they intend to improve circulation. Minorities will not only increase but will fill long-overdue jobs of importance. As an economic force, they will have to be catered to.

The technological advances reflected in the general interest in computers will mean a more educated audience. Newspaper readers will want education and newspapers can help provide it. In fact, those same technological advances can mean a tailormade newspaper. Any reader can buy a main section with an index, select from the index additional sections or more details on an event and purchase those, from the livingroom computer. Newspapers may be thinner and more compact, but the many tabloid (or whatever the size) inserts available on a cafeteria-style basis will ensure a newspaper that lives longer because its usefulness will extend beyond hard news. The newspaper will have a longer shelf life.

One of the major competitors facing newspapers is not television or radio but the changing technology that can put a low-cost two-way computer terminal in every home, allowing a person to summon forth news, advertisements and any other information at the touch of a couple of buttons on a keyboard. Who would need a newspaper?

Aware of the competition, news organizations have moved into the field of electronic home delivery. As noted, people with terminals at home can obtain all types of information, including news. Newspapers have joined databases and routinely make their files available to a central computer, allowing anyone with a computer and a telephone to receive information about any community whose newspaper provides information for accessing. The newspaper receives a royalty every time someone uses its information. Such a program, because it extends the shelf life and value of news, has attracted the interest of publishers, who are creating their own systems.

The next century looks interesting for newspapers. A person wanting to know where newspapers are headed would be advised to look to the skies. Up there satellites are taking over the distribution of news (and entertainment) as they beam information from one land base to another. The wire services already send their news reports to many subscribers equipped with a dish antenna that focuses on satellites parked more than 22,300 miles above the Equator. Back on Earth, any wire service subscriber can receive a wire report from a neighboring antenna via telephone lines. Thus, the news media of one city need only one dish antenna.

The major wire services, meanwhile, had to go into space to deliver their reports because of the increasing high costs and unreliability of earth-bound telephone lines. One satellite cannot monopolize the skies the way one company had monopolized telephone service; satellites don't require rate hearings. Besides, landlines are about 10 times as expensive as satellite transmission. Similarly, snowstorms and rainstorms don't wipe out satellite transmissions the way they knock down telephone lines. A satellite in space is easier to maintain than a telephone line on Earth. The wire services had no choice. Satellites offer stability.

Back on Earth, newspapers went to the air to beat traffic jams and to speed production. Metropolitan newspapers built printing plants some distance from their downtown offices. To get finished pages to those printing plants the newspapers send their pages via laser beams over microwave systems, above the traffic. The *Detroit News* beams to a satellite plant outside the city. The *News* built the plant to improve its distribution throughout Michigan.

The newspaper known for pioneering that technology is the *Wall Street Journal,* which transmits its pages via satellite to 18 printing plants around the United States. In effect, the *Journal* became a national paper, for it can be written, edited and printed on the same day everywhere in the United States. *The New York Times,* which once abandoned a functioning West Coast edition as too costly, returned to the marketplace about two decades later because it could beam its pages via satellite to eight printing plants around the United States, thus becoming a national newspaper. Before, the *Journal* and the *Times* relied heavily on slow-moving trucks and expensive airplanes. Satellite delivery enabled *USA Today* to establish itself not only in the United States but in Europe, the Middle East, North Africa and the Far East.

The ultimate use of satellite delivery depends on how easy it will be to persuade individuals to buy their own antennae to receive television programs, Hollywood movies, stock market reports, advertising, and their local newspaper in addition to one metropolitan newspaper.

Editors will have to package better, creating a more usable, functional product. A newspaper published in the morning might contain four sections, two of them filled with hard news (including sports) that the reader will absorb at the breakfast table. The other two sections will contain soft news—features, advice columns, opinion—which the reader can put off reading until later in the day. Thus, the newspaper will be useful to the reader at more than one time and for different reasons. The concept is not new: It exists already in the typical Sunday newspaper, which packages not only for reading that day but for days later. The magazine supplement of any Sunday newspaper can be put aside for reading later in the week, and the reader gets the bonus of midweek reading. That's extending the life of the Sunday paper, and it will happen to dailies too.

Naturally, newspapers will face competition, both from the usual and unusual sources. Newspapers will change to meet changing reader needs and new societal concerns. Radio adapted to television, and newspapers and television must adapt to a technology that challenges both. Look for more local news, especially in the form of narrowcasting on television and more analytical and specialized news in newspapers. The exciting thing is that editors burned by the declining readership of the 1970s are now more alert, more able to spot the trends and less likely to scoff when reader attitudes change. Intuitive editing should disappear. Newspapers of the future will adapt.

Sources and Resources

Anderson, Mary A. "The Health and Wealth of Sunday Newspapers." *Presstime* (November 1988): 28–34.

Bacon, Donald C. "Satellites Make Big Impact at Newspapers." *Presstime* (August 1988): 6–11.

Bogart, Leo. *Press and Public: Who Reads What, Where, When and Why in American Newspapers.* Hillsdale, N.J.: Lawrence Erlbaum Associates, 1981.

Constructing the Future. Reston, Va.: American Society of Newspaper Editors, 1989.

Fielder, Virginia Dodge, and Beverly A. Barnum. *Love Us and Leave Us: New Subscribers One Year Later.* Reston, Va.: American Society of Newspaper Editors, 1987. (This was followed by *Love 'Em and Keep 'Em,* 1988.)

Friedman, Barbara J. "P.M. Publishers Who Went A.M. Laud the Move." *Presstime* (February 1985): 16–17.

Meyer, Philip. *Precision Journalism*. Bloomington: Indiana University Press, 1973.

————. *The Newspaper Survival Book*. Bloomington: Indiana University Press, 1985.

Morton, John. "Newspaper Showdown: Metros vs. Locals." *Washington Journalism Review* (May 1989): 52.

The Next Newspapers. Reston, Va.: American Society of Newspaper Editors, 1988.

Rarick, Galen R., and James B. Lemert. "Subscriber Behavior and Attitudes in Response to PM–AM Conversion." *Newspaper Research Journal* 7, no. 2 (Winter 1986): 11–18.

Rykken, Rolf. "Readership Decline Brings Newspapers to Crossroads." *Presstime* (March 1989): 22–31. (This is a special report, which includes articles by *Presstime* staff members, academic researchers and publishers.)

Stamm, Keith R., and Lisa Fortini-Campbell. *The Relationship of Community Ties to Newspaper Use*. Journalism Monograph no. 84. Columbia, S.C.: Association for Education in Journalism and Mass Communications, 1983.

Appendix A

Editing Symbols

When relying on paper and pencil instead of a VDT, journalists use various editing symbols to tell printers what to do. The symbols shown and their functions are fairly standard in U.S. newspapers.

The circle indicates several things:

A word should be abbreviated: The (October) 12, 1944, meeting.

An abbreviation should be spelled out: the (Oct.) 1984 meeting.

A number should be a figure: (two hundred thirty.)

A figure should be spelled out: (2.)

The caret shows insertion:

A word: a day in May.

A hyphen: loose fitting clothes.

A dash: The meeting predicted to be volatile turned out to be short and quiet.

Commas, quotation marks, and apostrophes are marked as follows:

Comma: The meeting scheduled for later this month will be good.

Quotation marks: "I blame you," the speaker said.

Apostrophe: Those were the speaker's word.

Single and double lines function this way:

When a word is ~~cut out~~ deleted and you want the line closed up but with
one space between words, use a single line.
When letters are deleted within a word and you want the word closed up
with no space between letters, use a double bridge.
A double bridge is also used to close up two words, as in week end.

The transposition marker switches letters and words:

Sometimes letters within a word, or words within a sentence, are trans-
posed and the editor copy has to show the correct order.

Letters to be capitalized are marked with triple underlines:

tillie may williams

Letters to be lowercased are marked with slants:

The Wind ruffled the Trees.

A period is indicated this way:

P.T. Barnum

A separation is indicated with a vertical line:

When two words in copy are run together but you want to make them two
words, use a separation mark.

A new paragraph indent is marked as follows:

If you decide that a two-sentence paragraph should be two paragraphs, use
the paragraph indicator. Such a mark is not necessary, however, when
the writer has correctly indented.

If a paragraph is not wanted, connect the indented sentence to the preceding sentence:

Thus, you have the end of a paragraph and the start of a new one.⌐
⌐But later you change your mind and want the new paragraph to be part of the old. Connect the paragraphs with the line hook.

Other symbols:

Roman type: R or Rom

Italic type: I or Ital

Boldface type: b or bf

Boldface caps (all letters capitalized): bfc

Center, as in a byline:

⌐ By T.F. Williams ⌐
⌐ Journal Writer ⌐

Flush Left:

⌐ By T.F. Williams

Flush right:

Journal Writer ⌐

One other editing symbol is *stet,* a printer's term (derived from the Latin *stare*) to advise the person setting type to disregard a correction or to let a word stand as is even if it appears incorrect. The word has no use in a computer system, but every generation of copy editors should know what it means.

Appendix B

A Condensed Stylebook

This newspaper style book is based on the stylebook developed jointly by the Associated Press and United Press International, which you are encouraged to consult. The author's own style preferences are so identified.

abbreviations Some titles before names are abbreviated unless they appear in direct quotations. Abbreviate *Dr., Gov., Lt. Gov., Rep., the Rev., Sen.* and most military titles such as *Gen., Col., Capt., Lt., Adm., Cmdr.* When courtesy titles are necessary, use *Mr., Mrs., Ms.* See *courtesy titles.*

Using the first three letters, abbreviate the months of the year (except May, June, Sept.) only when used in dates: *Oct. 12* or *Oct. 12, 1984,* but *October 1984.*

Abbreviate the names of states in city-state combinations (*Joplin, Mo.*) with the exception of Alaska, Hawaii, Idaho, Iowa, Maine, Ohio, Texas and Utah. See *state names.*

addresses Abbreviate in numbered addresses (*326 W. Broad St.*) *avenue, boulevard* and *street* but not *alley, drive, road, terrace* and others. Spell out when no number is given: *West Broad Street.*

Always use figures: *8 Pilsdon Lane* rather than *Eight Pilsdon Lane.*

Numbers used as street names are spelled out: *First Street, Ninth Street;* above *ninth,* use figures: *10th Street.*

Directions that are part of an address are abbreviated (*1015 S. Terrace Ave.*) but are spelled out if no number is given: *South Terrace Avenue.*

ages Use figures at all times, even if the age is a single digit: *Tommy Thompson, 5, eats an ice cream cone for photographers.*

a.m., p.m. Always use lowercase letters and periods. Since *a.m.* means morning and *p.m.* means afternoon or night, avoid redundancies such as *9 a.m. this morning, 2 p.m. Wednesday afternoon, 10 p.m. tomorrow night.*

Bible   When referring to the Christian Bible, always capitalize. In other references, lowercase: *The wire services' stylebook is the bible at this newspaper.* Never capitalize *biblical.*

capitalization   In general, follow a down style, in which only proper nouns, names and formal titles before names are capitalized. Titles after names or standing alone without a name are never capitalized.

Work titles or job descriptions are not capitalized: *At the game's end, quarterback Fran Tarkenton threw a touchdown pass to wide receiver Ahmad Rashad.*

Lowercase common nouns that are part of proper nouns when used in subsequent references: *the Republican Party, the party.*

century   Always lowercase: *21st century.* Spell out *first* through *ninth* and use figures thereafter.

The 21st century, by the way, begins on Jan. 1, 2001, not Jan. 1, 2000, which begins the final year of the 20th century.

city council/governmental bodies/legislature   Capitalize full names such as *Houston City Council, the Tucson Fire Department* and *the Iowa Legislature,* and capitalize second references to them when it is clear what is being referred to. *Houston City Council* becomes *the City Council, the Tucson Fire Department* becomes *the Fire Department* and *the Iowa Legislature* becomes *the Legislature.*

Condensed further, though, it is *the council, the department.*

congress   When referring to the *U.S. Senate* and the *U.S. House of Representatives* or to a foreign body that includes *congress* in its name, capitalize. Lowercase *congress* when it is not part of an organization's name or when used as a second reference to a group or as a substitute for *convention.*

congressional districts   Always use figures and capitalize: *the 3rd Congressional District, the 23rd Congressional District.* But use lowercase in subsequent references: *the district.*

congressman, congresswoman   Acceptable gender-neutral references include *House member* and *senator* but not *congressperson.* (Author's preference)

constitution   Capitalize when referring to *the U.S. Constitution, the Constitution.* When referring to other states' or nations' constitutions, capitalize only with the state or nation name: *the Oregon Constitution, the French Constitution, the state constitution.*

An organization's constitution is always lowercase.

constitutional   Always lowercase.

county   Capitalize the names of counties and county governmental units: *Schuylkill County, the Clive County Sheriff's Department.* Subsequent references in a clear context always take capital letters: *the County Sheriff's Department.*

Lowercase *county* when it stands alone or as a subsequent reference to a proper name.

courtesy titles   Avoid courtesy titles. A person's gender or marital status has nothing to do with that person's newsworthiness. However, apply courtesy titles to situations where confusion might result, as when writing about a married couple and referring to one of them. Does the reference to *Jones* mean Mr. Jones or Mrs. Jones (or, if preferred, Ms. Jones)? Then a courtesy title is needed. (Author's preference)

datelines   Newspapers use datelines only on stories from outside the newspaper's immediate circulation area.

Generally datelines consist of a city name followed by the state name (abbreviated per style): *Laramie, Wyo.* Well-known cities do not need to be followed by a state name.

State names are not used in newspapers published in that state unless the city name by itself might cause confusion: *Washington, Pa., Cairo, Ill.*

In roundup stories, state names might be necessary within the story proper to make references clear: *Altoona, Iowa,* and *Altoona, Pa.*

(Datelines are so called because at one time they included the date the action in the story took place. The two major wire services now put the time element in the lead, but some newspapers still use datelines.)

dimensions/weights   Always use figures, but spell out *feet, inches, yards, meters, pounds, grams, ounces: The newborn baby weighs 8 pounds, 7 ounces, and was 21 inches long.*

The only exception to this rule is *millimeter* (use *mm*) when used in reference to film widths (*35 mm*) or weapons (*50 mm*).

directions/regions   Lowercase compass points when standing alone. Capitalize regions known specifically by direction: *the West, the South, the Middle West, the East, the Northeast, the Southwest.*

Lowercase general directions when part of a proper name, such as *southern Texas,* unless the section is well known, such as *South Philadelphia* and *Southern California.*

distances   Follow the general number rule: Spell out *one* through *nine* and use figures for *10* and above: *The proud parents of the 8-pound, 7-ounce, 21-inch baby took their child on her first trip—a five-mile drive to Grandma's.*

fractions   Below *1,* spell out; above *1,* use figures or convert to decimals. To convert 3¼ into a decimal, divide the 4 into the 1 and affix the answer with a decimal point to the whole number: *3.25.*

hurricane   Capitalize when part of a storm's name: *Hurricane Hugo.* A storm is not a hurricane unless the sustained wind speed is 74 miles per hour. Lesser blowing attempts are called *tropical storms.*

Although hurricanes have female and male names, all subsequent references to them are made with the neutral pronoun *it*.

incorporated   Although seldom needed in a corporation's name, *incorporated* when used is abbreviated and capitalized *Inc.* Do not set off with a comma: *NL Industries Inc.*

initials   When a person chooses to be known by his or her initials, respect that usage. Use periods but do not space between initials, because video display terminals and typesetters use space codes as guides in justifying lines and a space between initials could place them on separate lines.

it/she   Modern usage does not use gender pronouns to refer to neutral objects. Ships, nations and hurricanes are *it,* not *she.*

names/nicknames   Refer to people as they prefer to be known: *J. Edgar Hoover, Jimmy Carter* (whose full name is James Earl Carter Jr.).

The same guideline applies to nicknames, except when the nickname is intended to be derogatory: *"Fats" Olson.*

Some people acquire nicknames because their given names are uncommon. Thus, Amandus Lutz was always known as "Bud," which he preferred.

Nicknames are set off with quotation marks except on the sports pages.

No.   Always use the abbreviation for *number* when referring to rankings: *The No. 1 ranked football team in the preseason poll finished No. 19.*

numbers   Generally, spell out *one* through *nine* and use figures for *10* and above.

Numbers at the start of a sentence are spelled out if the result is not ungainly: *One thousand six hundred fifty-two students collected money to help fight cancer last year.* The sentence works better this way: *A total of 1,652 students* . . . However, don't carry that rule to extremes. It's all right to begin a sentence *Five people* . . . . *A total of five* wastes words.

For exceptions to the general numbers rule, see Addresses, Ages, Century, Congressional districts, Dimensions/weights, Fractions, No., Temperatures.

party affiliation   Three possible approaches form the basic application of this guideline:

Republican Sen. Barry Goldwater of Arizona said . . .

Sen. Barry Goldwater, R-Ariz., said . . . (note punctuation and abbreviation)

Sen. Barry Goldwater said . . . *The Arizona Republican also said* . . .

The choice often depends on what goes best with the rhythm of the sentence.

pope/pontiff Capitalize *pope* only in a formal title but never when used alone: *Pope John Paul II, the pope. Pontiff* is not a formal title and is always lowercase.

post office Do not capitalize; the correct name is *U.S. Postal Service,* although *post office* may be used when referring to the building from which mail is distributed.

president Capitalize only when part of a title, not when standing alone: *President Lincoln,* the president.

race Identification of anyone by race should be avoided. Consider the subjects of stories as individuals rather than as members of a race and avoid unnecessary racial references. (Author's preference)

seasons Unless part of a proper name, the seasons of the year are always lowercase.

slang Don't use. People may use slang when they talk, but when they read they expect precision, not flippancy. Given the generational differences in interpreting many slang words, their use impairs communication.

spouse When referring to marriage partners in general, use *spouse* to avoid the implication that only men occupy work roles and only women are homemakers.

state names Always spell out state names when they stand alone, but with the exception of eight states, abbreviate when used with town and city names in datelines and stories. Accepted abbreviations are Ala., Ariz., Ark., Calif., Colo., Conn., Del., Fla., Ga., Ill., Ind., Kan., Ky., La., Md., Mass., Mich., Minn., Miss., Mo., Mont., Neb., Nev., N.H., N.J., N.M., N.Y., N.C., N.D., Okla., Ore., Pa., R.I., S.C., S.D., Tenn., Vt., Va., Wash., W.Va., Wis., Wyo. (Do not use U.S. Postal Service abbreviations; they are confusing.)

temperatures Except for zero, all temperatures are given as figures. Use the words *minus* or *below zero* to report such temperatures. Do not use a minus sign.

time element Except when referring to the current day (the day of publication), use the day of the week. Thus, a Thursday newspaper would refer to *Wednesday* and *Friday* where appropriate, not *yesterday* and *tomorrow.*

TV Television is more acceptable, especially in noun usages.

United Nations/U.N. Use *United Nations* as a noun; use *U.N.* as a modifier: *The United Nations met today to debate a U.N. resolution.*

United States/U.S. Use *United States* as a noun; use *U.S.* as a modifier: *The United States sends many U.S. products overseas.*

vice president As a formal title, capitalize; standing alone, lowercase.

women/men   The two sexes are equal and should be treated as such. Copy should not assume a group of people is all male or female, or refer to a person's physical appearance: *attractive, muscular.* Copy should not mention a person's family relationship (*mother of five*) unless relevant.

In other words, treat men and women with equal respect and with a lack of condescension and stereotyping.

Appendix C

Glossary

A wire The main or major wire of a wire service, it provides the best news fastest. See also *Datastream, Datanews.*

access In computer jargon, a verb meaning to locate and process.

advance A story written and made available to an editor days before its publication date. Typically, such stories are features that do not have to appear immediately.

advertising The solicited and paid-for sales pitches that appear in a newspaper. The revenue from advertising helps pay the bills, but the work of the editorial department attracts the audience for the advertiser.

agate Five-and-a-half-point type. Frequently any small type, such as that used in box scores, is called agate, although the type may be slightly larger.

air White space intentionally placed on a page. It regularly appears around headlines and captions, between columns of type, and in other places of the page designer's choosing.

art Any graphics element on a page, including line drawings and photographs.

Associated Press, The A news-gathering cooperative.

attribution The identified source of information in a story.

banner headline A headline that runs from one side of the page to the other.

ben day A type of screened border used in boxes; a ben day border is a pattern of dots.

bleed The editing process of removing words and phrases as a way of reducing the length of a story rather than cutting paragraphs from the end.

body type Type sizes used exclusively for stories; sometimes called text type. Traditional sizes range from 8 to 10 points.

box   A border surrounding a story or other page element.

brite   A light-hearted or humorous story.

broadsheet   The format/size of a standard newspaper.

budget   A list of top stories. Also called directory, digest or schedule.

bullet   A dot used at the beginning of each paragraph that is part of a list. Some editors use dashes.

bulletin   A rapidly sent message that tells of an unusually significant or dramatic change in a story or of an important happening that probably will be a developing story.

bureau   A subordinate office of the main newspaper office.

butcher   A pejorative term used to describe a copy editor who does graceless work and makes stories worse rather than better.

byline   At the beginning of a story, the name of the reporter who wrote the story or of the wire service that provided it.

caption   The words used to complement a photograph.

char del   A VDT command for "character delete."

circulation   The number of newspapers sold, usually number of newspapers sold in a day. Advertisers are charged rates according to a newspaper's circulation; one with a large circulation can charge more for an advertisement than one with a small circulation.

cliché   A phrase used so many times it has lost the warmth and glow of originality. Avoided in good writing; removed in good editing.

close   A VDT command that tells the computer a reporter has completed a story.

cold type   The reproduction of type through photographic means. So called because the process does not require the melting of lead and the attendant heat found in hot-type methods.

column   A vertical arrangement of lines of type on a page; the width of such lines. Also, a short essay expressing a viewpoint.

column rule   Vertical rules used to separate columns of type. This design element is somewhat old-fashioned.

command   A function built into a VDT system and usually executed by pushing only one key.

computer   A piece of equipment capable of storing millions of pieces of information and processing that information speedily upon command.

computer printout   Information computer-transcribed from the computer to a printer, often called a hard copy printer.

copy   A VDT command for "duplicate." Also, newsroom jargon for "story."

copy schedule   An editor's listing of stories assigned for use in that day's issue.

CPU   Central processing unit, or the brains of the computer. The area of a computer where all the calculations take place.

crash   Computer breakdown.

credit line   The words at the end of a caption that give the source of the photograph. On wirephotos the credit line is no more than the name of the wire service providing the photograph.

crop   The process of marking any art to show which parts are to be reproduced and which parts are to be cut (cropped).

cursor   A blinking rectangular light that marks a VDT user's place on the screen. For example, a letter to be removed must appear under the cursor before the computer will delete that letter on command. The cursor moves in the four directions—up, down, left, right.

cutline   See *caption.*

database   An electronic library that can be accessed from a computer and over telephone lines.

Datanews   UPI's high-speed news service.

Datastream   AP's high-speed news service.

deadline   A date or time before which something must be done; the time after which copy is not accepted for a particular issue of a newspaper.

deck   One headline in a series of headlines stacked one above the other. It does not refer to a line in a multiline head.

dedicated   A computer term meaning that a piece of equipment can do only what it has been built to do. Some VDT systems are dedicated to processing text.

developing story   A story in which new information is added throughout a news cycle, thus creating an updated, new story with each transmission.

disk   The physical device on which information is stored. Personal computers increasingly use hard disks for main storage and floppy disks, which can be removed and stored elsewhere, for backup.

down style   Capitalizing only the first word and proper nouns in a headline.

drop headline   A subordinate, or secondary, headline that appears below a main headline. Also called a deck, a drop headline can be used when two stories appear under a main headline. The separate headlines on the stories are drop headlines.

dummy   A hand-drawn schematic of what an editor wants a page to look like when in print.

edition   A press run's worth of newspapers, not a day's worth. An edition is usually focused on a particular locale (city edition) or time of day (early edition). See also *zoned edition.*

evergreen   A virtually timeless story.

face   The type design; *face* is often preceded by a word telling which kind of face it is, such as Caslon.

feature   A human interest, or soft news, story written in non-news style.

filler   Short items used to fill space when a longer story comes up short.

floppy disk   A disk (similar to a phonograph record) on which computer programs or newsroom-generated information are stored for later accessing.

focus group   A gathering of newspaper readers brought together in an unsystematic fashion by a researcher looking for subjective analysis of a particular newspaper and for questions around which to build a readership survey.

folio   Found at the top of every page, it contains the newspaper's name, the publishing date and the page number. Often incorporated into the section flag.

format   The shape or form of the newspaper's contents.

formatting   Specifying through a VDT keyboard particular typographic requirements.

front end system   A computerized text-processing and type-generating system in which input is made at the initial point in the system (the VDT) and controlled from there.

graphic   A visual element designed to enhance the communication of a story. Drawings more than photographs qualify as graphics, although when editors refer to "graphic elements," they include photographs.

gutter   The vertical white space between columns or pages.

hairline   The thinnest rule available for boxes. The next larger size is 1-point.

hammer headline   An all-caps word or short phrase appearing above a headline where a kicker normally appears.

hard news   News that occurs and is reported within a 24-hour or shorter cycle; information that is timely. See also *soft news*.

hardware   Computer equipment.

header   A piece of information that normally appears on command at the beginning of VDT stories. The header might include space for a copy editor to indicate what edition the story goes in, which page it goes on, what size headline it gets, and so on.

headline   The larger type appearing (usually) above a story and telling what the story is about.

headline count   The maximum number of units a certain size headline will fill.

headlinese   Slang words in headlines that one would not use in normal writing.

hellbox A metal container in which printers threw lead to be melted down and recycled. A relic.

H&J See *justify*.

home A VDT command that returns the cursor to the top left-hand corner of the screen or to the beginning of a line.

index A list of stories and features in a newspaper edition.

insert A VDT command that allows a user to insert a word or letter without erasing other words or letters. When not in the insert mode, a VDT is in the overstrike mode.

International Typographical Union The union that represents members of the production department; at some newspapers the ITU also represents members of the editorial staff.

issue A single copy of a publication or the entire publication for a particular day; not to be confused with edition, which is a particular production run within an issue. "The local edition of Monday's issue contained fewer than the normal number of typos."

journalese The jargon of journalism; not fit to print.

jump The process of continuing a story from one page to another; the continued matter.

justify Alignment of lines of type on left and (especially) right sides. Also, a computer command that reformats a story on a VDT screen to show how the story will appear in type. Justifying a story will show where the end-of-line hyphens are going to appear, enabling an editor to check for incorrect hyphenation.

kicker A smaller headline that appears above the main headline.

label headline A verbless headline that gives the topic of a story but not the news.

lead The beginning of a story; usually only the first paragraph.

legend The (usually) all-caps beginning of a caption; also called a lead-in. The legend can also appear in headline type to the side of or above a caption.

legibility The clarity of appearance of type.

libel Anything published or broadcast that defames a person.

library A newspaper's collection of reference works and the newspaper's own stories. Older journalists call it the morgue.

localize The process of rewriting or editing a wire story so that the angle of interest to the newspaper's audience appears at the beginning of the story.

marketing The various strategies devised to sell a product.

memory The area of a computer that holds information, usually discussed in terms of capacity.

microcomputer Also called a personal computer; microcomputers began as standard home models but were taken on in newsrooms around the country, thanks to their increasing capability and low cost.

modem The device attached to a computer or affixed inside a computer that allows access to telephone circuits. *Modem* is the acronym for modulator-demodulator.

module A rectangle of any dimension in which a story or other page element is contained.

nameplate The name of the newspaper and other publishing information found at or near the top of Page One. Also called a flag.

new lead Fresh information transmitted by a wire service to replace the beginning of an earlier story.

news The timely content of a newspaper.

news hole The amount of space devoted to the news, usually determined as a percentage of total space after the advertisements are dummied.

Newspaper Fund A non-profit foundation supported by various newspapers and news organizations and dedicated to encouraging young people to consider careers in journalism. Two programs provide internships for minorities and students interested in copy editing.

Newspaper Guild A union whose members include journalists. At some newspapers members of the advertising staff also belong to the Guild.

newsprint The paper on which a newspaper is printed.

obit Journalese for "obituary." An obituary is an account of a person's death and facts about the person's life.

ombudsman A member of the newspaper staff whose main function is to process reader complaints against the newspaper and to serve as an in-house critic of the newspaper.

Open A typical VDT operation that commands a computer to produce a story from its files.

package The practice of putting related news items together for reader ease in finding them.

page A VDT screen full of type. A page equals approximately 20 lines, or what a reporter would normally type on one sheet of 8½ × 11 inch paper.

pagination The video-computer process of designing newspaper pages.

para A VDT command given at the end of a paragraph so that the following paragraph will be indented.

para del A VDT command for "paragraph delete."

peg A story's *raison d'être;* the main point on which the story hangs.

photojournalism The melding of words and pictures into a coherent story told mostly with photographs.

pica A printer's measure of type; 12 points; approximately one-sixth of an inch long. Pica measurements are applied to column widths and photograph sizes.

pica stick A printer's ruler. Also called a line gauge.

point The smallest measure of type; an inch contains 72 points. Point sizes are applied to borders, type, spaces or any other small area.

production See *shop*.

program Computer instructions.

proportional scale A wheel-shaped device used for scaling a photograph for reproduction.

publisher The chief officer of a newspaper. The publisher oversees all phases of the newspaper but does not get involved in day-to-day decisions in any one department.

Pulitzer Prize Journalism's most prestigious honor, bestowed annually on the best journalists and newspapers (and plays and books).

queue A dedicated space in the computer, set aside for a reporter to write a story or for wire service input or for copy editing.

ragged right Uneven right-side alignment of lines of type; sometimes called unjustified.

readability The clarity of the written word.

readership survey A systematic study of audience opinion about the content of a newspaper or magazine.

refer (REE-fer) Type within a story that refers the reader to a related story or photograph.

regional wire A wire devoted to serving a particular area, such as a state, half a state, or several small states.

reverse type Any type reversed from black on white to white on black through production techniques.

scratch pad A queue into which reporters write stories.

screamer headline A sensational headline that overstates the story and appears in an extra-large size.

scroll up/scroll down VDT commands that move lines up or down on the screen. On personal computers *Pg Up* and *Pg Dn* do the same thing.

second-day lead A lead on any version of a story except the first in which the news is originally reported; a second-day lead generally takes a feature angle or highlights a new and important action in a continuing story.

section flag Similar to a nameplate, except the section flag announces the section of the newspaper. Also called a logo.

sent del A VDT command for "sentence delete."

serif Additional strokes on letters that make type easier to read. Type lacking serifs is described as sans serif.

shop   The area of a newspaper building where stories are set in type and pages are put together. Also called production.

sidebar   A story related to a major story, but keying on one special point.

side-saddle headline   A headline situated alongside rather than above a story.

sign off   A VDT command telling the computer that the reporter or copy editor is through using the terminal.

skip   To start a VDT command key that sends the cursor to the beginning of the story, requiring the story to move with it so that the beginning of the story will appear at the top of the screen with the cursor. On personal computers, *Ctrl Pg Up* has the same effect.

slug   The name or identifying tag for a story. Usually the slug tells something about the story, such as "hotel/fire." Also called slugline.

soft news   The timeless or feature content of a newspaper that usually has some relation to a recent news event. Also, often a derisive term for stories of mass appeal but, in the opinion of the speaker, not of mass benefit.

software   A particular program, such as a spreadsheet or a word-processing program.

split page   Any page that begins any section (except the first); also called a break page.

split screen   The VDT capability of displaying two stories side by side. Also known as windows.

stack   A one-column breakdown of a longer story. A story spread evenly over five columns is said to have five stacks of type. Some editors refer to "sticks" or "legs" of type.

standing headline   A headline used unchangingly day by day to identify a type of news. May not be used as the main headline on a story. For example, "Weather" as a standing headline lacks the communicative strength of "Hurricane expected." Standing heads should not be used in place of an original headline.

stet   A printer's term (derived from the Latin *stare*) to advise the person setting type to disregard a correction or to let a word stand as is even if it appears incorrect. The word has no use in computerized typesetting, but every generation of copy editors should know what it means.

streamer headline   See *banner headline*.

style   The prescribed way of processing ambiguous usages in news stories. Style should always be consistent.

subhead   A subordinate headline appearing within the body of a story.

supplementary wire service   A service that complements rather than competes with the two major wires. Supplementary wires provide opinion columns, analyses and features not common on the AP and UPI wires.

tabloid   A newspaper format that is half the size of a standard newspaper. Also a phrase used to describe sensational newspapers.

take   A portion of a story, usually one page; for a wire story, 450 words.

time element   Usually the day of the week a news story takes place. Yesterday, today, tomorrow, last night, this morning, in addition to the days of the week, are acceptable time elements.

transition   A word or phrase that alerts the reader to a change of subject in a story.

typo   A typographical error.

United Press International   A privately owned news–gathering organization.

up style   Capitalizing the first letter of each word (except articles and short prepositions) in a headline.

VDT   See *video display terminal*.

video display terminal   A television screen connected to a typewriter keyboard; commands typed on the keyboard appear on the screen.

wicket   Similar to a kicker, it appears at the side of a headline.

window   A segment of the computer screen in which text appears. Using two or more windows simultaneously is a handy way of comparing related stories side by side or checking information at the end of a long story with information early in the story.

wrap type   Text that extends around a graphic element is said to wrap. Any display of type around a graphic element, whether in the news columns or in advertisements.

zoned edition   An edition of a newspaper that includes a page or section emphasizing news of a small area within the newspaper's larger circulation area.

Appendix D

A Budget for Beginners

Journalism students about to seek their first job usually don't know what constitutes a good salary, because they don't understand what bills they'll have to pay as they begin life on their own.

To help you as a first-time job seeker, I have prepared a checklist of typical items for which you will have to budget. If the job is in a strange city, talk to reporters on the staff about typical expenses so that you'll have an idea of what figures to put in the blanks. Try to find a reporter similar to yourself. If you're single and just beginning, talk to a single and fairly new employee. Other members of the staff will have different perspectives and may unintentionally provide misleading figures.

A typical budget:

rent	mad money
food, household supplies	minor medical
car payments	dental
car registration expenses	life insurance
car insurance	utilities
gasoline	travel to home or vacation
college loan repayment	professional memberships
clothing, laundry	magazine subscriptions
entertainment, hobbies	alumni association
savings	credit card payments
furniture payments	

Total (take-home pay)

To the take-home figure, add approximately 25 percent to find your gross salary needs. The 25 percent covers Social Security payments and tax deductions, both of which are especially heavy and burdensome on low-income, single people. This budget assumes that the company pays for medical insurance and all contributions to the company pension fund. If it does not, adjust accordingly. Be willing to compromise, but not to starve.

Appendix E

Workbook

Style Exercises

Correct the style mistakes in the following sentences.

1. Pilsdon City Council voted six to four to close the meeting to the press.
2. The attack appeared to indicate that the violence, which began September 5, was spreading.
3. Governor T. Thomas Williams today proposed a $1 million facelift for the Executive House, which is located at 341 North Second Street.
4. The Senate is one of two houses in the United States congress.
5. The President today called for a tax reduction as a way of spurring development.
6. When it comes to bragging rights in college football, usually the team declared number one by the wire services is the one that can do the bragging.
7. A sixteen-year-old person is considered a minor in many states.
8. If you've ever been to Des Moines, Ia., you have probably seen the gold dome on top of the state's capitol building.
9. Design Unlimited was granted a 5.5 million dollar contract to fix up the buildings.
10. City council meetings begin at 7:30 in the evening.

Spelling

I. Circle the correctly spelled word in each of the following sets.

roomate	roommate	discrepancy	discrepency
fundamental	funamental	dependent	dependant
grammer	grammar	seperate	separate
cemetery	cemetary	marshal	marshall
defendent	defendant	hemorrhage	hemorhage
liaison	liason	exhilarate	exilarate
drunkenness	drunkeness	consensus	concensus
yield	yeild	municiple	municipal
villin	villain	baroom	barroom
memento	momento	attorneys	attornies
permissible	permissable	imoral	immoral
guerilla	guerrilla	stupefy	stupify
harass	harrass	accommodate	accomodate
supercede	supersede	arguement	argument
liquify	liquefy	seige	siege
existance	existence	dissatisfied	disatisfied
accidentally	accidently	questionaire	questionnaire
coattails	coatails	unatural	unnatural
environment	enviroment	committee	comittee
goverment	government	believe	beleive
ectasy	ecstasy	gracefully	gracefuly
allege	alledge	agressive	aggressive
vilify	villify	propogation	propagation
sizable	sizeable	harangue	harrangue
precede	preceed	stubborness	stubbornness
occasional	occassional	development	developement
innoculate	inoculate	devisive	divisive
anoint	annoint	persistence	persistance

supressed	suppressed	a capella	a cappella
similar	similer	lambast	lambaste
occurred	occured	predominantly	predominately
tentativly	tentatively	diphtheria	diptheria
wondrous	wonderous	preferred	prefered
protesters	protestors		

II. Each sentence in this exercise contains at least one mispelled word for you to correct.

1. When the Chinese government declared marshal law in parts of Peking, the student was in Shanghai, where protests were mounting.

2. The new drugstore may need fewer partime employes, because the building is smaller.

3. The Mall's reflecting pool will seperate the two memorials.

4. It appears inevitable that Congress will lose its first domestic policy confrontation with the president if, as expected, he vetos the legislation raising the minimum wage.

5. The chief negotiater for the teachers union said both sides had made a committment to resolving the contract dispute.

6. Any discrepency in a public budget is bound to get a journalist's attention.

7. The ceremonys planned for Flag Day and the Fourth of July this year are more elaborate than any made in the past decade.

8. In any election, the incumbant has an advantage and usually recieves the most votes.

9. The injured man was given mouth-to-mouth recitation by a police officer.

10. Anytime a problem arises in a legal dispute before the trial begins, one attorney or another seeks a postponement.

11. The group that comissioned a memorial in honor of the Korean War dead recognized that the nation had forgotten that war.

Punctuation

Punctuate and fix any incorrect capitalization in the following sentences, using the editing symbols in Appendix A.

1. Waverly Township police have decided to change service weapons from a six shot revolver to a semi automatic pistol with a magazine that holds twice as many bullets.

2. "Thats what this program is really about getting artists and people together the festival representative said.

3. Charges against two inmates Ellis Weathersby 25 and Jonas Oliver 28 have been dismissed for lack of evidence prison authorities said.

4. While not as aggressive as the $40 billion a year plan pushed by his own Environmental Protection Agency, the presidents plan still was forecast to cost the economy between $14 billion and $19 billion a year by the end of the century.

5. Pictures of the two students were shown on national television and the announcer said Dont let these people flee They are wanted for counter-revolutionary crimes."

6. The court's four most liberal members John Paul Stevens William J Brennan Jr Thurgood Marshall and Harry A Blackmun dissented.

7. His 21 year old son Todd has just graduated from the University.

8. Foreign produced assault rifles have been banned from entering the country since March, when the president ordered the bureau to review the sporting value of the rifles such as Uzis and AK 47s that have become favorites of drug dealers.

9. The focus of the convention is the presidential election Tuesday afternoon with the 44 year old Daniel Vestal trying to unseat Jerry Vines 51 of Jacksonville Fla as president of the 14.8 million member denomination.

10. The American response needs to be flexible sensitive and committed to

helping the Poles and others continue on their way to more open societies.

11. Joe Banks the Clive resident who proposed the plan said the biggest stumbling block is political philosophy.

Language Skills

The following sentences contain typical language skills errors. Correct them.

1. Pilsdon Park Authority voted last night to increase their swimming pool fees for next year.
2. Sears sell many products, from screwdrivers to lawnmowers.
3. The preferential treatment afford the president's peanut business was revealed Wednesday by two directors of the bank in a special report.
4. Each of the members of our microcomputer club run four miles daily.
5. The article says journalism education inspires idealism in students that gradually fade away after the students work in the real world.
6. Last seen in the vicinity of Clive Avenue, police say the escaped bear is dangerous and could attack anyone without provocation.
7. Packard suggested closing the loopholes for the rich and rejection of salary increases for government officials.
8. The project requires cleaning and reconstruction of a water channel, repairing dikes and complying with anti-pollution measures.
9. Some firms expect their employees to start work at 7:30 a.m. in the morning.
10. The fact that there were children in the audience born since "Star Trek" stopped filming illustrated Nimoy's idea that the show reruns appeal to all generations.

11. A group of Johns Hopkins University scientists are studying human arteries to see whether arterial patterns can contribute to the disease.

12. The Spanish press, snarled by a web of restraints on what they can publish, faces new problems following the arrest of two journalists three days ago.

13. Proof that he was human came when he walked in here and talks about his pain.

14. The boy struck the ball. Which bounced over the pitcher's head and into center field.

15. The association recommended that the board consider adding two basketball games to the schedule, which increases it to 22 games, and to extend the girls' cross-country schedule to increase two meets with Pilsdon.

16. Using a radial arm saw and a variable speed drill, the bookcase was fashioned by her in three days.

17. Five persons with a rifle were shot by a police officer.

18. The Association for Intercollegiate Athletics for Women have stiffer rules than the NCAA.

19. As part of its study, the commission traveled through the state holding public hearings, took testimony from parents, teachers and administrators, and observing school activities.

20. The board includes seven volunteers, each of whom have a full-time job.

Editing Sentences

In copy editing the following sentences, fix all errors of spelling, punctuation, language usage, and redundancy.

1. More than one inch of rain fell this in one hour this morning in Waycross, Georgia, seventy miles northeast of Madison and in George, trees

were also blown down and a tin roof was blown off an old building, according to the National Weather Service.

2. (headline) Homocide spurs angry plea

3. Ambulance services would have to offer 24 hour coverage but those that do not operate 24 hours a day could make a mutual arrangement with another service to meet the requirement.

4. The author of a novel entitled "50" whose main character is middle aged, questions whether television is making life tougher for people having a mid life crisis.

5. In another development, the Soviet Union acknowleged at the United Nations on Monday that it failed to win support for a Security Council resolution calling for an end to the deadly missile duel.

6. Stewart Wilkins 6 of Fairfax Vermont eagerly awaits the return of his father from the ice cream stand.

7. Supervisor elect Lilla D. Richards said after her victory Tuesday night that she will be working between now and her inauguration in January to get ready "to get the job done."

8. Because both committees are controlled by Democrats, the final package will probably place most of any new tax burden on corporations and upper income individuals; a trait common to the pending bills.

9. United States officials say they destroyed at least two Libyan patrol boasts and made two attacks on a missile base on the Libyan coast.

10. In the report, a series of projections are made that vary according to possible economic developments in future years.

11. Trying to find its identity, the head of a little girl was reconstructed by a Calif. sculptor.

12. If anyone has legitimate problems and can't make a game, the Phillies will exchange their tickets for another game.

13. Tolls will riase from 80 cents to a dollar for two axle trucks with trailers.

14. The former mayor said Smith's race would not effect his own political plans.

15. The pig was returned by an unidentified youth on Thursday, who said he had found it at a nearby convenience store.

16. Samuel R. Pierce, United States Secretary of Housing and Urban Developement, said he has considered resigning as the only black in the Reagan cabinet if the president is reelected.

17. The study found that deaths rose in Atlanta when the temprature dropped below 32 degrees; Chicago, 11 degrees, Cincinatti, 15 degrees; Detroit, 16 degrees; Dallas, 34 degrees; Oklahoma City, 22 degrees, and Philadelphia, 23 degrees.

18. The late season storm caught many by surprise when it formed in the gulf on Saturday.

19. A Soviet sailor who was forced back to his ship twice after he apparently tried to defect was taken off the vessel Monday to be interviewed by U.S. authorities trying to find out if he wants to stay in the U.S.

20. The quake was felt along a 45- mile long stretch from Sacramento, California, to San Bernardino, California, and into western Nevada.

21. Under the Reagan administration plan, countries except Mexico and Canada would continued to be alotted a combined total of 230,000 emigrants a year.

22. The Soviets on occasion have sent new warplanes to Cuba, including a shipment last November of 17 jet fighters.

23. Last Thursday, a delegation from the U.S. Chamber of Commerce came in and encouraged the president to stick with his program of no tax increase.

24. The victims were taken to three area hospitals, where most were treated for minor injuries and released.

25. Following the session, Montgomery said in an interview that although at vote was not taken by the group, he felt there were enough Democrats on the House saide to join with Republicans and pass the budget plan Reagan has endorsed.

26. The boat's crew said they were abandoning the fishing vessel about twenty miles northeast of Jacksonville for a life raft.

27. She married Wayne Bentley who retired from grape farming in the early 1970s fifty-six years ago today.

28. Layoffs in the 38,000 member salaried force would offset Chryslers Aug. purchase of American Motors Corporation and an expect sales slum said sources quoted by the Detroit Free Press who spoke on condition of anonymity.

29. Chrysler chairman Lee Iacocca was expected to reveal the cutbacks at a news conference today where he was also expected to announce the company's 3rd quarter earnings, the Detroit News reported today.

30. Chief of Staff Lieutenant General Raphael Eytan, Foreign Minister Yitzhak Shamir and Brigadier General Amos Yaron, the Israeli commander in Beirut during the massacre were also harshly chastized in the report.

31. The defense attorney said he moved for dismissal primarily because the assistant district attorney failed to procede with his case, not because the alledged victim was late arriving.

32. An effort last year in the Senate to scuttle the project failed by only two votes.

33. The case of the explosion Monday aboard the 781 foot tanker, Ogden Argus, was not immediately determined.

34. Authorities would say little else about their investigation, other than the 54,000 acre Dayton Canyon fire was started by an arsonist and that an incendiary device had been found.

Editing Stories

In copy editing the following stories, fix all errors. Also list any questions you have.

Story 1

Two Clive County men are in the Mountinview Hospital today where they are being treated for injuries recieved in a plane crash at the Clive Air Park near Pilsdon yesterday at 1:50 p.m. Mary Weaver, 34, of Pilsdon was listed in serious cndition this morning with facial injuries and lacerations and Larry Stober, 30, of Leola, the pilot was listed n good condition with lacerations.

Witnesses told Mr. and Mrs. A. Garbrick, owners of the airport that the plane, a Piper Tri Pacer, appeared to be having difficulty taking off from the airport and failed to gain sufficient attitude to clear some trees at the end of an adjacent field, flipping over and landing upside down in a field.

It was reported that Stober freed himself from the wreckage and pulled Weaver from the passengers seat. Both persons were out of the plane when people at the airport arrived at the crash site.

The plane was owned by Keither Weaver of Toronto, Canada, and has been kept at the airport for several years, Mrs. Garbrick said. It was reported the airplane was being prepared for return to its owner in the near future.

The Federal Aviation Administration was expected to send represents to the crash site today to investigate the cause of the accident.

Story 2

Nicholas Tower is the new apartment condo project in Clive, planned for the corner of South Allen Street and Foster Ave.

James F. Nichols, project owner and developer said the six story building will contain 40 luxury condominiums, designed for buyers who will live in them instead of investors.

Features will include two or three bedrooms, a den, two and one half baths, storage, washers and driers, fireplace, patios, a security system and parking. Buyers will be able to cuttomize the interiors of their condos Mr. Nichols said.

The first floor will have parking and some commercial space, the other five floors will each contain four condos.

Nichols said the project is one that is aimed at those people who enjoy extensive living space, like a house, but don't want to fuss or bother with the upkeep of a house.

Story 3

Improving the street design and putting a limit on the types of vehicles that would have access to Calder Way is the most popular solution to the street's congestion problem, a study done by University students found.

The report, prepared by eleven undergraduate students was completed at the request of the Pilsdon Pedestrian Commission and presented by the students at the commissions meeting last night. It surveyed public officials and businessmen.

The students are in the Urban and Regional Planning Option of the Man-Enviroment Relations Program at the University.

The commission asked that the study be conducted after members observed conflicts between vehicles, pedestrians and bicycles in Calder Way, because of recent development in the alley, between South Allen St. and McAllister St.

The report will serve as a base for future studies, Comission Chairman Barbara Hardy said.

After surveying owners of thirty-eight businesses on Calder Way and intreviewing nineteen city officials and two developers of the street, the students reported that the prefered solution would be to improve the street design in order to provide such pedestrian amenities as trees and benches and to allow only local deliveries, emergency and service vehicles to have complete and full access to the street.

Of the 39 questionaires distributed to the businessmen, 31 were returned, Thomas Showalter, one of the students reported.

Of the 31 businessmen, 23 strongly supported improved street design and limiting vehicles, five moderately supported those modifications, one was indifferent and none were opposed, he said.

Among the officials and developers, ten strongly supported those solutions, three moderately supported them, were were indifferent and six opposed them, Diane Johnson, another student said.

Other solutions offered included making a pedestrian mall between South Allen and McAllister Streets, restricting the use of Calder Way as a thru street by blocking excess at the intersection of South Allen and Calder Way, the addition of sideswalks and reversing the one-way direction of the street.

The report also suggested that any improvements be done as a part of a long-range plan.

Monitoring the traffic showed that the peak period for traffic is between 5 and 5:30 p.m. Friday and that the alley has more pedestrians than other streets, Showwalters said.

Also, because Walker Way is narrower than other streets, pedestrians tend to walk on the street rather than the sidewalks, Showalter said.

Story 4

A Clive County crank caller persuaded a Pilsdon woman she was doing her part for modern medicine-and then indecently assault her.

Last month, the woman recieved a call from a man who said he was working for the University. She was asked a list of questions by him that gradually took on sexual overtones, said Rod Blundy, investigator for the Pilsdon Police Department.

Blundy would not release the woman's name, but the Bugle learned that she is Anne Jenkins, wife of Pilsdon dentist Keller Jenkins.

As the interview continued, the man said he was working on a new invention to detect breast cancer. He said that this invention, connected to the telephone, he could detect lumps if Mrs. Jenkins rubber her breast with the telephone receiver, according to Musser.

Mrs. Jenkins, 29, followed the mans' instructions and was told that he found evidence of a few lumps. He set up an appointment to examine her at her home, police said. Later that day the man arrived at her door.

"She said that when he came to the door she was too scarred to tell him to leave. She felt she was going to be hurt," Blundy said.

Mrs. Jenkins opened the door and the exam began. The man took of her blouse and bra, rubbing her breasts with baby oil and layed his head on her breast and began humming. He told her he found lumps and gave her a phone number to call to set up another appointment.

After he left, Mrs. Jenkins called police, embarassed that she had been so naive, police said.

The man was described as in his 20s, 5-foot-8, white and 210 pounds with a beer belly. His short brown hair was combed straight back and he was wearing a light blue jacket. The phone number he left with Mrs. Jenkins was not his number, police said.

Bundy said police received 2 other complaints about calls that may be releated. In one instance, a caller told a woman he was working for the University Medical Center. The Bugle learned that the woman is Elaine Sanders, a graduate student at the University. After questions became suggesstive, she hung up.

In the second complaint, the caller said he was doing a study on sexual problems for University Medical Center. When the woman asked for the caller's name and phone number, he hung up.

A well place sourced, who asked not to be named, identified this woman as Grace Metcalf, an accountant in Pilsdon.

Johnathan E. Cartwright, director of the University's Office for Protection of Human Subjects, said that the best way a person can protect themselves from a unscrupulous questioner is to find out the caller's name and get the project director's phone number.

If legitimate, the caller also should explain the nature of the interview and indicate that answering any of the questions is voluntery.

Crank calls, which include everything from obscene calls to "hang ups" are reported to Clive county police departments daily. Blundy estimated that between 150 to 200 complaints of harrassing calls a year are received by the Pilsdon police.

Callers often use the guise of University researchers to trap innocent residents who want to help with the "research project," he said. Other crank calles have been known to say their doing research for Playboy or Penthouse magazines.

"The questions don't start off color," said Blundy. Eventually, however, the questions reach the point where most women say to themselves, "If this was for real, he wouldn't be asking me this stuff," he said.

At that point, suggested Blundy, the woman should hang up and call police.

Story 5

David J. Rothballer, Jr., dean emeritus of the University's College of Science died today at Clive County Hospital.

Dean Rothballer, 75, is credited with creating the College of Science twenty years ago and bringingit national stature within five years. He did that by hiring some top rate faculty from other universities, but most he concentrated on hiring young professors and giving them free reign.

Those young professors include seven winners of the President's Award for Exemplary Research.

Rothbaler, who also had a law degree, once worked as an attorney 40 years ago in Chicago. While there, according to the Chicago Sun-Times, he served a year in prison for blackmailing a Chicago police officer. A librarian at the newspaper said today that Dean Rothballer was not the main person in the crime.

After prison, Rothballer went ont to his his PhD in chemistry at the University of Stanford. He came immediately to the University asn an assistant professor and rose rapidly through the ranks, becoming head of the Department of Chemistry within five years. He retired as dean emeritus.

Dean Rothballer was an active member of the community, he helped start the Volunteers for Prisoners Society, which aids prisoners in their rehabilitative efforts, he served as chairman of the Clive County United Way dirve three times.

The dean also helped start the Clive County Legal Aid Society and served as its parttime director during some difficult financial times after he had retired as dean.

He served the city of Pilsdon with two terns on the Civil Service Board and one on the Police Pension Committee.

He is survived by his wife, the former Janet Tobin, a daughter, Deborah Rea Manchester of Virginia Beach, Va., a son, Roger, of Bridgeport, Connecticut, and three grandchildren.

Bleeding

Reduce the length of this 531-word story by 20 percent without rewriting the story or altering the writer's style. (Copyright 1985 The Washington Post).

Family, friends, colleagues and top Army officials gathered yesterday in a military chapel at Forth Myer to honor Maj. Arthur D. Nicholson Jr. and eulogize him as a man who had volunteered for a stressful assignment because he wanted to be on "the cutting edge."

Nicholson, 37, a liaison officer to East Germany, was shot and killed by a Soviet sentry near a garage-like storage shed one week ago. Nicholson, whose home was West Redding, Conn., had been attached to the 14-member liaison mission in Potsdam since 1982.

As several hundred people honored Nicholson with a service in Fort Myer's Memorial Chapel and a military burial in Arlington National Cemtery, Secretary of State George Shultz and Soviet Ambassador Anatoliy Dobrynin met at the State Department and agreed on discussions to prevent similar incidents.

In the chapel, family, friends and colleagues sat silently as the muffled beats of a drum corps outside signaled the arrival of the major's flag-draped casket.

Col. Roland LaJoie, commander of the liaison mission, recalled Nicholson as man who "not only passed the tests, he set the standards."

Nicholson was "my officer, my professional colleague and, most importantly, my personal friend," LaJoie said. "I was the last of us to see Nick alive and the first to see him dead."

LaJoie praised Nicholson's heroism and decried the circumstances of his death. "It was not a battle, it was not a fair fight; he was unarmed, in uniform, in broad daylight . . ."

And he stressed that Nicholson believed in the value of his work. "He constantly sought ways to increase contacts with Soviet officers so we could get to know each other better. Nick immensely enjoyed what he was doing, and I can tell you unequivocally, he was very good at it.

"He wanted to be out there, and he needed to be out there, close to what he considered the cutting edge," LaJoie said.

Following the chapel service, the funeral procession wound slowly through the cemetery. The horse-drawn caisson bearing Nicholson's casket came to rest near the Tomb of the Unknown Soldier.

More than 200 people ringed the grave site under ashen skies, listening to the music that resounded for minutes before members of the U.S. Army Band marched into view. Six white horses pulling the caisson halted near the grave site, and Nicholson's family stood behind—his parents, his wife Karyn and his 9-year-old daughter Jennifer, who clutched a sprig of flowers in one hand and a dollar in the other.

Riflemen fired three volleys into the chilly air, and a single bugler played Taps.

After a brief, quiet service, Deputy Secretary of Defense William Howard Taft IV presented flags to Nicholson's wife and father; Army Secretary John O. Marsh Jr. gave the Legion of Merit Award, and Army Chief of Staff Gen. John A. Wickham presented the Purple Heart.

Nicholson's family rose and one by one, placed roses on his casket. His daughter, then his wife, bent to kiss the lid. The funeral party dispersed quickly, and a few people drifted down from the hillside from the Tomb of the Unknown Soldier to stare at the casket, the mounds of flowers and the empty chairs.

Index

(Quotations, *cont.*)
  as leads, 69
  libel and, 46
  paraphrasing, 28, 36, 80
  pomposity in, 28
  see also Attribution

Racism, 56–59
Ragged right, 210
Rape victims, 47–48, 49
Readership, 271–277, 283
Reading copy, 24, 61
Redundancies, 104–105
Refers, 217
Register and Tribune Syndicate Inc., 254
Reinhold, Robert, 13
Relative clauses, 126–217
Repetition
  for clarity, 117–118
  deleting, 108
  for transition, 85
Reporters
  demand for, 1
  duties of, 25–26
Reuters News Agency, 253, 254
Rewrite editors. *See* Copy editors
Robinson, Thelma, 228–229
Ross, Madelyn, 148
Roundup, 261
RSI (repetitive strain injury), 20
Rules, 208, 214–215
  as half-box, 215
  Oxford, 215

San Diego *Evening Tribune,* 11
San Francisco Chronicle, 14
San Jose Mercury News, 12, 216, 228
Satellite transmission, 282
Scanlan, Christopher, 139
Science news, 186, 273
Seattle Times, 202, 205–206, 209, 227
Section editors, 251
Section flags, 208, 217–218
Self, stories about, 273
Self-checking, 61
Semantics. *See* Word meanings
Semicolon, 130, 132

Senior citizens, 60
Sensationalism, 48–49
Sentences
  average length, 30, 82
  breaking, 29
  direct versus indirect, 99–100
  editing exercises, 312–315
  fragment and run-on, 82
  long, 29–30
  news story, 81–83
  number of thoughts in, 65
  precision in, 36–37
  transition, 65, 83–86
  word order in, 64–65
Series
  false, 125
  semicolons in, 130, 132
Serif, 174, 209
Sex
  community standards and, 51
  double entendre, 35–36
Sexism, 56, 58, 120
Sidebars, 207, 261
Skyboxes, 219
Slang, 81, 164–165
Slot, 25
Slot editor, 251
Slug line, 258
Society news, 33
Soft news, 33, 191–192, 274
Sources, testing, 53–54
Spanish language, 40, 278
Spelling, 135–136
  computer correction of, 135
  errors in headlines, 170
  exercises, 308–309
  names, 39, 136
Sports editor, 9
Sports news, 275
  photographs, 226
  from wire services, 252
  writing styles, 94
Sports scores, 17–18, 210, 258
Spot news, 256
State College *Centre Daily Times,* 12, 228
State editor, 8
State news, 8, 186–187, 268
Statistics, 68
Stepp, Carl Sessions, 139